IS
GOD
A
GAY
BASHER?

Memoirs of a Christian, Gay Affirming Lesbian

Jan Liebegott

DEDICATION

Mom: for your love, strength, patience and support. Most of all I thank you for bringing me up in the Word of God and in the discipline of our Lord and Savior, Jesus the Christ. You were God's greatest earthly gift to me; my dearest friend and closest confidant. Though you went home with Jesus in February 2001, I feel you with me always. I miss you dearly, but will serve our Lord Jesus till He comes to take me home to be with you again, for eternity. Till then, never forget how much I love you.

CONTENTS

Introduction

Book One: Chapter 1-32   Early Years: 1946-1972

Book Two: Chapter 1-14   Wild Gay Years: 1972-1976

Book Three: Chapter 1-12   Gay Married Years: 1976 - 1994

Epilogue

Book Four: Gay Affirmation   Scripture and Homosexuality

Bibliography

MilJan Publications, New York

c) 1989/2002/2015

INTRODUCTION

"It's a world full of beauty. It's a world that is ugly.
When it's beautiful, Heaven is close at hand.
When it's ugly, it's full of agony; you cry alone.
Some say it's wrong, sick and unnatural.
Everyone involved in this beautiful/ugly world is fighting
an inner conflict.
Deep within everyone cries to be free.
Yes, it's full of joy; it's full of sorrow.
It's called beautiful; it's called ugly.
It's called Gay."

   I wrote this piece in September 1973, five months after I "came out" of the closet. I was going through Hell; the Hell most, if not all, gay people visit and oft times become residents.
   All too often the gay world is ugly because it is difficult to cope with the condemnation the Christian Church casts upon us. Even if, as in my case, a person feels freed by coming out, she/he must continually deal with the Church, which negatively influences our feelings towards ourselves; a Church that, instead of perceiving us as decent, God-fearing people, believes us to be perverted, sick and sinful.
   Unfortunately, many gay people crumble under such pressure, escaping into alcohol, drugs, indiscriminate sex and general emotional retardation. This reinforces negativity, making positive attitudes of morality towards gay people virtually impossible.
   What then is the "cure" for this destructive vicious cycle?
   We gay people cannot look for an easy solution, nor can we expect acceptance to come from the straight world unless we find peace from within ourselves. Without this inner peace we will not have the wisdom and strength to deal with the destructive forces.

Indeed, change must come from outside our world, but we gays must lead the way. Only then is there hope for freedom.

Hopefully, by exposing my guilt, fears, shame, suffering and subsequent peace, others will be able to affirm gay love and gay people will affirm their love for each other and for God. Hopefully, a bridge between the two worlds can be built, bringing more avenues of communication and understanding. Hopefully, the barrier will be lifted allowing gays to live the fulfilled, productive and peaceful life in which God intended.

Gays and straights cannot continue to live in worlds separated by fear, ignorance and hatred. This is destructive. This is inhuman. This is sin!

BOOK ONE: Early Years: 1946-1972

Chapter 1: 1972

My heart throbbed within my head. It felt as if a vice was squeezing the life out of my lungs. My nerves were so taut I thought they would snap like an icicle. My mind was a mass of colliding emotions struggling to become organized, wanting to express and repress simultaneously.

My sense of hopelessness was as heavy as the humidity that August night, as I ran from my house, raced my car out of the driveway and sped to the local drugstore, the place that had become my refuge of late.

It hadn't been the first, nor had it been the worst fight I'd had with him, but tonight I was at the end of my rope and didn't know if I could tie another knot and keep on hanging. I'd been hanging so long and was tired; tired of having intelligent discussions turn into irrational arguments; tired of having to kiss him goodnight when I wanted to tell him to go to Hell; tired of him preaching the Word of God while he sat drinking himself into damnation; tired of being crucified because I had a mind of my own.

He, my adoring father, didn't understand what was happening to me. Dammit! Neither did I! At twenty-six I was still living at home. Unlike my childhood friends, whom had all married and were raising families, as I believed all normal people should, I sat, day in and day out, a recluse in a house that, except for my Mom, I hated. Hated yet could not leave because my dependence on her

was life supporting. Mom was my world and if I wanted her I had to accept the presence of my father. Why hadn't she divorced him years ago? Life would have been utopian without him. She was the nearest thing to Heaven, but because of him my
Heaven was being destroyed as I passively sat, watching my happiness burn away.

  How in God's name had my life gotten so bent out of shape? Where had I lost control?

Chapter 2: 1946-1955

Despite the barren side-walked streets, copulating houses and limited playgrounds, Hollis, Queens wasn't a bad place to begin life, in 1946, when I was born. The war was over and a sense of peace permeated our community as families returned to rebuilding their lives.

My home was a Christian one, filled with the love of Jesus. Mom & Dad, who had met at church, instilled their faith in Paul (my brother, 3 years my senior) and me from the start. We attended church every Sunday, said grace at mealtimes and read our Bibles daily. Respect for one another was strictly enforced and foul language was prohibited (punishable by a scrubbing of one's mouth with the most awful tasting soap). I never heard my parents curse or argue and Paul and I got along better than most siblings.

My father was a hard working white-collar man who spent long hours away from home. Sometimes I didn't see him until the weekend because his job forced him to commute to eastern Long Island. Consequently, he had little time to spend with either Paul or me and since I displayed a desire and a talent for baseball, at a very young age, most of the time Dad had was monopolized by me. Dad was a frustrated ball player who would have tried out for the major leagues had not the depression obstructed his dream. I always felt I was chosen to fulfill his thwarted dream and strove to acquire perfection in the sport.

Paul never seemed to mind Dad's lack of attention, preferring solitude and a good book. He was obsessed with learning. I don't want anyone to get the wrong impression of him, though. A bookworm, yes; boring, no! Always there for me when I had a problem and always ready to wrestle with me, Paul's sense of humor and enjoyment of life was a constant source of inspiration.

In spite of the wonderful times spent with Dad and Paul, my deepest devotion and happiness lay with Mom. She couldn't throw a baseball like Dad or pin me to the ground in a wrestling hold like Paul, but she had other talents that I found more than necessary.

A pretty woman with a small, hour glassed frame, medium length brown hair, vivid blue eyes, set deep above high cheekbones, a warm smile and a personality that captured your heart, Mom exuded warmth the minute she walked into a room and if her warmth didn't get to you her sense of humor would. Quick and somewhat dry, she could make you laugh during your worst moment.

Mom was a woman of great faith. She lived her life according to God's rule, letting the light of Jesus shine through her every deed. Her sensitivity to the needs of others won her love and respect. She was a strict disciplinarian, but fair. In my youth I was slightly overactive, prone to bouts of mischief and unable to ignore a dare. When I was five, my friend Jerry dared me to throw a rock through the window of our neighborhood witch's house. Naturally, I had to accept. Though I had a good throwing arm, nurtured over the years by Dad, no one was more surprised than I when the rock I hurled went crashing through the old witch's front window.

Jerry and I withdrew quickly from the scene, retreating to the safety of our homes. Later that day the old witch came to my house demanding payment for her broken window and severe punishment for me. Mom paid the old woman and promptly sent her away, but I was never punished for my crime. Mom merely explained that even if a person was not nice, like the old woman, it did not make it right for me to do something destructive to her.

On other occasions I felt the sting of Mom's discipline. One of my favorite pastimes was playing at the local railroad track, in spite of the exposed third rail. Aware of the danger, Mom would try to dissuade my escapades with a spanking, but even when I felt the sting of the bristled side of the hairbrush on my bare behind, I knew that Mom loved me and cared for my well being. My journeys to the railroad tracks were short lived.

Nobody had a more compassionate mother than I. When I entered Kindergarten, at the tender age of 4, I missed her terribly. Each day, while playing in the toy doll house, I would call her on the play telephone. When I returned home from school I'd enter the house screaming, "Mommy, I called you today. Did you hear me?" Sensitive to my needs she'd play along, saying how wonderful my call had been

Yes, indeed, I had the greatest Mom in the world. She was my protector, comforter, friend and the love of my life.

* * * * * * * * *

It was in Kindergarten that I experienced a phenomenon I would later come to recognize as sexism. I loved playing in the doll house at school, but I also liked playing with the more rugged toys, like blocks. I had not been prohibited at home so never thought school would be any different. When I saw some boys playing with the blocks I didn't hesitate helping them build a large skyscraper. We were having a terrific time until my teacher came over and told me I could not play with the blocks because they were for boys only. Despite my protestations that the boys were allowed to play in the doll house so I should be able to play with the blocks, my teacher turned me away from the blocks towards the doll house. Her message was clear and I became livid. Later I returned to the boys, who were beaming with pride over the skyscraper I had helped them build and with one swift kick the great building crashed to the floor. My behavior shocked me, for I had never asserted myself with such hostility. However, the feeling of triumph was exhilarating, even when I saw my teacher walking towards me, eyes ablaze at the destruction my foot had caused. Anger turned to fear as I prepared to be royally punished, but to my surprise she merely turned me toward the ever-familiar doll house, without speaking a word. Despite the grave injustice I felt had been dealt me, I never had the nerve to play with the blocks again.

 Realizing that by being a girl I would not be allowed to enjoy certain toys or activities, I buckled down and tried to be a good student. However, I had one major problem. I loved to talk and as a result spent many hours at my desk writing, "I must be a good girl", one hundred times on a piece of paper. This behavior brought me much attention from the boys, especially those who sat writing as I.

 Boys had always taken to me and I loved their attention. However, when it came to girls I had trouble making friends. This puzzled me, but girls were sissies and I was better off without them. This line of reasoning satisfied me until Bonnie entered my life.

 Bonnie was visiting her Grandmother who was our next-door neighbor. When Mom saw her playing by herself she urged me to join her. Hesitantly, I obeyed.

 As Bonnie and I played I realized that, though she was just another sissy girl, I was having fun. I couldn't explain the difference between her and other girls, but it was there. Bonnie's inability to throw a baseball didn't matter. In spite of herself, I liked Bonnie and the feeling was reciprocated.

 The afternoon seemed to fly by, the two of us giggling as all seven years old will. I'd never had so much fun with a girl so when Bonnie started kissing me, I kissed back. I'd never kissed any girl on the mouth, except for Mom and was vaguely aware that what we were doing was reserved for boys and girls only; however, this logical thinking didn't sway my behavior or my enjoyment of it.

I suppose we would have kissed forever had not Bonnies's Grandmother called her in to go home. The only sissy girl I had known, who liked me exactly as I was and with whom I had not felt awkward, was leaving. I would never forget Bonnie or her lips on mine, but I never shared my wonderful afternoon with anybody, not even Mom. Something inside warned against such candor.

By now I was beginning to realize, more deeply, that I was somehow different from other girls. This fact made me feel proud because I didn't want to be considered a sissy girl. Maybe it was OK for the other girls, but not for me. I took pride in my ability to play ball and my rough and tumble manner. Yet, I longed to find another girl who was like me. I prayed for such a girl and my prayer was answered.

One rainy afternoon when I was restless from being shut indoors, Mom took me to see a movie about a frontier woman named Calamity Jane. I loved western movies so watched quietly and intently. As the movie progressed I noticed a similarity between Calamity Jane and myself. She was no sissy and the realization that I was not alone gave me a feeling of elation. I couldn't believe my prayer was being answered and reveled in the wonderful warm feeling that spread throughout my body.

On the trip home from the movie and for weeks to come I could not get this fabulous frontier woman, or the actress who portrayed her, out of my mind. However, as with Bonnie, I never spoke my feelings to anyone. Again, something told me I should remain quiet.

* * * * * * * * * *

Les was the new boy in my fourth grade class. I couldn't resist his pretty baby face and clear blue eyes. The fact that he was tiny, like me, only enhanced my feelings.

As we walked to school each morning our affection grew. Considering our feelings it was only natural that we decided to get married. Only the class dunce stood in our way.

Walter was a fat kid who stuttered, spit uncontrollably, always appeared dirty and was madly in love with me. Les and I had to think fast or our future would be ruined so we decided to kill Walter. Our plan was for me to marry Walter just to keep him quiet. At the wedding reception Walter would eat the poison cake Les and I would make and die. Les and I would then be free to marry and live happily ever after.

Each day Les and I sat at our desks preparing the poison for the wedding cake by scraping rubber erasures on our desks and mixing the shreds into the inkwells. Our plan couldn't fail.

Being brought up in a strict Christian atmosphere I knew that Les and I were committing a grave sin. I should have merely told Walter I didn't love him instead of committing such an act of violence, but I couldn't assert myself in this manner. It seemed kinder to kill Walter than to hurt his feelings.

Fortunately, God must have been keeping careful watch, for my evil deed was never committed and my marriage never actualized. Shortly before the wedding to Les was to commence my parents moved the family from Queens to eastern Long Island where my father had been permanently transferred by his company.

Chapter 3: 1955

   Moving can be a traumatic experience for a child of nine, but not for me. I had few friends to miss and though I was saddened at the thought of leaving my beloved Les, I quickly forgot him, consoled by the fact that my family was moving to the country, which I had come to love from our weekly visits to Grandma Liebegott's. We would not be living on a farm, as she, but the same fresh air and open space was there for me to devour.

   Sixty miles east of Queens, on the north shore of Long Island, lay the tiny rural town of Shoreham, our new home. Our six-room ranch was one of only ten houses standing in the newly developed community. Streets, which bordered every lawn, aroused my curiosity. How anyone could get around without sidewalks to lead the way, I thought, feeling wonderfully free from the dried out pieces of concrete.

   Every direction I looked brought the feeling of communing with nature. Trees and dense woods surrounded our house, which sat on one third of an acre of land. I could hear the trees beckon me to live among them and my heart quickened with the thought of the many adventures awaiting me.

   Suddenly I realized that riding my bike was going to be thrilling because the one lane, narrow road undulated with hills. It would be like riding a roller coaster and my excitement intensified. Within walking distance of my new home lay the most wonderful benefit of living in our new community. Beneath five hundred feet of sand dunes lay the clear, blue-green water of Long Island Sound. Its pebbled beach and clean air enticed all to love and enjoy its beauty and respite from the hot summer sun. I felt like Adam and Eve must have, for this place was truly paradise.

   A house almost identical to mine stood across the road. As I walked to the road for a closer inspection, a little boy, whom I would come to know as Jason, darted from the back door of his house. He was no older or bigger than me and I was filled with joy at the thought of making a new friend.

    Jason peered curiously at my house and then at me, as if he knew I belonged. I waved to him and he returned my friendliness by jumping in back of a nearby bush pretending, with his hand, to shoot a gun at me. I took his cue and without saying a word fired my finger gun in his direction, joyously thinking, "This truly is the Garden of Eden." Yet, even Eden was destroyed.

* * * * * * * * *

    It was through Jason that I met his sister Carrie and that's when it happened. Perhaps it was caused by my ever-present shyness with girls or maybe it was caused by Carrie's confident manner. Whatever the reason, I could not cope with what was happening. My legs felt like jelly, my heart raced within my chest and the strange tingling sensation that ran through my entire body was frightening. I prayed my skinny legs would support me as the "funny feeling" persisted.

    Carrie was a pretty girl; the prettiest girl I'd ever met, despite her baby fat. She was a couple of inches taller than me and about a year older. Her brown, wavy hair was cut just below her ears and her eyes, spaced wide over a tiny pug nose, were the same color as her hair.

    She seemed in a hurry that first meeting for she quickly and confidently said "hi" and disappeared. I was grateful our meeting had been brief because I didn't think I could take anymore of the "funny feeling" shooting through my body, but I vowed to have more control in the future for I knew I had to have Carrie for my best friend.

* * * * * * * * *

In the weeks that followed I tried, without being obvious, to be around Carrie as much as possible, obsessed with making her my friend. However, this wasn't easy and the result of my endeavors was depressingly fruitless. The "funny feeling" appeared at the slightest thought of her and talking to her was almost impossible. I managed to say "hi" each morning while we waited for the school bus, but I didn't join her as she stood with her girlfriends. As usual, I was drawn to the boy's group where I felt comfortable and could observe Carrie from a safe distance.

Our bus stop was at the corner of a small farm from where we could see a pasture containing a small pond and some horses. After a couple of days of observing Carrie talking to the horses, trying to make them come close enough so she could pet them, I worked up the courage to leave my boy friends and go to the fence where she stood. The "funny feeling" surged through my body. I could hardly breathe, but I did manage a few words in the direction of the gray mare, trying to act cool, as if I was only interested in the horse.

When the mare moved towards us I started to panic. She was enormous and I was afraid she'd come through the barbwire fence. Outwardly I remained calm, for it would not have helped my battle to win Carrie's friendship if she saw my fear. She'd have thought me a city slicker and I couldn't make her think negatively about me.

Carrie was ecstatic when the horse came to the fence where we stood. She leaned forward to stroke its head, eyes filled with delight. Then she turned and smiled at me. I thought my heart would leap from my chest. I had pleased her, at least for the moment.

The school bus came down the road and without a word Carrie returned to her girl friends, leaving me to bid farewell to my gray comrade. For a moment the chasm between Carrie and me had been closed, giving me hope that someday we would be good friends. However, I knew someday would be a long way off and I'd have to be patient, accepting the few close moments I was allowed to share with her.

The growing friendship of Hank and Brett helped me handle the situation with Carrie. The boys couldn't stand any of the girls. I suppose because they couldn't play baseball like me. With Hank and Brett I was an equal. I was one of them and I loved the freedom it brought. In their company I could forget Carrie and concentrate on the activities that, up until she came into my life, had been foremost in my mind.

* * * * * * * * *

School was out for the summer giving me time to explore my new surroundings. About one hundred feet behind my house lay a sand pile, flattened by many hours of children's play and a large 'V' shaped tree just perfect for the tree house that Hank, Brett and I erected in one day. Hank had supervised its construction while Brett and I did the hard work, but we hadn't arranged it this way just because Hank was the smartest. He was also the most inept. With one swing of the hammer he'd struck dead on his thumb and could not do anymore manual labor.

Besides playing in our tree house or playing baseball, we spent every summer day rollicking at the beach. My city pallor turned brown and the soles of my feet hardened from running on the pebbled beach.

Carrie was at the beach, too, playing sissy games with her girl friends, making it difficult for me to concentrate on Hank and Brett. Sissies though the girls were I wanted to join because I had to be a part of Carrie's world.

I began to show off, hoping to impress Carrie so she would ask me to join her group, but hard as I tried, nothing seemed to penetrate her aloof barrier. It was Janet, the smallest of Carrie's friends, who, unknowingly, came to my rescue when a brightly colored beach ball, with which the girls had been playing, flew onto my blanket. Janet came to fetch it, smiling at me as she drew near. She waved 'hi' and I coyly returned her friendly gesture. We began exchanging pleasantries. Janet was easy to talk to; actually you listened, most of the time, for she was a chatterbox.

After a couple of minutes of conversation we heard Carrie yelling for Janet to hurry up with the ball. Janet turned, then stopped and asked me to come along. The "funny feeling" shot through my body at the thought, but before I knew it I had said yes. Two seconds later I was laughing and screaming with pleasure, forgetting about Hank and Brett.

All the girls in Carrie's group were nice and though I could never feel as close to them as I wanted to be with her, I enjoyed their company. They made it easier to be around Carrie.

Janet was the smallest and youngest girl in the group. Her happy giggle and bright personality brought the group to life. Next to Carrie I liked Janet the best, not only being drawn by her cheerful personality, but also to her tom boyishness. She made me feel less conspicuous.

Penny was a little younger than me, but bigger in height and weight. She was the quiet one, almost as shy as me. Nevertheless, she was a sweet girl and made me feel welcome.

Nora was my age and a bit chubby. Her face was pretty, but her personality was sometimes irritating because she was a Pollyanna. Whenever the girls made a remark that Nora thought unkind or naughty she'd become indignant and scold them.

I spent the remainder of the summer dividing my time between the boys and the girls, each of whom couldn't stand the other, but both of whom accepted me. My shyness began to fade, although it was still almost impossible for me to relate to Carrie. She was pleasant and sometimes I could feel shreds of friendliness from her, but for the most part she remained reserved and aloof, leaving me frustrated. The "funny feeling" subsided some within the safety of the group, but left alone with Carrie or whenever she singled me out in conversation, the "funny feeling" surged, making me feel self-conscious and strangely frightened.

Chapter 4: 1956

   The days were filled with school and homework leaving little time for socialization. Days turned into weeks and before I knew it another summer of lazy days in which to grow closer to Carrie, who with the warmth of the summer sun had become a little friendlier. It wasn't much, but I clung to hope.
   This was the summer I was elected secretary to the "Bird Brain Club" over which Carrie presided. We met everyday to plan our summer activities. The bake sale at the beginning of summer gave us the funds to plan a camp out in the woods behind my house, where a grove had been cleared by the constant activity of the boys and me. Sometime before a tree had fallen, providing us with fabulous wooden horses when we played cowboys or the most modern space ship for our more scientific play. At the base of the fallen tree we made camp.
   The day had been warm and as dusk neared the sun blazed red-orange in the sky. We ate cold chicken for dinner and when the night turned dark we sat around the campfire toasting marshmallows. The atmosphere was light and I felt relaxed within the safety of the group, where I could show off without Carrie knowing it was for her benefit and without letting her know she was my favorite.
   The night turned black and the stars shined brightly. We were all exhausted from the events of the evening so we turned in. Soon everyone was asleep; everyone except me. All had gone so well. Carrie has been exceptionally friendly to me. I should have slept like a baby, but I lay awake unable to control a strange feeling of fear.
   A few hours before dawn, exhaustion took over and I fell asleep. I woke shortly after, feeling the same fear I had felt earlier. All I could think about was Mom, my own bed and my desire to be home.

Quickly I rose, got my things together, careful not to wake the girls and left for the safety only Mom could provide. She never questioned why I'd come home so early and I never told her of my fear. How could I when I couldn't explain it myself?

* * * * * * * * *

With the camp out safely tucked away in the past, the "Bird Brain Club" undertook a production of "Rumplestilskin". Since we had a limited supply of willing boys to act, I cheerfully volunteered to play the part of the charming prince.

Rehearsals were a lot of fun and I found myself becoming a ham. All the girls seemed to enjoy my antics, including Carrie. I relaxed more, loving every moment of the play and Carrie's directorial attention.

Sometimes I'd drive her crazy with my excessive joking, especially during the scene in which the prince was to kiss the lovely heroine, played by Janet. Actually I was quite nervous about having to kiss Janet, remembering how much I'd enjoyed it with Bonnie. I didn't want the girls to know my secret. By fooling around during this scene I never actually kissed Janet.

The night of the play I was in a state of hysterics for it finally dawned on me that I couldn't joke my way through the kissing scene as I had during rehearsals. Our performance was a serious matter and I wanted it to be a success. Again God came to my rescue for as the kissing scene drew near I was engulfed by a brainstorm that would solve the problem. I spoke my lead-in lines, bent down to kiss Janet and quickly put my hand over her mouth, kissing the back of my own hand. The audience never saw my clever distortion of the scene, the play was a success and my baffling secret remained in tact.

Chapter 5: 1956-57

Weeks turned into months with little progress in winning Carrie's friendship. As soon as I felt us becoming close she seemed to back away. I grew tired of the constant frustration she had brought into my life and found myself drifting away from her into a fantasy world in which the two of us were inseparable. At night, before I went to bed, my thoughts were filled with Carrie and sometimes I'd sit in my room playing my ukulele, singing to her.

This new behavior perplexed me. I knew that no other girl behaved as I. Even Calamity Jane didn't sing to another girl, at least not the kind of songs I was singing. Mine were songs of love.

My difference was becoming more confusing. There was no use in rationalizing anymore. The fault lay in me, not other girls. This fact became unquestionably real not only because of my new behavior, but also by the ridicule some of the boys at school threw at me. I heard them laughing at me, calling me "boy" or "tomboy" and could not deny the truth in their mockery. I'd always known I acted more like a boy, but until now I'd been proud of this fact. Shame became integrated with my pride and the vague fear that had surfaced a few times in the past became my constant, unwanted companion.

My language began to reflect my distress. With my parents and other adults my demeanor remained angelic, but among my peers I cursed like a truck driver and acted tough, hoping to soften the sting of the insults and gain some respect through this hard, impenetrable façade.

I felt terrible guilt because I was behaving the total opposite of how I'd religiously been raised. I hoped and prayed that God would understand and forgive. I wanted to be a good Christian, but people just wouldn't let me be myself. This became crystal clear one summer afternoon as Hank, Brett and I play a game of war, in Hank's backyard. We were portraying the men who held the flag at Iwo Jima, climbing over each other, arms and legs interwoven.

At the point when we fell on top of each other, playing dead, Hank's mother yelled out the kitchen window, "Be careful boys. Don't play so rough. Jan is a girl and you'll hurt her."

I felt as if a truck had hit me. What difference did my being a girl make? I wasn't getting hurt, never had, so why was Mrs. Gregory getting so upset? I couldn't play anymore so I made up an excuse to go home, hoping my friends had not noticed how upset I was. I hated any show of weakness in myself and to let anyone see it was unthinkable.

On the short walk home, which seemed an endless journey, I couldn't rid my mind of the events that had taken place. I knew I was a girl, but I hated being treated like a fragile doll. In some ways I wanted to be a boy. They had no restrictions. I was at ease with myself and my body did what I wanted it to do. It was just that people, like Mrs. Gregory, treated me like a weakling just because I was female. I felt as strong and as capable as the boys. Why couldn't others just leave it at that?

The vague fear reared its horrible head telling me something was definitely wrong. What though? Was there really cause to worry? No! I would not allow myself to be swayed by other people. I was merely diversified in my talents and if people couldn't accept that in me then something was wrong with them. Why couldn't people just leave me alone? Why did I have to choose between boy and girl behaviors?

"Dear God in Heaven, help me! I hurt. I don't know what's wrong and I don't want to be a bad person. I don't want to hurt you, Lord. Please tell me what's going on. Tell me how I can stop what's ripping me apart." I prayed, but no answer came.

* * * * * * * *

On a hazy summer afternoon as Brett and I played by our fallen tree, Wally Harris, a tough kid from school, barged in on us. I had never liked Wally because he had a dirty mouth matched only by his dirty appearance.

With his usual bravado he began carving in our fallen tree, desecrating its beauty. Brett and I looked at each other full of curiosity, but Wally would not let us see his carved masterpiece until it was complete.

The minutes crawled by as Wally diligently worked. Suddenly he stepped back proudly, allowing us to read the words he had carved:

FUCK THE CUNT

I was shocked and disgusted at the words, but laughed to maintain my tough façade. Neither Brett nor I knew what the words meant, except that they were dirty, so Wally graphically told us, "You see, the man lays on top of the woman and sticks his prick into her cunt. Then he shoves it in and out and then his prick shoots out creamy stuff into her cunt. That's how she gets knocked up."

Up until that moment I believed that when a man and a woman married, babies automatically appeared without any kind of mechanics. Apparently Brett was as unaware as I for he looked at me in astonishment and we uttered, in unison, "Oh no, that can't be!"

* * * * * * * * * *

The frustration I was feeling outside my house was matched by the tension growing from within my home. Dad's brother, my Uncle John, had admitted himself into a hospital and was receiving some kind of therapy called "shock". Dad must have gone into some sort of shock, too, for he had changed. He spent less time with me now, preferring to sit with a couple of bottles of beer, staring out the living room picture window. Most nights he'd go to bed before me, talking to himself in a whisper as he walked, unsteadily, to his room.

At first it wasn't too bad watching him succumb to the beer, but the night of his office's annual Christmas party my naive eyes opened to the seriousness of his drinking.

Paul and I had been sent to bed around 10 pm, but I couldn't sleep. Dad had promised Mom he'd be home early and as the night grew late and Dad didn't come home, Mom became angry. From my bedroom I could hear her pacing in the kitchen, slamming the cabinets. I'd never seen her so mad and prayed Dad would hurry home so she'd calm down.

I drifted into a restless sleep, waking around 2 in the morning to the sound of men singing outside my house. As I started to get out of bed, to see who it was, Paul came into my room, obviously upset, rambling on that it was Dad and his boss and that they were very drunk. Paul and I ran into the living room where we saw Mom bent over the front door steps. She was trying to lift Dad off the stoop. His nose was bleeding from his fall and he was crying, "Forgive me."

Mom turned to Dad's boss and in a harsh voice, one I'd never heard before, told him to get out of her house. When he left she helped Dad into the bedroom, stopping in front of Paul and me to tell us to get back to our rooms.

Wide-awake in my room I could hear Mom getting Dad into bed. Her voice was high pitched and angry as she threatened to divorce him if he ever did this again.

Dad became quiet so I opened my bedroom door to go out and be with Mom, whom I could hear in the living room, but when I saw her pulling out the sofa bed I thought I'd better leave her alone.

That was the first time I'd heard my parents fight and the first time I'd seen them sleep apart.

Chapter 6: 1958

It was a dreary Friday the thirteenth, just one week after I'd begun eighth grade that I stayed home from school with a cold.

Sick days at home were a favorite time for me because I had Mom all to myself. She'd take such good care of me, bathing me with the kind of attention I craved. It was like having an all day picnic. We'd watch TV, play games and eat sandwiches that Mom cut into "soldier boys" attempting to entice my picky appetite. Every couple of hours she'd rub my neck and chest with Vicks to help me breathe easier, singing a silly song about three men in a tub all stuffed up like me. I just loved being home with Mom, even if I was sick.

By night my cold worsened and I fell into a trouble sleep. Sometime during the night the shaking of my bed wakened me. Fear turned to panic as I realized that the shaking was coming from inside my body.

"Dear God, it's my heart!" It was pounding so hard and racing so fast I could feel it in every part of my body. "God in Heaven, please don't let me die!"

Mom heard me the first time I yelled for her and came into my room.

"I can't stop my heart from beating", I said hysterically.

Mom walked to my side and took my wrist in her hand, calmly telling me not to worry. I followed her instruction to hold my breath in order to slow my heart rate, but each time I exhaled it would accelerate. Minutes ticked by slowly and my heart would not return to normal. Mom took me into her bedroom, ordering Dad to sleep in my bed.

At this point I knew I was seriously sick, but gained some comfort from lying next to Mom. If I was going to die I wanted the person I loved the most to be with me. With Mom's hand on my wrist, monitoring my heart rate, I drifted into the darkness of night.

I awoke at dawn and the pounding was gone.

"Thank God," I thought with relief, "I'm better."

I reached for my wrist so I could feel the slowed heart beat, but when I touched it I began to shake again. My heart was racing so fast it felt like one continuous beat. In panic I woke Mom. Again she tried to calm me, but I didn't feel confident when she called Dr. Seth. I knew Mom wouldn't do this unless she was worried, too.

Mom returned to the bedroom with the news I fearfully expected. Dr. Seth wanted me at the hospital immediately. Mom dressed me in warm winter clothes over my pajama, despite the fact that it was only September, while Dad started the car. All this rushing intensified my feeling that I was surely going to die.

As we drove to the hospital I began to think that soon I would wake from this horrible nightmare and be safe at home, cradled in Mom's arms, but the medieval form of Mather Memorial Hospital loomed into view forcing me to abandon my comforting fantasy. A chill shot through me as I contemplated my impending separation from Mom, a thought that caused as much fear as the pounding in my chest.

Smiling warmly, Dr. Seth greeted us at the door of the hospital and, with the help of an orderly, place me on a gurney. Mom and Dad stayed with Dr. Seth while the orderly wheeled me into a ward in the corner wing. The room was immense, containing six beds, two of which were hidden behind drawn curtains. I had never slept anywhere but in my small, one bed, room and I knew I wasn't going to like the present crowded surroundings. The pastel blue color of the walls did nothing to make me feel comfortable and the groan from behind one of the drawn curtains made my blood freeze.

The gurney stopped beside a bed in the corner of the room next to a window that overlooked the parking lot where our car sat waiting for me in vain. The bars on the gurney were lowered and the orderly lifted me onto the starched white hospital bed. I felt as if I had been laid into a casket and my body began to shake more violently. I wanted Mom, but she was nowhere in sight. Tears rolled down my cheeks as scores of doctors and nurses tended me. From the hallway I could hear Dr. Seth yelling at a nurse because she had been tardy with my medication.

"Dear God in Heaven," I thought, "I must really be in serious shape for him to yell like that."

Technicians came in taking blood from me by what seemed like the gallon. They put tiny metal buttons, attached to a wire that ran to a large machine, on my chest. Nurses came in every few minutes to swill pills down my throat. Prior to this I had been incapable of swallowing pills, but after chewing my first dose of quinine and subsequently vomiting, I easily swallowed any pill given.

After what seemed an eternity, Mom appeared. With a smile on her face and no sign of crying or worry, she came towards my bed and embraced me. My fear subsided. As long as she was near I'd have the strength to hold on and fight. I wanted her to hold me forever.

Dad came in for a minute, but looked stiff and was red in the face like I'd seen him, many times before, when we visited Uncle John in the mental hospital. I knew Dad didn't like hospitals or sickness so understood when he kissed my cheek and said goodbye. It didn't matter. All I needed was Mom.

I talked little, trying to gain comfort from Mom's words, hoping that her optimism was true, depressed with the reality that she would soon have to leave me, a prisoner in my sterile coffin.

A few minutes after Mom's departure I looked out my window and waved weakly at her diminishing figure, though she couldn't see me. As I watched her car speed down the road, away from my grasp, tears streamed down my face. The pounding in my body made the sheet that covered me quiver violently. I knew that even if I was lucky enough to live, I'd surely be an invalid the rest of my life. I didn't know which thought I liked better.

The hours drifted by under a barrage of tests and pills. I was getting used to the pounding in my chest and the pills had eased me. Though drowsy, I could not sleep so I played a game with the water in the pitcher next to my bed. Sticking two fingers into the water and then placing the drops on my wrist, I pretended the drops were men racing to the finish line which was the crease in my elbow. A silly game, that was to lead the nurses to believe I was delirious, but it made the time pass.

During my play I noticed a window about twenty feet across from my bed. I peered through and realized it was a private room occupied by a young woman. As I wondered what this woman's illness was a nurse entered pushing a glass object that looked like a fish tank. When something moved within it I gasped. I'd never seen a baby that small. He was no bigger than my foot.

Hospital grapevines are a known phenomenon so it wasn't long before I learned that the mother and baby were sick and there was little hope the baby would live. All day I watched the baby, hoping and praying that his tiny body would have the strength to fight his illness, feeling a bond form between this helpless child of God and myself.

Two days passed with no decrease in my heart rate. It kept pounding at a speed of 220 beats per minute, 140 beats above normal. All my tests had returned negative and Dr. Seth was encouraged, though confused. Medication was changed every few hours with no positive results. My spirits descended as I worried how long my heart could race at such a speed.

I looked toward the room where the wrinkled, red baby lay fighting for his life and was shocked to see two orderlies washing down the walls. It was evident. The baby had died. I cried out for him and for myself as I wondered if my fate would be the same as his.

Tears burned my cheeks as I pleaded and bargained with God, "Dear Lord, I know I've been bad, cursed too much, acted too tough, but I promise to be good, change my ways, never curse again, if only You will make me well."

On the third day of my hospital stay my heart slowed to 90 beats per minutes. Dr. Seth had given me a medication made from the root of a snake plant and this sedative worked. When Mom came to visit that night I greeted her with a long awaited smile.

Dr. Seth told us that with time, rest and medication I would get well, although he could not tell how long that would take. He didn't know what had caused my illness, but guessed it was merely nerves associated with puberty. I would recover, but had to lay off sports for an indeterminable period of time. I was happy to be alive, but the thought of even a couple of weeks without sports in my life was unbearable.

On the fifth day of my hospital stay a young girl was admitted to my ward, leg heavy laden with plaster. Patty was only a year older than my twelve years, but well into the pubescent stage of life that had, thus far, eluded me, despite what Dr. Seth had said. I was flat as a board, had not begun to menstruate and had the fuzz of a peach between my legs.

Patty's short, dark, straight hair accentuated her pretty face. Her smile was warm and quick, occasionally twitching from the pain in her broken leg. Feeling as lonely as I, we reached out to each other and became friends. I hadn't the strength to negatively react to her sissy nature. I needed someone to talk with and Patty was there for me. With her companionship my spirits began to skyrocket and my heath improved.

Seeing the healthy effect Patty had on me the nurses pushed our beds together so we could play cards. The dreariness and isolation of the hospital began to fade. In spite of the fact that Patty was a girl and we were not playing baseball, I was having a good time. She was a breath of fresh, non-antiseptic air.

The second day after Patty's arrival a young doctor came into our ward. I'd seen him before and had instantly disliked him, not knowing why. He walked over to Patty's bed and without drawing the curtain, pulled her hospital gown down and proceeded to tap on her breasts. Instantly I knew why I had disliked him. I'd always thought he looked at the female nurses in a dirty way. Anyway, Patty turned beet red. I was revolted, not by the sight of Patty's breasts, for they were soft and womanly and I felt somewhat guilty for enjoying them, but by the nerve of this doctor. After all, Patty had a broken leg not a busted boob so why was he giving her a feel? I felt like puking at his forceful entry and vowed to kick him in his balls if he ever tried that with me.

Patty was discharged from the hospital on Friday morning, the day before I was scheduled to go home. I felt sad, but took comfort in the knowledge that the next day I would be as lucky as she.

Our good-bye was a tearful one. We had grown into such good friends during her short stay and I was going to miss her. Patty came to my bedside, leaned down, for she was now on crutches and touched her lips to my cheek. I threw my arms around her returning her warmth.

Minutes later I was alone again, but with the thought of my wonderful friend and the reality of going home I was content.

That night when the lights were out my hand drifted between my legs. I knew this was an awful sin, but I'd been doing it for years. Furthermore, I knew I shouldn't do it because it would make my heart go fast, but I was going home in the morning and it was a time for celebration. Surely a little would not hurt.

After I was satisfied, despite my usual feelings of guilt, I fell into a deep, restful sleep.

The next morning I awoke, excited about going home, when suddenly the pounding began.

"Oh no, not again," I thought hysterically.

I called the nurse and after a while Dr. Seth came in, checked me over and said I'd have to stay a few more days. Then I heard him, off down the hall, yelling, "And get her out of that ward. It's too much for her nerves!" I began to cry.

Resting in my semi-private room with a lovely, quiet woman for a roommate, I began to relax and my heart returned to a normal rate.

I turned towards the wall and prayed, "Dear God, this is what I get for celebrating last night and I deserve it. I have sinned against You after I'd promised to be good." My heart was penitent as I vowed never to commit this dreadful sin again.

My recuperation continued in the peacefulness of my new room and on Tuesday I was discharged, with instructions to rest, stay in bed and avoid excitement. It was a depressing way to live, but at least I'd be home with Mom.

Chapter 7: 1958

My convalescence was a slow one. The first two weeks I was bedridden, except for bathroom privileges. Four times a day Mom would check my heart rate, reporting to Dr. Seth every few days.

By the end of two weeks Dr. Seth, pleased with my progress and the apparent success of the medication prescribed, lifted some restrictions. I was now allowed to watch TV and walk around. Also, I was to be taken out of the house.

Since another girl, whom I knew from church, was also convalescing at her home, only ten minutes from mine, Mom would drive me over so Jessica and I could have some same-aged companionship. Mom and Jessica's mother, Rebecca, were acquainted, but while Jessica and I talked and played gentle board games, they became close friends.

Jessica was a remarkable girl. She was a year older than me, but in the same grade. Jessica had contracted polio when she was five; so severe she required an iron lung for a time. Her right arm was completely paralyzed and had atrophied over the years, but it was amazing how much she could do with her lifeless arm. It seemed not a handicap at all.

Jessica was recuperating from spinal surgery to alleviate a severe case of scoliosis brought on by the polio. Her body, which was fragile and painfully thin, now lay immobilized in a cast that went from just below her neck to her waist. I couldn't imagine how she lived so confined, but she never complained. She was never anything but happy and grateful to be alive. Her positive attitude made me ashamed of the self-pity I had wallowed in of late and she gave me the spirit to start fighting back.

We talked of many things, but mostly about the spiritual side of life. Jessica believed in God and was a follower of Jesus, as I, but her faith was far more mature than mine or anybody else our age.

Her constant optimism, humor and joy filled me with a sense of confidence. The going would be rough for me, but it was rougher for Jessica. If she could remain optimistic I could, too. At least I'd try. Jessica's faith and courage were an inspiration that I would draw upon all the days of my life.

Chapter 8: 1958-1959

Returning to school after a month long convalescence was a traumatic experience. The weeks of solitude combined with the devastating effects of my illness made it difficult to relate to my teachers and classmates. I felt isolated in a school full of healthy kids who were all too aware of my demeaning limitations.

Though Dr. Seth assured me that, in time, I would be able to return to participating in sports, he could not give me a specific date. Furthermore, he cautioned that I would always have to set limitations on my activities. It was good to be alive, but the thought of a life full of limitations kept me in a state of depression I had to continually battle.

What was even more depressing was the knowledge that even when I was allowed to return to sports I would never recapture the life I had once known and loved. I learned that you couldn't go back when Hank and Brett came to visit me on my return home from the hospital. I guess they sensed my loss, too, for my buddies couldn't relate to me, acting tense and all too gentle.

I couldn't blame them, though, for by virtue of my illness I had joined the ranks of a sissy girl. Without sports in my life even I wondered what good I was. Surely they must have thought the same. I was now a weak, fragile girl, just like Hank's mother had said a short while ago and I hated the reality that had been forced upon me.

I was out of the hospital, back with Mom and going to school. I was back among the living, but unable to accept my half existence, despite the encouragement and love I received from Mom and Jessica.

During those early weeks of school I was forever panicking, afraid my heart would race out of control, sending me back to the hospital, this time never to return. By now I was so aware of my heart I could feel it beating all the time and could instantly tell how fast it was going without looking at a clock. Sometimes, in those early weeks, it would beat as fast as 130 times a minute, which was much slower than when I was in the hospital, but I'd start to shake with fear that it would go faster. All I could think of was Mom and I'd walk, as fast as I was allowed, to the nearest telephone. Hearing Mom's tender, reassuring voice gave me the courage to push myself through the day despite my burning need to go home to the safety only Mom could provide.

The days dragged on, but somehow I grew accustomed to my heart's frequent outburst of speed and my panic began to fade, along with my racing heart. My confidence grew, but it was to be short lived, for as my heart calmed and ceased to upset me, my stomach began to trouble me. By first period I'd be sick. Soon after, I'd be in the nurse's office. I began to spend more time with her than in my classes. Not only did I feel nauseous, but sometimes I'd feel faint and other times I had a strange feeling of not being real. It felt as if I was dreaming.

Sometimes the nurse would send me home thinking my symptoms were caused by a virus, but the minute I set foot in my house I'd feel fine and would devour the lunch I couldn't have eaten an hour earlier.

My grades began to suffer and, even though it was still early in the school year, I worried about graduating because I saw no release from the ill feelings that inhibited me. I feared I had cancer, but the doctors could find nothing wrong. Nothing helped except being home with Mom. I lived in terror, praying for weekends and holidays so I wouldn't have to leave the safety of Mom's world.

Halfway through the school year, which was becoming a complete disaster, I met Heather. With long, straight, shining black hair, surrounding a face of olive complexion and piercing black eyes, Heather's Greek heritage was beautifully displayed. Inside, Heather was just as beautiful. Sweet and understanding, she made me feel secure.

A child of a broken home (Heather's father had left a year before our meeting), Heather had as many problems as I. I suppose it was our problems that drew us together, for our friendship grew fast. Everyday we'd have lunch together, talking about the difficulties in our lives, gaining strength from each other. It felt good to unload the confusion and fear that had overcome me the past couple of years; feelings I'd never even discussed with Mom. Heather empathized with my anguish over Dad's drinking, his berating of women, which made me feel cheated in life and his sudden interest in peaking at my naked body, which had finally begun to develop. Heather's caring attitude helped me from completely yielding to the frustration and loneliness that loomed over me.

Yet, as close as I felt to Heather I could not bring myself to tell her of the "funny feeling" that had plagued me the last three years. Part of my silence was due to my inability to understand or verbalize it, but the other reason for my silence was because the "funny feeling" had hit me the first day I met Heather. In addition, the fact that I felt so comfortable with Heather confused me. How could I grow close to her while experiencing the "feeling" when it had inhibited my relationship with Carrie? Nothing made sense to me so I kept this one secret locked away, lest I upset Heather and send her running from me.

The days passed swiftly and my health improved. I attended school regularly, anxious to see Heather. My grades improved and in June of 1959 I miraculously, though barely, graduated from eighth grade.

Contemplating a summer of separation from Heather, who lived miles from me, made me fearful. I still saw Jessica and gained strength from her, but Heather was different. I needed Heather by my side as I faced the first summer in my changed condition. I was scared that I wouldn't be able to relate to Carrie, the girls, Hank and Brett. Also, I worried I would not be able to adapt to a summer as passive onlooker instead of active participant.

* * * * * * * * *

 I couldn't tell you how it began or why. Maybe Heather's influence stayed with me, despite her absence. Maybe it was Jessica's love. Maybe it was my forced life of gentility. Maybe it was just the warm, therapeutic summer sun. Whatever the reason, my summer started off on a good note. Hank and Brett no longer came to my door yelling for me to come out and play ball, but they still wanted me for their friend. Like me, they had changed. Hank had developed a strong interest in the game of chess, among other board games and we spent many hours involved in these games. He still occasionally played ball, but seemed more content to spend his time with me, engaged in mental competition. Hank had always been different than the other boys. Now I could communicate with him on his level.

 Sometimes Brett joined us, but when he tired of our tedious and ever so gently play, he would call on my brother. A strong friendship began to grow between them and this meant the world to me. Paul had always been such a loner, content to read and, of late, work-out with barbells. I worried about him because of his shy, introverted way, but when he started hanging out with Brett, who was quite an extrovert, Paul's personality grew. The two of them were inseparable and their antics kept me joyfully occupied. At the beach they became acrobatic clowns, diving off each other's shoulders into the water. Sometimes Hank would join their masculine play, but his lack of grace and inability to be rough made me laugh till my sides ached.

 When the hot sun cooled, Brett would spend his evenings in our backyard continuing his comical routines with Paul. Life certainly wasn't the same since I couldn't participate; however, it wasn't as frustrating as I thought it would be.

 As in the past, I divided my time equally between the boys and the girls. However, it was easier to enjoy the girls now. My illness had forced me to give in to the more gentle side of life.

Cake sales and lazy days chatting under a cool tree were more in line with my physical abilities. It didn't seem stimulating at first, but as the days passed I found myself at ease, even with Carrie. The "funny feeling" had strangely vanished and I could finally talk to her without discomfort.

Carrie had changed, too. Sometimes I'd thought that my inability to get close to her was due to a snobbish streak that ran through her, but as I spent more time with Carrie I realized she was just a very quiet, shy person. A warm friendship began to burgeon. My dream of the past three years was finally coming true and I vowed to be the best friend Carrie would ever have.

Carrie and I drifted away from the other girls and I drifted away from Hank and Brett. The inseparability I had dreamed of was becoming a reality, but it was sealed on a muggy August day as Carrie and I walked on our beach, surveying the damage a hurricane had ravished the day before.

"Jan, I've got something to tell you that I want kept a secret." She paused for a long moment and then continued, weakly, "My mother is pregnant. It wasn't planned, but it happened."

Her statement stunned me for Carrie's mother was over forty years old.

"Promise you won't tell a soul?" She pleaded.

"I promise."

"Thanks, Jan. You're the only one I'd ever tell this to."

At this statement I was so happy I wanted to wrap my arms around Carrie and kiss her, but the strange fear that lived within forced me to control my physical emotions. It didn't matter for at that moment I knew Carrie and I were friends for life. Nothing could come between us, for the sharing of such a confidence was an eternal bond.

* * * * * * * * *

The months passed quickly in joyous union with Carrie and her baby sister, Jenny, who was born in December 1959. Carrie was in high school now while I was still in junior high and since the schools were a few miles apart we didn't get to see each other during the day. However, we spent almost every night together taking care of little Jenny. She was the most adorable baby in the world. Her eyes were green, like a cat's and her strawberry blonde hair was straight and silky. She was extremely intelligent and never ceased to amaze me. I felt this child was ours. She was an extension of our friendship. We shared her, loved her, watched over her and helped her grow. The happiness that came into my life with Carrie and Jenny spilled over into my physical and mental health. I was still not allowed to participate in sports, but Dr. Seth has lifted more restrictions. No longer did I feel like an invalid. I knew it would not be long before I could play baseball again, although the thought of no more baseball was not quite as devastating as it had been. There were other things fulfilling me.

I attended school regularly and my grades improved remarkably. Jessica had returned to school after her year of recuperation and we spent most of our free time, at school, together. Our relationship became closer than ever. It was different than any I had ever experienced. I suppose that lay in the fact that with Jessica the spiritual part of me grew. I had always been a Christian, but Jessica inspired me by her close relationship with God. I admired her faith and prayed that the peace she'd found would be mine, too. Jessica had an influence on me that I could never adequately put into words, but one I would always cherish.

I still saw Heather everyday, but she had changed. She wasn't sweet anymore and neither were her new friends. She'd say "hi" when we passed in the hallway, but then she'd be off with her friends smoking in the bathroom or flirting with the boys. It amazed me how one short summer could make so many changes. Good ones for me, but not so good for Heather. I felt terrible for her and prayed God would help her find someone like Jessica to show her the way to Him.

* * * * * * * * *

An odd turnabout was happening during my ninth grade year. Prior to it I'd had no trouble attracting boys. Now I was acquiring an abundance of girls for friends while the boys drew away. Furthermore, boys and girls now wanted to be with each other in a way foreign to me. I couldn't understand why boys acted differently towards me than the other girls. When I was with the girls I'd try to conform to their preoccupation with boys, but it was difficult because I just didn't feel the way they did. Nonetheless, I kept on trying to get a boyfriend so I wouldn't be thought of as weird.

There was one nice boy in my math class, named Robbie, whom I decided to zoom in on even though he had a crush on Jean Garabaldi. I couldn't blame him if he ended up choosing her over me for Jean was very pretty. There was no contest. Regardless, I was determined to have this boy like me the way he liked Jean. I tried dazzling him with my sense of humor. He'd laugh at my jokes and clown-like behavior and tell me how funny I was. He seemed to like me, but didn't give me the kind of attention he gave to Jean.

The night of our class dance, which Jean did not attend, Robbie looked gorgeous in his light blue tuxedo. I tried to wait for his invitation to dance, but lost patience and started walking in his direction. Face to face with him I nervously asked him if he wanted to dance with me. To my horror he declined, saying that he didn't know how to dance.

I felt like a fool and withdrew to the bathroom. Later that evening I saw Robbie dancing, quite adroitly, with a very pretty girl. I was crushed. I couldn't imagine why he had rejected my invitation and then lied. I was a good catch. I was athletic and fun to be around. Robbie liked me, wasn't repulsed by me, so why wouldn't he dance with me?

I took my problem to Mom.

"None of the boys like me the way they like the other girls. They're friendly, but don't want to dance with me, much less date me. I must be the ugliest girl on the face of the earth." I said in desperation.

Mom's eyes turned angry and before I had a chance to retract my statement I felt the stinging slap of her hand across my face. Never before had she hit me in the face.

"Don't you ever say that again!" Mom was fuming. "That's an insult to me. I gave birth to you and I do not make ugly children!"

I was stunned, but she was right. My light brown hair, with its natural wave, light green eyes set above high cheekbones, just like Mom's, my cupid lipped mouth which broke into a warm smile and my slender yet well proportioned body did not spell ugly. Yet, if I was pretty why didn't the boys want to date me?

There were always questions with no answers.

Chapter 9: 1960

With ninth grade successfully completed I looked forward to the pleasure of spending the warm, sunny days with Carrie and Jennie. Each day I rose bright and early and ran to Carrie's house where we'd begin planning our adventurous day. Since Carrie's mother worked, our top priority was the care of little Jenny, a task that remained pure delight for me. I adored this little child and cherished the tender, loving moments she constantly supplied. More than this I loved the warm moments Carrie and I shared in our surrogate mother roles. Whether on the beach, watching Jenny as she splashed in the refreshing water of the Sound or sprawled on a blanket in Carrie's backyard, teaching Jenny social graces, we took pride in raising her. I could have lived this way forever.

* * * * * * * * *

This was the summer I became a member of Luther League, along with Jessica, a group comprised of all confirmed youth in the church for the enrichment of our spiritual lives and for plain old fun. It was a time for boy, girl mixing and the awful feeling of being left out overwhelmed me. The boys had a good time with me, but when it came to dancing I was left sitting in the corner. My feeling that there was something wrong with me grew more intense. Had it not been for Carrie and Jessica who, like me, lacked for male attention, I would have felt completely desolate.

Then Jim started coming to League. Jim was a city boy who spent his summers in our town. A big-framed kid with a mouth to match, I thought he was nothing but a conceited blow hard with the mentality of a two year old. However, Carrie felt differently and when Jim started paying attention to her, she responded. It wasn't long before they were dating. How could Carrie do this to me? How could she push me out of the number one position I had worked so hard to attain? Yet, Carrie was growing up and I couldn't begrudge her a boyfriend. I wanted Carrie to be happy. It's just that I thought she had been with me.

I never discussed these feelings with Jessica, sensitive to her position. She seemed to handle the situation so much better than I and I was ashamed. I hoped and prayed I could be happy for Carrie and Jim as I'm sure Jessica was.

The pain over the loss of Carrie was eased some when I met Cindy, the newest member of our community. Cindy was two years my junior and looked like a typical twelve-year-old kid, but her actions were those of a worldly woman. With flaming red hair, blue eyes and the flattest chest in town, she was soon to earn the reputation of town tramp. Nevertheless, I liked her. Actually it was more than this for the moment I laid eyes on her I was gripped by the "funny feeling". Eagerly I prepared to make Cindy my friend and since no other girls liked her, she responded to my warmth.

Where Carrie was conservative and quiet, Cindy was wild and extroverted. I found her exhilarating, though she represented everything I believed to be sinful.

Cindy made me the center of attention, even when she began dating Carrie's brother, Jason. I never felt second place when the three of us were together. However, Jason and Cindy intensified the fear that something was wrong with me because a few years before I had tried to make Jason my boyfriend, but he wanted no part of me. I wondered what Cindy had that I didn't.

Lately, to dispel these negative feelings I'd begun to think to myself, "Why do I want a boyfriend anyway? All boys do is treat you like a weak girl, unable to take care of yourself and the girls behave all frilly and helpless when they're with their boyfriends. It makes me sick and I'm thankful I don't have to go through such humiliation."

Truthfully, I couldn't see myself acting the way girls did with boys; behaving in such an inferior way. Yet, this kind of rebellious thinking made me feel guilty. According to the Bible women were to be submissive to men; respecting them as their "head". Dad had preached this to me since I was a child. I sincerely believed in the infallibility of God's Word, but I couldn't accept an inferior position. I fought God blindly, disagreeing with the omnipotent Being, growing sick at heart for my uncontrollable sin.

* * * * * * * * *

An infamous bar-room preacher, Dad made no bones about his beliefs. On many occasions I'd accompany him to the local bar where he'd down a few beers while I sipped a cola. At first I enjoyed these trips, feeling very grown up, but after a while I questioned Dad's preaching, wondering what right he had telling the men at the bar that they must mend their evil ways, while he sat drinking, more than modestly. Wasn't drinking in excess a sin, too? The Bible said so. How could Dad be so hypocritical and judgmental?

Dad's hypocrisy was beginning to show at home, too. It was a daily ritual for him to come home from work and go directly to the refrigerator for a beer. My jaw would tighten as I heard the bottle top pop from the pressure of the bubbly brew. By eight o'clock he was feeling the effects and so was I.

It would only take something on TV or a bad day at the office, when one of Dad's co-workers who "didn't know his ass from his elbow" had irritated him and he was on his soapbox. Sometimes I started him off by disagreeing with him and lately I was beginning to disagree with most everything he said. A discussion would ensue, which at first was quite friendly. I loved this stage because it was communicating on an intellectual and mature level, where I could state my opinions, which I, if not Dad, thought were valid.

As Dad drank his logic waned and my anger rose. The intellectual, rational discussion turned into a critical, demeaning argument. Dad never laid a hand on me in my life, but his tongue cut like a razor.

Our arguments went on for up to two hours with Mom off in another room avoiding our fireworks. At the time I felt she should have told Dad to lay off me and I resented her lack of interest in my welfare. When Mom took me aside and told me she agreed with me, most of the time, I grew confused. If she felt I was right why didn't she tell Dad to stop harassing me? Then my mind would stop as I remembered that women were to remain passive because the man is the "head" of the woman. Mom was only adhering to the Word of God. The Word I could not obey.

Dad and I had most of our arguments on the subject of men and women and the roles they must assume by virtue of God's Divine Will. Man, according to my father, who was full of divine wisdom, was the head of woman. I was a true believer in the Bible, fundamentalist too, but this one area caused me much anguish. When I'd tell Dad that something had to be misunderstood about these Biblical passages, he'd become irate. Not having the knowledge on how to interpret the Bible I could only argue in a vague and immature fashion, but I held firm, coming away from our battles feeling guilty and hopeless, praying for forgiveness, hoping that somehow I was right, but fearing I was truly inferior because of my gender.

All our arguments ended on the same note. Dad would be enraged and tell me there was something wrong with my faith. Then he'd go to bed, sometimes mumbling, "I don't get any respect" or "What's wrong with her?"

One night, after an especially heated fight, as Dad bent to kiss me goodnight, I turned my face from him. There was no way I would or could kiss someone who had just crucified me.

When I turned away from his kiss, Dad got angrier and started preaching the Bible, saying in his righteous voice, "Never let the sun go down on your anger."

This was a wonderful Christian attitude, one I believed, but coming out of his hypocritical, beer soaked mouth, it sounded like garbage.

* * * * * * * * *

There seemed no way to avoid my growing feelings of inferiority and guilt. In addition, my "funny feeling" was becoming more frightening. Not only was I experiencing it more frequently, but also a new dimension had appeared.

On a rainy afternoon, confined to the house by the dreary elements, Carrie and I amused ourselves by listening to the radio, dancing rhythmically to the inspirational rock and roll music of 1960. As we sat, regenerating our bodies for the next round of dancing, a slow song began to play. Despite a strange feeling of guilt running through my head, I asked Carrie if she'd like to dance with me.

"I don't know," she paused, looking at me nervously, "but I guess so."

We stood up and I timidly took Carrie in my arms, trying to remember how the boys danced with their girlfriends.

We hadn't danced more than a few steps when Carrie frantically said, "Stop! I don't like this!"

"What's the matter?" I asked, knowing what she'd say.

"I can feel your chest and it's not right." She explained as she gently pushed me from her.

I was crushed and ashamed, for I was enjoying the feel of Carrie's body close to mine. I couldn't understand why she had not felt the same. After all, we were best friends. What was wrong with holding each other? I'd seen my mother dance slowly with her women friends at our neighborhood block parties. She always hugged her female friends, too. It was an expression of love. What could be wrong with that? The vague fear reared it horrid head, making me uncomfortable with my feelings. I left shortly after, angry with myself for upsetting Carrie. Why did I do these things? Just because I enjoyed holding Carrie was no reason to think she'd feel the same.

A few days later I went over to Cindy's house, still upset over the incident with Carrie. Cindy and I walked to where a new house was being constructed. As we played, Cindy noticed a girl, about our age, watching from a house about twenty feet from where we stood.

"Jan, I think that girl thinks you're a boy." Cindy said with a mischievous giggle.

It wasn't' hard to see how someone could make that mistake. Even though my figure had developed, I wore such loose fitting clothes no one could see my slim, almost fully developed female figure.

"Why don't we put her on and act like you're my boyfriend?" Cindy pressed, but I didn't need coaxing.

"OK, that sounds like fun. We'll pretend you're my girl and then that girl over there will get jealous because she can't have me." I teased conceitedly.

We giggled cautiously, lest the unsuspecting girl become wise. I began to act gallant, protecting Cindy from the dangerous terrain while Cindy acted helpless, holding on to my shoulders, the way girls do. We were having a ball, trying to hold in our laughter, for the other girl seemed to be buying our premise.

Cindy was really going crazy with our game, stroking my face and shoulders. Suddenly my genitals became warm, much the way it felt when I masturbated. The sensation was enjoyable, but I was scared and wondered how this could be happening when my hand wasn't between my legs.

Terror overpowered me. I wanted to run home, but my legs wouldn't move. Cindy was engrossed in our game and I couldn't tell her I didn't want to play anymore. That would have hurt her feelings and I didn't want to do that, nor did I want Cindy to know what was happening to my body.

Fortunately, the young girl gazing at our play-acting walked away. Our game was over, thank God and Cindy and I decided to go home.

As I walked home my body began to return to normal. I prayed for answers to the forest of questions, all undefined, that sped through my mind. I ran to the safety only Mom brought, but never told her what I'd done or felt. With Mom I was safe from the fear that ripped my insides.

However, safety didn't last long. My fear turned to panic the night of Cindy's pajama party. It began with high hopes, for this was the first time since my camp out in the woods, with Carrie and the other girls, that I'd tried to sleep away from Mom. The thought terrified me, but I had to test my independence.

Cindy's party progressed nicely and my fear was minimal. I was having a good time, acting cool and making this new group of friends laugh. Suddenly Cindy jumped from the bed and told us to stay where we were; she had a surprise for us. We all waited eagerly, joking about crazy Cindy and her games.

With the record player blasting, Cindy made her entrance, her body gyrating like a stripper. As she danced she proceeded to take off her clothes. I became uncomfortable. The other girls were laughing hysterically, but I couldn't. The ache in my groin made if difficult to laugh. I could feel my pulse pounding rapidly between my legs. It felt as if my insides were going to burst. I wanted Cindy to stop so I could rid myself of this sensation that made me feel sinful.

Cindy finished her performance when her mother unexpectedly came home and, upon finding Cindy stripped to her underpants, with the belt from a bathrobe covering her non-existent breasts, pulled her out of our view. I was afraid for Cindy, but very glad that Mrs. Harris had stopped the performance before something terrible happened to me.

Shortly, Cindy returned, dressed and apparently pleased with herself, despite the unfortunate incident with her mother. She was ready to continue the party, but I couldn't share her enthusiasm. It was only eleven o'clock, but the party was over for me. I wanted to go home. My fear of being away from Mom had intensified so I made my apologies and excuses and left, longing for the safety of home where I could relax, sleep and keep my mind from questioning what had happened.

Chapter 10: 1960-61

The summer, which, along with the friendly warmth of the sun had also brought a terrifying warmth from within, was over and I concentrated on the pleasures of returning to school, pushing aside the distress of the past few months.

High School began with the hope of great things to come. I was pronounced healthy enough to return to gym class with only a limitation on long distance running. This bothered me little for I never cared for the boring activity.

The first day progressed smoothly. Each class excited me more than the one before. I was making new friends, experiencing less shyness. My personality was becoming more outgoing and pleasant, exchanging the tough façade for a healthier sense of confidence.

The day was more than half over when I walked into my Business Arithmetic class, excited because this class was the first in my journey towards my newly acquired desire to become a career woman.

Everyone scuffled to their seats as the bell sound, eyes fixed on the teacher, anxiously waiting his words. As he began to speak a girl walked through the door smiling sheepishly for her tardiness. I looked at her and was hit by the "funny feeling" so intensely, I almost fell off my chair.

The girl had straight white teeth, beautifully accentuating her wide mouth, making her round blue eyes sparkle within her gentle face. She was a bit shorter than my 5'4" frame, but her body was heavier and more solid than mine, as it would have to have been to hold her extremely broad and square shoulders. She wore her straight brown hair short and parted on one side. It was plain, almost boyish. She so captivated me I forgot about the "funny feeling" shooting through my body, concentrating on how to make this girl my friend.

Her name was Lauren and I was pleased to find that she had been assigned to the same gym class as me. As I watched her on the athletic field my "funny feeling" went crazy. Lauren was truly Olympic material and my admiration overpowered the sharp twinge of envy I felt towards her superior athletic ability. I never thought any girl could be more athletic than me, but Lauren outshined me in every area.

I found it difficult to be friendly with Lauren for she intimidated me, more than Carrie had. Occasionally we exchanged amenities, but this was merely brought about by sharing gym class. Whenever we talked, though, I'd get so nervous my words became tangled so rather than make a fool of myself I avoided conversation whenever possible. It was apparent I would not win Lauren's friendship with my dazzling verbal display so I set my sites in other directions.

Babs Leonard, a Luther League acquaintance of mine, had become friends with Lauren so I decided to pump her for information, hoping it would give me a clue as to how to get close to Lauren. Instead of helping, Babs made me feel terrible because she'd had no trouble becoming friends with Lauren. I cooled towards Babs, envious of her friendship with Lauren.

One day in study hall I thought I felt eyes on me. When I looked up, Lauren was staring at me, but turned away when she saw me look back at her. Taking this as proof that she was interested in me, but perhaps too shy to act upon her feelings reinforced the validity of my pursuit.

Adding to my optimism was another factor. One weekend Mom and I went to see a movie about a family that had twin daughters, but before the twins were a year old the parents divorced, each taking one of the twin daughters in the settlement. Coincidently, the twins met at summer camp and were astounded when they saw their duplicate. One scene showed how they would look at each other in exactly the same manner Lauren and I had done that day in study hall. Since the movie ended with the twins finding out the truth and becoming inseparable, I knew it was a sure thing that Lauren and I would end up the same way.

As the movie progressed, though, I stopped thinking of Lauren because I found myself getting the "funny feeling" for the actress who portrayed the twins. In the weeks and months that followed I bought every movie magazine I could, reading and daydreaming about the actress, admiring her and wishing we could be friends.

Many people go crazy over movie stars, but something told me my feelings were different. I kept telling myself I just wanted to be friends with the actress, the same as I had with Calamity Jane, Carrie and Lauren. I could have lived my life with all of them. It was a wonderful feeling in one way, but the obsessiveness gnawed at my insides.

I went to Mom to allay my fears, mentioning only Lauren and the actress for I didn't feel right telling Mom I had once felt this strange feeling for Carrie. Mom listened patiently and told me that everyone had 'idols'. Hers was Judy Garland and she, too, dreamed of having her for a friend.

"I think a person feels the way you do when she wants to be friends and either the other person doesn't choose to or, like movie stars, the person is out of your reach. It's perfectly normal, sweetie."

Though Mom's feelings about her movie idol were similar to mine, I don't think she understood what I was trying to convey. Small wonder; neither did I. My confusion increase, as always, but I hung on to Mom's words, trying to believe.

* * * * * * * * *

One Saturday in October, Cindy, Jason and I went bowling. Taking my turn on the alley, determined to prove my athletic prowess, I began my stride, but with the wrong foot. Halfway through the stride the bowling ball came back on my right knee with a blood-curdling crack. I fell to the floor writhing in pain. My knee felt like a balloon with splinters inside.

Once the pain subsided some I realized that Cindy was at my side holding me. An unidentifiable, yet pleasant feeling swept though my body. She put her arm around my waist and helped me to a nearby phone so I could call my mother. Mom came down to the bowling alley and wanted to call Dr. Seth, but I said no. I was afraid he'd put my leg in a cast and I couldn't stand the thought of another restriction. Mom acquiesced, but said if I wasn't better in a day she would take me to the doctor.

Later that day Cindy and Jason came to visit. Though in pain, I was thrilled over my accident because Cindy was extra attentive to me. I thoroughly enjoyed her pampering.

When they left I realized that Lauren was in charge of taking attendance in gym class. On Monday she'd see my bandaged, swollen knee and rush to comfort me. Friendship would be ours.

I sat in the gym class sick room with two other girls, waiting the entrance of Lauren, reveling in the thought of the victory that was soon to be mine.

She entered, looking beautiful in her white starched gym uniform and my heart fluttered as it always did when she was near. Turning to the other girls first, Lauren asked why they weren't playing today and they gave the typical sissy answer I'd come to hate; they had their monthly distress. How ridiculous, I thought. Though I had not begun to menstruate, when I did I wasn't going to be a sissy about it, like them.

Lauren turned to me, looking sensitively down on my handicapped position. She wouldn't think I'd make up a flimsy excuse like the other two had for Lauren knew I was different. As she opened her mouth to ask what had happened my hands began to sweat and my skin was on fire. She listened patiently as I explained, softly said she was sorry and hoped I would soon be on my feet. Then she turned and left the room.

"What happened? This isn't the way she's supposed to act. She was warm, but she didn't rush to my side to comfort me. She just walked away as if I didn't matter." I was devastated.

In the days that followed, Lauren remained friendly, but aloof as usual. I could not speak to her without breaking out in a sweat. My behavior was uncomprehendable. Though the "funny feeling" was not new to me, my ability to stay outwardly cool had always been in control. Now Lauren was the cool one. On the athletic field I tried to impress her with my ability, but the minute she looked in my direction I'd make an error. I sure wasn't winning her with my athletic prowess, which up until she entered my life had astounded everyone, so I began to show off again.

During study hall I would sit close to Lauren's table so she could easily observe me. If the teacher made me stand in the corner for talking too much, which happened often (a habit I could never break), I'd be in Heaven, knowing I was more visible to Lauren. Soon I realized how ineffective my efforts had been for one day Lauren came into study hall, went directly to the teacher, had a pass signed and left. I found out she was spending her study hall time in the gym and was angered by her indifference. The thought that she would rather play in the gym than watch my antics depressed me terribly.

I had tried everything, but nothing had worked. Lauren drifted into her cliché of friends and I was left outside.

* * * * * * * * *

Lauren was only one aspect of my ever-growing number of frustrations. Carrie still had her stupid boyfriend, Jim. I tolerated the situation only to hold on to my friendship with Carrie no matter how limited I felt it had become, constantly consoling myself with the knowledge that she and Jim couldn't last forever and I would be back in the number one position.

In addition, sexual reality was squeezing me into a corner. I hadn't even kissed a boy and had no burning desire to do so, but all my girlfriends talked endlessly about the joys of making out. I was an outcast desperately wanting to be part of the norm, somehow knowing I was asking too much of myself.

I drew some consolation by identifying myself as a non-conformist. My brother was always that way; it probably ran in the family. There was nothing wrong with Paul so there was no need for me to worry. Paul was 17 and hadn't dated a girl. We were two of a kind.

Lauren wasn't interested in boys either and that eased me. However, for some strange reason I felt her lack of interest in boys was the antithesis of mine. I had a gnawing feeling that Lauren was one of those lesbians. I don't know where this thought came from. I knew nothing about those kinds of people except that they were perverted and sick. To think that Lauren fit into this category was totally ludicrous. She was so nice and never showed any perverted behavior; not even in the locker room where girls walked around naked. Surely, if she was a lesbian, she'd attack. But her behavior remained exemplary.

I knew little on the subject of homosexuality except what I'd read in the Bible and that was all negative. The first time I heard the proper name for such people was on a TV talk show I watched with Mom, in which two men, hidden behind masks, discussed their homosexual relationship. As I watched and listened I realized that, aside from their choice of bed partners, they were no different than anyone else. They weren't even effeminate. They didn't appear to be sick or perverted. Their love was as real as any man and woman couple.

When the show was over I said to Mom, "I can't see anything sinful in their loving relationship". Mom replied, "Neither can I. There must be something the Church is misinterpreting in the Bible." I hoped we were right because I couldn't bear the thought of the Biblical punishment awaiting Lauren, if she was a lesbian.

* * * * * * * * *

The terrible shyness of my youth continued to abate and I was becoming more extroverted. I was always clowning around, trying to make people laugh, devouring the positive attention my actions received and happy that my antics could lift people out of their misery, if only for a brief time.

However, I had a very serious side to my personality and that lay in the area of religion. I went to church every Sunday, led Bible studies at Luther League and read my Bible daily. I was a devout Christian, obsessed with the desire to save souls for Jesus. My faith was strong and inflexible, like my father's, although I couldn't see this fact, then.

Believing adultery and pre-marital sex (and that included anything more than benign kissing) was the deadliest sin, I began a crusade for chastity and with this crusade I found a reason for my distaste and lack of interest in sex. Without the benefit of marriage I could feel no other for that would have been a sin. I was merely obeying God's commandment and doing His Will. My commitment was to Him and my desire to remain single was a result of my dedication to God. There was no room for sex.

With this logical explanation, I turned my attention to souls in need. Carrie caused me much concern for sometimes I'd see hickeys on her neck and that meant she and Jim were doing more than just kissing. I was irate because he tainted her. I never spoke to Carrie about my fears for her because I was scared I'd lose what little relationship we had since Jim entered the picture, but I prayed for her. She was a good Christian, a faithful churchgoer so I knew she would eventually change her sinful ways.

Cindy was another story. She had become our town tramp. Even though she stayed true to Jason, she'd helped him grow up fast. The few times I'd caught them kissing they didn't look like innocent thirteen year old kids, for they kissed with mouths wide open, consuming each other's tongues.

When I spoke with Cindy she agreed that her behavior was sinful, but she just couldn't control herself. Frustrated over my inability to change her I could only feel sorry and forgave. After all, Christians were to try to love and forgive, like God. I prayed for Cindy, hoping she'd come to love God and receive the strength to control her sinful appetite.

I worried about Lauren, too. Not because of sex since I knew she was not interested in anything but sports. However, I had to know if she believed in Jesus. Babs Leonard helped me this time, telling me that Lauren was a devout Catholic. That relaxed me.

My Godly purpose was the mainstream of my life. I enjoyed the responsibility of helping people. The martyr syndrome or the halo effect became my style though I never thought of it as such. Nor did it ever occur to me that my desire to save souls was almost exclusively directed towards females.

Chapter 11: 1961

I missed Lauren terribly when school was over, but filled the void by becoming more involved in Luther League, putting my energy into being a model Christian to the new kids who had become members, hoping to enrich their lives and bring them closer to God.

Carol had lived around the block from me for a couple of years, but we had never been close. She was extremely intelligent and traveled in a different circle than I. When she entered League we were pleasantly forced into the same circle and I discovered that she was a lovely girl with a wonderful sense of humor. I didn't have the "funny feeling" for her, but I had come to realize that the origin of the "feeling" was not caused by an inability to make friends with a girl. It was brought on by my need to help the troubled girl. This explained why I didn't feel it for every girl. It was merely part of my Christian love for the unfortunate.

Carol and I quickly became friends. Popular and capable of fighting for her own rights, Carol would never be an underdog. Her ability to be a person unto herself attracted me as did her vast knowledge on the subject of boys and sex, acquired through books, not practice, for Carol was chaste.

Evelyn and Debbie were two other new member with whom I become involved. At first I gave my attention to Evelyn, a tall, slim, brown haired girl with blue eyes and an infectious laugh which needed little to unleash. Evelyn instantly brought on my "funny feeling" and it remained as our friendship grew. Yet, it didn't worry me for I knew it was present because Evelyn came from a bad family and was in need of help.

For weeks we hung around together, enjoying each other's company and talking about God. Evelyn was still chaste, but I knew she could easily go astray for her faith was weak. I hoped and prayed that God would use me as His vehicle to help Evelyn find the strength to resist temptation, but I was to be disappointed. As suddenly as our friendship began, it ended. Her personality changed and she became wild. Now more than ever she needed help, but much as I tried she'd laugh at me. There was nothing to do except pray for her and turn my attention on ears that would listen. Debbie responded.

A cute blonde haired, green-eyed girl with a personality that attracted everyone, my "funny feeling" hit immediately. However, I couldn't explain it away with my new theory. Debbie was anything but an underdog. She was intelligent, popular and had a strong faith.

My confusion returned as to the cause of my "funny feeling". I found it difficult to believe in the validity of a theory if there were exceptions and there always were. Nonetheless, I had to continue to believe there was another facet and when I discovered this missing link there would no longer be any exceptions and my mind could stop questioning the origins of this terrifying, gnawing "funny feeling".

Chapter 12: 1961-1962

I will remember my junior year as the best year of my high school life. The physical limitations set by Dr. Seth were so minimal I had no trouble adjusting. Actually, the limitations were advantageous, in that, I could use them as an excuse to rationalize any inadequacy I had in the athletic arena. If I made an error or if I didn't have the ability to perform some athletic feat (I was terrible in gymnastics) I could and would blame it on my physical handicap, escaping the reality of my imperfections; a reality I could not tolerate. With the confidence I sucked out of this logic, I put my all into sports, to impress Lauren, in a continuing effort to win her friendship.

My skinny body turned to muscle, positively accentuating my maturing female frame, of which I was very proud. I enjoyed my womanly body and dressed in a way that would display the curves, modestly of course, so I would not sin against God's laws on modesty.

However, even with my feminine figure boys were still unaffected. Other girls were not as pretty as I, but the boys chose to date them. The lack of male attention hurt my ego, but I held firm to the belief that I was blessed. Boys would only interfere with the work God had for me.

It was a year of outstanding scholastic achievement. I had always been an above average student, but my grades improved and I was making second honor roll. I felt no inadequacy for not making first honors because those who did were basically egotistical eggheads. They may have been smarter, holding positions of authority, but they were no better than anyone else. I refused to feel inferior to them as many of my friends did.

More and more I turned to the underdog; the unpopular or troubled girls. I preached the values of the Bible in an effort to uplift them.

One of my "flock" was a rather heavy, unattractive girl who slept with anyone who'd have her. I'd tell her the evil of her ways, explaining that one need not have sex to be loved. She never listened and I worried about her soul, but there was nothing I could do except pray that she would find God's Way.

Salvation was the focal point of my life and I preached fervently, feeling devastated if I failed to convert people, which was the general outcome.

Yet, I kept on preaching, "God is forgiving, but you must accept Jesus as your Lord and Savior and turn from your sins before forgiveness and salvation can be yours. It is not good enough just to say you believe. You must back that belief up with purity and that means little sinning, especially with sex." I was firm, unaware of my fanaticism or the neglect I gave the other nine commandments.

Other girls, who were unwilling wall flowers, would seek my companionship. I'd try to help by making them realize they should be thankful they didn't have to deal with the sinfulness that came with being pretty and popular. I told these wallflowers that being unpopular was really a blessing in disguise; that they should concentrate on helping others instead of feeling sorry for themselves. They'd nod in agreement, but I didn't feel victorious when they continued to look unhappy.

That year my relationship with Dad deteriorated more. My hatred grew and so did the intensity of our arguments, but I didn't perceive this as bad since I'd grown sophisticated in the art of arguing and took pleasure in using my newly acquired knowledge to run Dad into the ground. I felt righteous, as if God was on my side. I perceived Dad as an irrational, fanatical, ignorant man in need of my fifteen-year-old wisdom. With my biblical knowledge and verbal acumen I could enrage him to the point of hysterics. He would turn red, then purple and storm off to his bedroom muttering words of anger, disapproval and frustration. His emotional reaction proved I was right and he was a fool.

It was a year of increased sexual arousal. Despite my promise to God three years before, I began to masturbate again (without sexual fantasies – never entered my mind.)

That year I entered the final stages of womanhood. I was shy of my sixteenth birthday by four months when I began to menstruate. Although all my girlfriends complained about their monthly "curse", I felt proud. At least in one area I was now like them.

It was a year of feeling more comfortable with Lauren. My desire to be friends had not diminished nor had the "funny feeling", but I began to accept the probability that we'd never be close. Lauren was special. I had placed her on a pedestal inaccessible to me and all I could do was admire her from afar, gratefully accepting the fragments of friendliness she bestowed upon me.

It was the year I turned sixteen. Sweet sixteen and never been kissed. Outwardly I was proud. Inwardly I was upset, but kept remembering that it was hard being a Christian. My chastity was pleasing to God and I'd do anything for Him. Self-righteousness became my middle name, although I was unaware of this fact. I felt so much better than those who gave in to the weaknesses of sex, drinking, smoking and other evils. I knew I was a sinner, but believed I was closer to God than most of the other kids. When I'd get down about my lonely state or my difference I'd tell myself this was the price one paid for being a dedicated Christian. Perhaps a high price and certainly a frustrating one, but it was God's Will for me to be this way. I knew that all people of faith suffered, but had also found peace and fulfillment of a higher nature. I would find that peace, too, for God would not desert me. He would show me the reason for my difference and my place in His plan.

The highlight of my junior year was the graduation of Carrie. I joined the "Daisy Chain", a prestigious ritual given by the junior class to the graduating students to show respect.

I worked for two days, along with about 100 other juniors, picking and then attaching thousands of daisies to a light metal frame. On graduation night we juniors would form two parallel lines, holding the daisy chain on our shoulders, making a threshold through which the seniors would march.

This was not an act I normally would have done for it meant getting dressed up in a sissy gown, but I wanted to show Carrie the depth of my friendship and love.

"When she walks by me," I thought, "I will look at her and smile. Carrie will feel my love and smile hers back." It was going to be a most tender moment between us. No one would realize the love and loyalty within our smiles.

The night of graduation I held my part of the daisy chain, anxiously awaiting Carrie's arrival.

"There she is!" I screamed to myself as I saw her walking towards me, looking beautiful in her cap and gown. "Soon she'll turn her head, our eyes will meet and our smiles will seal our covenant of friendship." I was aglow.

"Wait! Wait! She's staring straight ahead and there's no smile on her face. Doesn't she see me? She's rejecting me! No. Calm down. She's merely nervous." I tried to convince myself, but I hurt.

I had gone out of my way to do this sissy ceremony for Carrie and she didn't even appreciate my sacrifice. Yet, I couldn't stay mad. Carrie wasn't like me, whatever me was like and I had to accept that fact. After all, I was different. But, dear God, how?

Chapter 13: 1962-1963

Hidden behind the hopes I held for senior year, the volcano that had long churned within clandestinely prepared for another more volatile eruption.

Naturally, I was excited about seeing Lauren after a long summer separation, but, in addition, the President's Physical Fitness program was in effect. I worked my body into peak condition for it was imperative that I pass the fitness test and earn my "letter". Then my athletic prowess could not be denied. I could accept the fact that Lauren was a better athlete only if I had a "letter" proving that I was at least in her league.

Along with my pursuit for an athletic "letter" I ardently pursued my goal to land a boyfriend. I had to attend the prestigious activities inherent in senior year, proving beyond a doubt that I was a regular girl.

I'd met a boy at League that passed summer who gave me the kind of attention I wanted from a boy. At the time I was friendly, but kept my distance because he had a girlfriend.

Don was a stocky 6'2" boy with a stuttering problem that made him appear below average in intelligence. He wasn't the greatest catch, but I was in no position to be choosey. When he broke off with his girlfriend and started coming on to me, in his awkward boyish way, I responded. Don was my ticket into normal society and I was buying.

Our first date was the football game victory dance at school, although our team lost. Don wasn't much for talking and I was so uncomfortable my tongue was tied, but the presence of his sister and her boyfriend saved the evening from being a complete disaster.

Don and I danced all the slow dances for he didn't know how to dance fast and we held hands. I was delirious with the joy of having a boyfriend, despite the fear that Don would want more physical affection than I could or would offer.

The weeks drifted by, Don and I earning the reputation of being a couple. He never tried to kiss me. I thought this odd for I knew he had gone pretty far with his last girlfriend, but I wasn't upset. I guessed that Don had learned from his sinful past experience and would continue to be respectful of my unspoken wishes.

Christmas grew near and Luther League organized their annual caroling to the neighborhood shut-ins. I was feeling uppity because Carrie, who was home from college, was joining our festivity and I wanted to flaunt the fact that I had a boyfriend, too. Once again I couldn't understand my hostility towards Carrie and was sorry for my sinfulness.

Don's mother drove us around the neighborhood, with my mother sitting in the front seat. Driving from house to house, occasionally getting stuck in the newly fallen snow, I sensed that Don was working up to a kiss. Excitement flowed through me with the knowledge that a kiss would transform me. I would be like the other girls. Yet I was terrified. Afraid that one kiss would make Don lose control. Dad's words kept running through my mind, "Kissing leads to other things, so beware." Since both our mother's were in the car I felt safe, but what would happen on other dates?

The moment arrived and I felt Don's full lips cover mine. I kept my mouth shut and my head still. Don's head moved slowly back and forth as his mouth devoured mine passionately, but gently. The sloppiness of his kiss repulsed me and I was angry for having to submit to passivity. To kiss back would cause Don to lose control of his sexual appetite and our relationship had to remain chaste.

Don kept kissing me the entire night and I grew more repulsed. Fortunately he seemed to want nothing more than kissing so I endured rather than lose my chance for further social prestige.

* * * * * * * * *

The physical fitness program at school was under way. I performed each task perfectly and was on my way towards earning the treasured letter. Till now I had done equally as well as Lauren, but the next event, the softball throw, would put me behind. I showed her I didn't throw like a sissy, receiving one of the top marks with my long hurl, but I knew Lauren would do much better.

Lauren tossed her first ball 175 feet. Everyone wanted her to break the 200 foot mark and I was no exception. She fell short of the mark by a few feet on her second try. As she stepped up to the line for her final attempt, I screamed as loudly as the other girls. Lauren's arm drew back and the ball streaked through the air as if it was fired from a cannon. All was quiet as we waited for the measurement.

"202 feet," the judge yelled.

The crowd was on its feet, going wild. I was filled with a sense of victory, pride and admiration. No girl had ever thrown a softball that far. Lauren's great accomplishment was for all women. She was an inspiration.

Sit-ups were the last event in the President's Physical Fitness program. I worried about this event because sit-ups had always been difficult for me. Fifty sit-ups was a perfect score, but you only needed seventeen to pass. Despite my weakness I felt I could muster that many.

I entered the gym anxiously as our teacher called off partners. When I heard my name paired with Lauren's I thought I'd die. Excitement and terror collided as we exchanged the familiar pleasantries.

I declined Lauren's offer to go first. I was too nervous and needed some time to get over the shock of being paired with the best athlete in school.

Lauren quickly lie on the floor, staring at me with a look of bewilderment for I was having trouble performing the simple task of holding her ankles. Hands shaking and clammy, I finally took hold of her ankles and she began her sit-ups, barely using any energy. I watched in total amazement, trying, without success, to avert my eyes from her bare, muscular legs.

Suddenly a spasm shot through my gut and I felt weak. Through all 50 sit-ups I fought this sensation, unable to shake it.

With Lauren's spectacular accomplishment finished I positioned myself on the floor anxiously awaiting the touch of her hands upon my ankles. The spasm persisted and my body was too weak to move. More than ever I wanted to do well, but much as I strained I only did 11 sit-ups. When I told Lauren I could do no more she released my legs, got up and walked away, leaving my ego as flat as my position on the floor. I had failed.

With my last ounce of energy I stood up and as I did I felt my chest drop to my stomach. Quickly I put my head between my legs to avoid fainting. When I felt better I went to my teacher and asked her if I could have another chance at sit-ups, explaining that I had felt ill. Understanding my need she set a make-up date for after Christmas vacation, allaying my despair.

* * * * * * * * *

Christmas had always been a joyous time, with presents piled high under our moderately sized, but beautifully decorated tree. Mom made Scotch shortbread, a traditional recipe handed down from generations and we'd devour it till we were pleasantly full. The spirit of the Christ child permeated our home as we gathered around Dad, singing carols while he played the organ. After we opened our presents we'd prepare for candlelight service at church. If there were any problems in our lives, they were forgotten amidst the gaiety.

With Paul home the house was filled with shrieks of laughter as we caught up on our shenanigans, desperately missed while he'd been away at college. I confided the fears I had relating to Don, hoping Paul's wisdom would help. He told me to be more open with my affections, assuring me I would be able to control any unwanted advances, should Don try. With the confidence gained from Paul's words I set out to change my behavior and not be so frigid. As always, Paul came to my rescue.

* * * * * * * * *

I skipped my period that December, but worried little about it until the day we made our Christmas visit to Grandma & Grandpa Adickes.

It had been a pleasant day. Nana was in a festive mood and Grandpa engaged in his usual mischievous antics which brought a scornful look to Nana's eyes. However, the love she felt for this gentle man could not be hidden.

Paul was off in his own world, as usual, reading on the merits of some way out philosophy while I played schoolteacher, avidly marking the TV guide as if it were a test paper.

Towards late afternoon I began to feel funny. My stomach was tight and an awful tickling sensation spread throughout my body. I told Mom and, upon determining that I had no fever, she instructed me to rest on the sofa, assuring me that it was probably due to the skipping of my period.

Within the next hour the symptoms intensified. Now I was feeling light headed and I was having trouble breathing. I was worried about all sorts of terrible things. Maybe I was dying. All I wanted to do was go home.

Mom must have read my mind for she entered the living room and told Paul and me to get our coats.

On the way home Mom sat in the back seat of the car, cradling me in her arms. The sensations had grown worse. I wanted to scream from the maddening tickling throughout my body, but there seemed no air in my lungs to do so. It felt as if thousands of ants crawled under my skin. I was scared to death, unable to stop gasping for air. I kept asking Mom if I was going to die and she kept telling me there was no reason to worry. I wished I could have shared her confidence.

Shortly after we arrived home the symptoms quickly vanished, but the fear of their return stayed with me and because of this, although I tried, I spent most of the remainder of the school year at home. My last chance to win my letter for physical fitness was gone.

Every time I attempted school I'd feel as if nothing was real, including me. It was as if I was dreaming. I felt like I was going to faint and I couldn't breathe. When I managed to get to school, more times than not, I'd go to the nurse and she'd send me home.

My social life faded. Don called asking me out, but I declined. He was totally confused and I felt bad, but couldn't explain to him what was happening. I just couldn't seem to set foot outside my house without feeling like I was dying.

In January I skipped my period again and Dr. Seth referred me to a gynecologist. After the humiliating examination was completed, Dr. Gilbert prescribed hormones to alleviate my problem, gently scolding me for running away from school. I hated him! Did he think I manufactured my symptoms? Did he think I had any control over them?

Weeks passed marked by bi-weekly humiliations with Dr. Gilbert, but no period. The hormones were making me nauseous and every week, like clockwork, I would violently vomit.

Three months after I began taking the hormones I started to menstruate. However, it lasted only two hours and stopped as quickly as it had begun. A few days later I began to bleed again, only the bleeding was heavier with abnormally large clots. I had never bled this much and was terrified. As before, the bleeding stopped within a few hours.

A week later the bleeding reappeared, but this time it didn't stop within a few hours. For eight hours I flowed heavily, growing weak and pale. Mom had me lay on the sofa with my legs elevated while she called Dr. Gilbert and made an appointment for the next day.

In his office my humiliation was matched only by the fear that rose within me when Dr. Gilbert told me I needed a D & C. He suspected some kind of growth, probably a cyst, had caused the cessation of my period. At his words I immediately thought I had cancer. My life was over at seventeen. I had beaten death five years ago, but it was going to claim me now.

On May 17, 1963 I entered the hospital for surgery. Pastor Andy, the minister of my church whom had confirmed me and whom I'd adored since the age of ten, when he first became our preacher, came to visit, but even he couldn't stop me from thinking the worst. The only light thought that entered my mind was the fact that this operation would "de-flower" me, making my wedding night less traumatic.

Dad had a different train of thought on this subject. Totally concerned with the fact that my physical virginity would be destroyed he requested a written statement from the doctor verifying that I was a virgin at the time of surgery. He was trying to protect me, for my future husband might be upset when he found that I was not a virgin, but I didn't see Dad's motive at the time. I was angry and hated him for it.

After surgery I was wakened by a slap in the face. I looked up and saw clear liquid dripping through a tube attached to my arm, from a bottle a few feet above my head. I had survived the operation. Now all I had to do was wait for the verdict. Again I turned to God.

Shortly after I was returned to my room, Dr. Gilbert came in. My heart quickened as I thought, "This is it. The big "C"!

Dr. Gilbert leaned over my bed and said, "You're going to be fine. You had scar tissue growing inside you and it was benign."

He left and I turned my head and wept in happiness, thankfulness and repentance to God for my weak faith.

* * * * * * * * *

The afternoon after my surgery, Carrie came to visit. I had forgotten it was her vacation from college and was deliriously happy to see her. We talked a few minutes, mostly about her new boyfriend Bob. She told me he was in the waiting room and asked if I'd like to meet him. At this moment I was in no mood to share Carrie, but what could I say? She was so happy. How could I deny her?

Bob was a tall, well-build, blue-eyed blond, with a warm personality, but nice as he was I could not bring myself to like him.

We talked for a few minutes, but I sensed that Bob was as uncomfortable as I so I told them I was tired and asked if they'd mind leaving.

Alone in my room, lost in depression, I again questioned my inability to accept Carrie's boyfriends. Bob was not a creep, like Jim, so why couldn't I be happy for her? I was angry with myself and vowed that Carrie would never know I didn't like Bob.

A week after my release from the hospital I returned to school with a six week restriction on any physical activity. With the operation a success and the return of my period I thought I'd be free from the debilitating physical symptoms, but was wrong. I still felt sick. My depression grew with the knowledge that despite the restoration of my physical health there seemed no way to escape these ill feelings. Nothing, not even my desire to see Lauren, could pry me from my home.

I was sent to the school psychologist, but he couldn't help, either. He seemed not to understand how earnestly I wanted and tried to attend school; how hard I battled the symptoms. I wasn't using them as an excuse to skip school, as he stated. I loved school. Nobody seemed to understand that I didn't enjoy being the way I was.

I couldn't concentrate on anything except my inability to function. My teachers were understanding and sent my work home, but I had little desire to do it.

Don kept calling asking if he could come over. I saw him on these terms, tried to converse with him, but the feeling of faintness, unreality and the inability to breathe made it impossible to be good company. Soon he stopped calling.

Pastor Andy tried to help by hiring me to baby-sit for his two children. It was his attempt to draw me from my seclusion. However, when I baby sat I was alone, not far from home and it was night-time when, for some odd reason, I felt better, so I'm not sure what good was accomplished.

One night, when the kids were asleep, I became restless with the tons of homework piled before me. I had an urge to play "American Bandstand" so I turned on the radio, grabbed one of the kid's dolls and began to dance, pretending I was Matt, the most popular boy on the show. He was, in reality, a conceited young man who thought he was God's gift to women, but I admired his confidence and ease. It felt strange pretending to be a man, but by portraying this strong, confident ladies man I could forget my weak, nothing personage.

Chapter 14: 1963

Through the cooperation of the school board I passed, although barely, all my subjects and was ready to graduate. I'd plowed through the last day of school since it only lasted an hour and was to go up to the football field for graduation rehearsal. As I looked up the one hundred steps that led to the field, feeling faint and breathless, I knew I'd never make the climb.

I walked into the school and phoned Mom to come pick me up. When she got to the school we had a scene. She desperately wanted me to go to practice instead of running, telling me there was nothing wrong with my health, but after much pleading she took me home.

I couldn't stand myself for being so weak. I prayed for the strength to get through the actual graduation ceremony. Much as I wanted to avoid going, I couldn't hurt Mom anymore.

God was with me that night for after the first horrendous hour I began to relax. The climb up the hundred steps was a slow one, thank God.

My eyes filled with tears as we sang our class anthem, bringing to mind the reality that an important part of my life was ending. More so, it meant I wouldn't see Lauren anymore. She was joining the Air Force. Three years of high school had not been enough time to achieve my goal of winning her friendship. That was the saddest part of graduation night.

* * * * * * * * *

The summer days ahead had always meant daily adventures at the beach or in the woods, but not this summer. Five years earlier I'd had to adjust to a life of limitations. I'd fought back only to become more limited than before. Now I retreated into the safety of my home, scared to venture out even to be a spectator. Walking to the mailbox, fifty feet from my back door, became a monumental accomplishment. Outside the confines of my house my heart would race, my lungs seemed unable to suck in air and my head felt faint and in a dream world. I lived in fear all my waking hours, finding relief from the myriad of devastating ills only within the walls of my home.

My social life came to a complete halt and I began a mad love affair with TV. Game shows, soap operas and late, late movies became my world. I went to be at 4 AM and woke at noon, unconsciously avoiding as many daytime hours as possible. Strangely, I felt healthier and more relaxed when the rest of the world slept.

As I journeyed with my TV friends my "funny feeling" went berserk, tearing my insides with pleasure and terror. My theory that the "feeling" occurred when I saw a girl who was in need of help was of no consolation. It began losing its credibility when exceptions moved in and while I watched the soaps, with their forest of independent, capable women, any faith I still had in my theory went out the window. There seemed no logical explanation to my "funny feeling" and I grew more desolate.

Seeing my secluded and depressed state, Mom took me to a psychiatrist, much to the dismay of Dad who preached that if I had faith in God I wouldn't be so weak and need a head doctor. I gagged on his words, but feared he was right. Penitently I prayed, asking God to forgive my faithlessness. I needed His forgiveness for I could not forgive myself.

Dr. Kruger was a short, stocky, bald man with a German accent so thick I spent half of our therapy sessions saying, "What?" He prescribed a very strong tranquilizer and diagnosed me as having psychosomatic disorder. In other words, my emotions were making me feel sick. The tranquilizers calmed me so I was able to get out a little more. I could breath easier and my giddy head seemed to return to reality. Talking in therapy was a waste of time, but the tranquilizers made me feel better so I continued the treatments.

A few weeks after I began therapy I started experiencing eye-rolling attacks. Without warning my eyes would pull up in their sockets. Despite attempts to bring them down, they would automatically roll back up.

I discussed these episodes with Dr. Kruger and he told me that since my other symptoms were disappearing and since they had kept me from facing reality, this new symptom was occurring as another way to keep me secluded. This was the plight of a psychosomatic person, until cured. I couldn't accept his logic because my eyes rolled at home as well as away from home. Yet, Dr. Kruger persisted in his diagnosis and I was forced to follow his advice to relax when they started rolling.

The next few weeks in therapy were spent talking entirely about my terror over the eye-rolling attacks. At night I'd have to hold my eyelids closed with my fingers, even though they weren't rolling, in order to go to sleep. When they did roll no sleep could find me and they were rolling about twice a week now. The episodes intensified, lasting up to five hours.

Dr. Kruger and I talked little about my home life, relationships or things that had disturbed me up until the eye-rolling had started. Now nothing bothered me except these dreadful attacks. Dr. Kruger's constant explanation that these attacks kept me from facing reality made me sick. I knew they rolled because of the tranquilizers and told him, but he wouldn't listen.

Through my eye-rolling attacks Mom stayed supportive. She'd sit by my side, as I lay in bed, holding me and encouraging me to get my eyes down. She never panicked and that gave me the strength to endure.

Dad remained firm in his belief that my faith was weak. There was no compassion or willingness to help. All I got from him was his damnable fire and brimstone sermons. In one of his attacks on me, during an especially serious eye-rolling episode, I struck back.

"If you had faith in God you wouldn't need your damn beer!" I yelled hysterically.

"Beer is different. I can stop anytime I want," he said, obviously irate at my impudence.

As I lay in my bed, eyes rolled up, neck pulled back, heart pounding wildly, I wanted to kill him.

Seeing my distress, Mom yelled at Dad and pushed him out of my room. Tears of victory boiled in my rolled back eyes for I knew Mom was on my side. I guess I'd always known.

The final straw hit in September when I had such a severe attack I thought I would die. Mom told me she could not see the color of my eyes, so far had they rolled. The pain in my neck and back, from the arching, was unbearable. After six hours of torture and four futile hot toddies, Mom called Dr. Kruger's office. He was not available so the answering service referred Mom to another psychiatrist, who, upon hearing the situation and ruling out the possibility that I was having a seizure, told Mom to stop the tranquilizers for they were causing a muscle spasm.

At last, a doctor who confirmed that I wasn't crazy!

The tranquilizers were discontinued and my eyes stopped rolling. However, the fear that they would roll again, despite the knowledge that the medication had caused it, stayed with me for years.

Mom stopped taking me to Dr. Kruger, much to my relief and Dad's and I started to regain my senses. Life became real gain, without medication.

* * * * * * * * *

As a graduation present Mom and Dad bought me a cream-puff, two-toned green 1956 Chevrolet. Now that my eyes had ceased to roll and I was feeling better, although not well enough to get a job, I put my new found freedom into gear. I drove around town, showing off my car, getting kicks from speeding. I don't know how I escaped death given my careless driving.

Feeling healthier and with time on my hands I began to think of Lauren. I had heard that Lauren was scheduled to leave for the Air Force that October, so I took a chance and went to visit "Ma" Gracey, my old high school gym teacher, in hopes that Lauren would also be visiting, as I heard was a habit of hers.

As I entered "Ma" Gracey's office my heart leaped when I saw the familiar broad shoulders. Lauren turned around and smiled at me. We exchanged a few amenities, "Ma" sensitively leaving us alone and then Lauren asked me about my illness. I couldn't believe this was happening. Nervously I told her about my operation, only and received the compassion and attention I'd tried to acquire all through high school.

We talked incessantly, getting to know each other better in one hour than in three years of high school. Lauren was a warm, sensitive person, not at all stuck up.

However, our friendship was doomed. Lauren was leaving for Texas the next day. Funny, how you hope and plan on something for so long and when it finally begins to materialize it's too late. Lauren was leaving and the reality left me empty.

I walked with Lauren to her car and she took my hand in hers, warmly saying good-bye. I held fast to her hand, not wanting to let go.

Tears welled up in my eyes as I watched her drive away. Lauren had to live her life as I had to live mine. I had to let go. Let go of what? I never had her anyway.

Chapter 15: 1963-1964

The loneliness of Lauren's departure was filled when Charlie entered my life. Charlie was twenty-sex years old and a janitor at our local elementary school. Possessing a sixth grade education, due to a childhood bout with rheumatic fever, Charlie wasn't the brightest of men. Nonetheless, in an unsophisticated way, he was quite charming.

However, Dad was not so charmed and had a fit when he found out I was going on a date with Charlie.

"The man is nine years older than you," he ranted, "You can't date a man that old!"

"You're nine years older than Mom, so what's the difference?" I tried to be rational.

"Your mother is different. Besides, Charlie is a Catholic (a fact I had mentioned, much to my regret) and you can't date a Catholic. Mixing religions is wrong." Dad was adamant.

"I know, but if anything serious happens I would make Charlie change his religion so you don't have to worry. Anyway, you've got nothing to worry about cause I don't intend to marry Charlie." I tried to appease him.

The conversation was at an impasse.

Mom objected, too, but for a different reason.

"Honey, I know this will sound unfair, but Charlie's lack of education is what bothers me and someday it will bother you. I don't want to see either of you hurt."

I didn't understand and thought Mom was being a snob. I told her I was going to date Charlie whether they liked it or not.

Dad kept on complaining and we fought even more. Mom allowed me my independence and was always pleasant towards Charlie.

It was a great experience dating an older man. Charlie doted on me, making me feel special. After a few weeks of dating I knew he was quite taken with me. One part of me loved his feelings, but the other part wanted nothing to do with a serious relationship. I knew Charlie wanted to marry me, but because of my age and because he was aware of my father's negative feelings about him, Charlie kept silent. He never pressed me for any kind of sex, for which I was eternally grateful. All I wanted was a boy to be my steady friend. However, Charlie was puzzled by my total lack of sexual interest. I tried to explain to him, as well as to myself.

"It's because I don't believe Catholics and Protestants should get serious. It's like mixing milk and vinegar. Apart each is fine, but mixed they sour."

"Jan, I haven't asked you to marry me. You won't even kiss me."

"Kissing leads to other things (I quoted Dad unconsciously) and I don't want that."

"I like you a lot, Jan. So much that I'd change my religion if anything serious happens between us."

I was stunned. Charlie wasn't going to yield. I had to think fast.

"Charlie, I like you, too, but I'm too young to get serious. Can't we just stay friends?"

"I understand and I'm not trying to rush you." He sounded so pathetic. "I'll stay your friend, but there's no reason I can't hope, is there?"

He was breaking my heart, so I lied, "There's always hope."

* * * * * * * * *

The months passed quickly and I became a night owl, constantly out with Charlie, who had kept his promise and remained a friend.

Arguments with Dad grew more intense. Now he nagged at my sleeping habits. He insisted I wasn't getting eight hours sleep a night. Going to bed at four in the morning and rising at noon added up to eight hours to me, yet Dad kept harping on my abnormal behavior.

"Why don't you get a job like a normal person?" He'd constantly come down on me and I couldn't argue. He was right, although I would never tell him. I just couldn't work, yet. It scared me. I needed freedom. All my life I had obeyed rules for bedtime, meals and health. I had obeyed without question and was sick of rules and authority. I wanted my own wings and I would fight for them. However, juxtaposed with my desire for freedom was my growing dependence on Mom. Where Dad gave me nothing be injury, Mom took care of my wounds. She was my world and I couldn't bear the thought of living without her. She may not have had all the answers, but she was always understanding, supportive and non-judgmental. I wanted freedom, but Mom had to be near.

Chapter 16: 1964

A year after graduation a new romance entered my life. I was to meet Charlie at the elementary school for an informal date. The school was having a slide show and a lot of young people gathered. I greeted Charlie and as we sat watching the show, David Devine came in and sat beside me.

I had known David for years. He lived a few houses from me and his family went to our church. David was two years older so we had never been friends, but I had always thought him to be a nice boy.

I quickly forgot that Charlie was devotedly sitting next to me and gave all my attention to David, who responded. I enjoyed his college intellect and his good looks. He wasn't tall, but had a muscular physique. His light brown hair fell across his forehead, reminiscent of Elvis and his blue eyes reflected the warmth of his nature. Had David not looked so ruggedly handsome many may have thought him a little feminine, for he spoke with a gentle voice and his personality radiated sensitivity. David was as different from other men as I was from other women and I was attracted to him.

I knew David was going to ask me out and a few days later my premonition came true. I accepted, easily forgetting Charlie. Mom had been right. Nice as Charlie was, I had tired of his lack of education and, as gently as I could, broke off with him.

David took me to the movies on our first date. I'd never had so much fun with a man. David was the first man I'd ever had a desire to kiss. However, it took him three dates to work up the courage. When he finally kissed me, it was gentle, closed mouthed and dry. I was in Heaven.

* * * * * * * * *

During the time I dated David I got a job as a typist at a Title Insurance Company. With David's loyalty and affection my fear of working disappeared, along with most of the psychosomatic symptoms. Now I wanted the independence a job would bring and I reset my goal towards becoming a successful businesswoman. My parents were supportive, David gave me encouragement and, best of all, both my parents liked David very much. I was a happy woman.

The office where I worked was small and sparsely staffed, but I did make a good friend in Kate. She was the funniest woman I'd ever known. A farm girl with a naïve sense of humor, we hit it off right away and for the next three months, between the hours of nine to five, we were inseparable.

By the end of the summer the job was strangling me. Kate was getting married and moving upstate and I had to move on to better employment.

On her last day of work, Kate and I stood outside for an hour, hugging each other, saying farewell. If felt good to know she would miss me, to hear her say she loved me and for me to express those feelings to her. I had never spoken words of love to anyone but my family. I loved Carrie, but couldn't say the words to her; why I didn't know. Kate was such a warm, sensitive person, she made it easy to express my feelings.

That day was the warmest of my life. Kate helped me express my emotions and revel in the feel of love's exchange.

* * * * * * * * *

David and I spent all of August together. Never did I have to worry about sexual advances, for he seemed quite satisfied with our innocent kissing. He was the man I'd always wanted; a male companion satisfied with the only affection and sex I could morally give.

Just before David returned to college we went out for our farewell dinner. At the table we stared into each other's eyes as the jukebox serenaded us with love songs. I felt like I was falling in love and David's eyes told me he felt the same.

The next day David left for college, with the promise to write. A few weeks later his letter arrived, much to my relief. I'd been upset because he had taken so long. After our last night together I'd expected him to write sooner and, after I opened his letter and read it, more romantically. Dejected, I wrote back. It was two months before another letter came.

When I took out the letter a newspaper clipping fell to the floor. David's letter was filled with the same pleasant amenities as his first one and then it read, "Enclosed is a picture of my fiancée. We met at school and plan a spring wedding."

Disbelievingly, I picked the clipping off the floor realizing I wasn't dreaming. David had found someone else. I couldn't imagine what had gone wrong. Our last evening had been so beautiful. I thought David was falling in love with me.

Tears fell from my eyes blurring his printed words. David had been unfaithful. He, whom I thought different from other men, had hurt me deeply.

A short time later I found out that David had to get married for his girlfriend was pregnant. My feelings began to change and my anger waned. In my mind David had been victimized. I blamed his girlfriend for his predicament. She had led him astray, probably gotten him drunk. David had merely been sucked into committing a horrid mistake and, being a wonderful person, was doing the honorable thing.

Chapter 17: 1964-1965

Absorbed in my new job as an assistant bookkeeper at a local car dealership my broken heart quickly healed. I was making $3.00 more per week and happy with this small step up the ladder of business success.

Owned by a domineering man and his two equally domineering sons, my negative attitude towards authority grew more adamant. Working for people like these became tedious and nerve wracking. Had I not needed to feel financially independent and had I not requested the responsibility of paying Mom rent, I would have quit a week after I'd been hired. And if I had quit I would have missed the experience of Felix.

Felix was a young man, newly arrived from Germany, who had purchased a car from us and was forever hanging around. A strikingly handsome man of twenty-three, who openly admitted to being an infamous ladies man, living for love making, he made a dichotomous impression on me.

With light golden brown hair, piercing blue eyes and perfect, gentle facial features set atop a small almost fragile frame that smelled of delicious cologne, he appeared almost feminine. I was quite attracted to him, but was also scared because I knew I would have no control over this man as I'd had over all my other boyfriends. I was sure Felix had never heard the word "no" from a woman.

The part of me that wasn't afraid of him was challenged and I guess my constant rejection of his charming offers to make love challenged him, too. Though persistent in his desires, Felix remained a gentleman.

We constantly discussed our differing opinions on sex and Felix would shake his head over my belief in chastity, saying, "What a waste."

His statement floored me. With my strong Christian attitude against the immorality Felix practiced, I shouldn't have been so affected. God help me, a part of me envied Felix and wanted to be like him.

Four months after I was hired I had a scene with the boss that was to end my relationship with Felix. I was getting sick of the hassle at work, feeling I deserved more respect. I blew my stack at one of the boss's sons and became so irate I left his office swinging the door wide open, knowing it would slam into one of the floor's model cars. I never looked back to see if the car had been dented, but I couldn't have cared less.

The next day, after discussing the problem with Mom and getting her approval to quit, I went into my boss, told him to buy another slave and quit.

My outbursts of temper were few and far between, but when I got harassed something would burst inside me and I'd lose my head and my sense of morals. I'd try to control my language, for swearing was still a grave sin to me, but my actions spoke louder. The incident at work had been my first publicly seen tantrum, but it was only a sign of the frustration pleading for release.

For three months I remained peacefully unemployed, enjoying my vacation. Despite my motivation to be a success in business, I needed this time to regroup myself. Happily, I fell back into my beloved night owl routine.

Carrie came home from college one weekend and we spent some time together, but she angered me with her constant talk of Bob. They had been going together for two years, now and it looked serious. I still couldn't accept their relationship, especially after the day when I accompanied Carrie to the city so she could get a pre-employment physical.

On the way home Carrie asked if I would mind if she stopped at the gas station where Bob worked. Certainly I minded, but she was doing the driving so who was I to stop her?

At the station Carrie left me in the car while she visited with Bob. My blood boiled as I waited. How dare she be so inconsiderate? She saw Bob every day and I got to see her so little.

When they emerged from the station office Bob waved at me and I forced a cheerful greeting. They stopped by the side of the car and proceeded to kiss. I couldn't see much, but I could hear their lips smacking wetly. The whole incident disgusted me, but worse, made me wonder how far Carrie and Bob had gone sexually. I was determined to get an answer the next time I saw her.

A short while later, after a movie, as Carrie and I sat eating ice cream, I slyly turned the conversation towards sex. Carrie was a bright girl and sensed what I wanted to know. Hesitantly she told me that she and Bob had been making love for months. Though I'd expected this response, I was upset.

"How is it?" I asked.

"It's all right." Carrie answered blandly.

She was so vague I had to press her. "Didn't you enjoy it?"

"You get used to it." Her reply was emotionless.

You get used to it, I thought angrily! Wasn't sex supposed to be enjoyable? Then I checked my line of thinking for Carrie's attitude towards making love seemed similar to mine. I could see no reason to get excited over making love with a man, either. Yet, making love was to be special and enjoyable. Was I destined to "get used to it" as Carrie had?

What bothered me even more was the fact that Carrie was sinning. Surely she would be punished for having premarital sex. I was torn between my Christian beliefs and the knowledge that she and Bob loved each other very much. Why should their love have to wait? I couldn't punish Carrie for her sin. Maybe God wouldn't either. I hoped and prayed God would forgive Carrie, never realizing I wasn't the least bit concerned for Bob's soul.

Chapter 18: 1965

St. Charles Hospital majestically sat atop a hill overlooking the gaily-lighted harbor of Port Jefferson. A blend of old and new, one side, built in the early 1900's, housed all out patient facilities and the large conservative, but beautifully adorned chapel. A somewhat dilapidated stairway led from the chapel to the mysterious convent which cloistered no more than twenty-five nuns who ran the merciful institution.

Attached to this traditional building stood the modern extension containing six floors of immaculately clean rooms which rose above green grass and a blacktopped parking lot. Above the first floor, designated for the business aspects of the hospital, lay four floors of private and semi-private rooms. The basement contained x-ray and lab facilities, surgery and the ever-busy emergency room. The top floor was used for storage and led to the roof on which stood a multi-bulb cross that spread its message of peace for miles.

It was here, on a muggy summer day, that I parked my car and walked briskly to the accounting office, anxious to begin my job as an assistant bookkeeper/biller. The job not only paid $15 more a week than any prior job, but also provided a great avenue for attaining my goal of success as a businesswoman. So absorbed in acquiring this success I remained oblivious to the informal education I received from the many diversified people who were touching my life.

William, the office comptroller, was a tall, slender man with thinning brown hair and blue eyes that twinkled mischievously. He was a fair, good-humored boss who instilled in me a sense of accomplishment for he never held back praise. Through him I grew confident in my business acumen.

Sister Amy, our office manager, was a crazy nun. In her mid forties, her blue eyes, one of which was fixed looking outward, making it difficult to know when she focused on you, sparkled.

She had an infectious laugh and a sense of humor I thought unusually ribald for a nun.

Elly was a large framed, green-eyed Irish woman in her late thirties. She was single and quite shy, speaking almost in a whisper. However, covertly she possessed a dry wit that, once she got to know you, was hilarious.

In her late thirties also, Rhoda was short, dark and homely, with a personality reminiscent of chalk squeaking on a blackboard. Like Elly she was single, but unlike Elly, Rhoda was the typical neurotic female who felt incomplete without a man. She had the "hots" for our boss William, who was aware of the fact and since he couldn't stand her, took advantage of the situation by leading her on to a dead end. Not very nice, but it made the office break into gales of covert laughter.

Selina, lovingly dubbed, by herself, "the gorgeous Greek" was a dark haired, olive skinned woman pushing forty. A spitfire lady, divorced from a "bastard" of a man whom had left her sole supporter of three children, she was a woman of great compassion. At first she thought I was a real serious kid and, in many ways she was right. I was slow to open up to strangers. However, it didn't take Selina long to bring me out of my shell, with the help of the last member of our office.

Judy, a second rate, ex-show biz band singer, working on her third marriage at the age of thirty-nine, was the epitome of extroversion and sacrilege. A blonde, blue-eyed woman of large stature, she was never lost in a crowd. Loud talking, loud laughing, blasphemous in every area of life, including religion (she was an avowed atheist), I grew to love this woman, who would say of herself, "beneath this rough exterior beats a heart of rock." In reality her heart was sensitive.

In the beginning of my employ I was assigned to handle the emergency room billing with Judy as my mentor and for the first few weeks was actually stationed in the emergency room, with all its blood and suffering. Many times I'd run to the bathroom because my dormant symptoms surfaced.

During this time I met Doug, a nineteen-year-old man working as an aide to help pay his tremendous medical college expense.

Not too tall, which was the way I liked men, with dark hair and sky blue eyes, set in a pretty boy's face, Doug was an absolute doll. I wanted this Adonis for myself and set out to conquer him.

Shortly after, Doug asked me for a date. We went golfing and I think I intimidated him. Doug beat me by a few strokes, but the competition was stiff and I don't think he liked such competition coming from a woman.

On a golf course there are two tees, one for men and one for women. The woman's tee is closer to the green, giving them a handicap because of their lesser driving power. I told Doug I wouldn't play from the woman's tee because I didn't need a handicap. I was equal to a man. I don't think he liked this statement and when he never asked me for another date I knew he just couldn't handle my equalitarian attitude. Men just couldn't accept woman who didn't know their place, but that was their problem. I grieved over my loss, but wouldn't compromise my beliefs for anyone.

After my date with Doug I was moved upstairs into the Accounting Office, much to my relief. I couldn't cope with facing Doug on a daily basis given his prejudice. If he couldn't accept me as an equal I didn't want to be around him.

It wasn't long after I joined the office staff that Selina and I were getting an infamous reputation for being the office clowns. We were always joking about her great beauty or having rubber band fights. When Sister Amy left for lunch, either Selina or I would yell "Battle Stations" and begin to bomb everyone with rubber bands, causing the entire office, even stuffy Rhoda, to become totally unprofessional.

Selina and I became good friends and our relationship filled me with pleasure. I would tease her that someday I would be as lovely as she. With stern face, belying her desire to laugh at our spoof, she assured me that, with age, I would grow lovelier, "but never as lovely as I."

Some days we'd go on for hours, entertaining the office with our antics. Even Sister Amy, who would sit and shake her head in disapproval, could not hide her pleasure.

My innocence struggled to stay alive within this new environment. Through all, I remained pure of language and action, in spite of Judy's constant harassment. In the beginning I didn't like her. Judy was too tough, cursed too much and was anti-God. Yet, they say opposites attract and we soon became close friends. In fact, she became my closet confidant.

We had lunch together almost every day debating the merits of her life compared to mine. It was a battle between good and evil. Judy put me down, just like Dad, but coming out of her mouth it didn't hurt. She acted as she believed and though I disapproved of her lifestyle, at least she wasn't a hypocrite. Blasphemer though she was, I loved her dearly. Lord only knew why.

* * * * * * * * *

During that first summer at St. Charles my brother was working at a surveyor's office around the block and we'd occasionally have lunch together.

On one afternoon Paul's co-worker, Gary, joined us. Gary was thirty-two years old and about two inches shorter than my 5'4" frame. He talked in a high-pitched, almost womanly voice and looked like a fourteen year old kid. I learned that when he was fourteen he'd had brain surgery to remove a benign tumor lodged around his pituitary gland and this had caused retardation in his physical development. The operation was a success, but Gary would never look like a grown man. However, he was a normal man in every other way.

Gary took a liking to me and I was attracted to him by his crazy sense of humor. It wasn't long before we began to date. Again, I was thrilled to be dating an older man, especially since Dad approved. I think he felt I was safe with Gary because of his lack of manliness and I never told Dad otherwise, deciding it was better for all if Dad stayed in his fantasy world.

Gary was a gentleman and I had no trouble keeping him in line. We'd kiss, but they were platonic and he made no other demands. As with all my other boyfriends, I had no sexual desire outside of simple kissing. We were merely buddies exchanging occasional shows of affections which I thought satisfied Gary as they did me.

One day, while Paul, Gary and I played darts, Gary made an attempt to touch my breast. I was abhorred and told him, rather curtly, "If you ever try that again, I'll deck you."

Gary laughed, obviously not taking me seriously, but Paul assured him I was quite sincere and capable. Gary backed off and never tried it again.

As a result of this event I knew that Gary was becoming too serious. I didn't want to hurt him, but I had to break off the relationship. I tried to explain to Gary that I couldn't get serious because it would interfere with my career plans. He was heartbroken and baffled as to why I couldn't mix both. I had no answer, holding firmly to my decision.

I was relieved, but felt guilty because I thought it was my fault Gary had become serious. Then I checked myself for such misguided thinking. Though I had been affectionate with him I never teased or led him on in any way. Gary was just like every other man; a constant source of confusion. Men couldn't be satisfied with friendship. Serious thoughts and sex always came up and there was no way I would deviate from my
career plans, which were coming along nicely. My probation period was over at the hospital and they had asked me to continue

my employ. My hard work and steadfast conviction was paying off and it showed in my paycheck, too.

   My life was going in the direction I had planned and nothing, not even a man, would alter my course.

Chapter 19: 1965

    Early that fall Troy Donahue and Joey Heatherton were making a promotional appearance at a local movie theatre. Since I was an avid fan of Troy's, nothing could stop me from going. I also wanted to see Joey, a rising newcomer whom had triggered my "funny feeling" the first time I'd seen her on TV. Continuing to rationalize that she was an inaccessible movie star, whom I wanted to befriend, as the reason for the "feeling", I accepted its existence. It never occurred to me that the same situation applied to Troy.

    After what seemed an eternity of sitting in the front row of the theatre (I had gotten there about an hour early to insure a good seat), Troy walked onto the stage. He was absolutely gorgeous. I was thrilled, but anxious because Joey hadn't entered. Troy sadly explained that Joey had taken ill and had to cancel her appearance. A frightening disappointment overwhelmed me.

    Troy continued with a question and answer period that was wonderful; he was so kind and sincere. I just loved him! I only wished Joey had been there, for the evening was incomplete without her. However, when the movie began I forgot my disappointment over Joey's absence, captivated by her on screen. Captivated, yet filled with the vague fear I had come to know so well.

* * * * * * * * *

    In November an unexpected visitor dropped by my house. I hadn't seen my high school sweetheart in almost two years, since he'd joined the Army.

    Though still stocky, Don had grown quite handsome. Also, his stuttering problem was almost unnoticeable and there was a maturity about him that I found attractive.

We talked for hours. No longer was he boring. Don had improved his mind through experience. Perhaps he bragged a bit too much, but I understood.

Don asked me for a date and I accepted. Why not? He was married to the army as I was married to my work at the hospital. There would be no need to become serious. Don would shortly return to his base in Germany. We would merely have some companionship and a few laughs.

Three weeks after we began dating Don began to act strangely. I asked him if anything was wrong and, as he hemmed and hawed, I became fearful. I had the feeling he was going to ruin everything by getting serious. We'd had three lovely weeks of casual dating. There had been good-night kisses, which I now reciprocated, not fearing my aggressive affection because I was confident in my ability to handle men. Now Don was changing and I didn't understand why things couldn't stay the way they were.

After two hours of playing a game of twenty questions and after two attempts to French kiss me, which I averted (French kissing before marriage was too permissive for my Christian morals), he popped the question.

Don was such a nice guy and I didn't want to hurt him, but I couldn't marry him. Gently I told him I just wasn't ready to settle down. Hard as it was, I think he understood, for we parted friends.

* * * * * * * * *

I was becoming proficient at my job and soon my boss assigned me to learn the NCR posting machine. Every morning I'd sit at the machine posting the daily hospital charges to the patient account cards. It became so rote an assignment I found my mind wandering, becoming introspective.

During this time tragedy hit a family I'd known for years. Sara Sullivan was the ten-year-old daughter of a family in my church.

Sara had leukemia and the doctors were not optimistic, although she remained unaware of the extent of her illness.

Day after day, while posting her charges, I would read the lab slips that monitored her white blood count. Some days were hopeful for her white count was low, but usually that was the result of a blood transfusion the previous day. For the most part her white count was extremely high and I was terrified for her.

Everyday I went to the hospital's chapel and lit a candle, staying fifteen minutes to pray for her recovery. It was a time for soul searching. I couldn't accept her fate and questioned God's reason for allowing this to happen to such a good Christian family. Sara was an adorable child, not old enough to realize the sinfulness of life. The why's persisted, but I continued to trust God.

Sara died in March, a year later. Our church was bursting with people at the funeral; not a dry eye to be found. The day before had been a cold, winter-like day, but the day of Sara's funeral was warm and bright. The flowers and trees, which had been barren the day before, began to bud. It seemed as if God was telling everyone that, as the trees come back to life, so would Sara.

My questions as to why God had allowed Sara to die were answered by a deep feeling in my soul that God was getting His message of eternal life across to all who attended, trying to strengthen our faith. You might think this feeble, but not if you'd experienced the peace that day brought me.

* * * * * * * * * *

At Christmas a new woman was employed by the medical records department of St. Charles Hospital. Diane was a year younger than me with short brown hair, brown eyes and a cute freckled face. Though small in statue, she had a beautifully proportioned figure and a personality as attractive as her appearance. Sweet and kind, with a sense of humor that delighted me endlessly, I could not help becoming friends with her.

It had been almost a year since I'd experienced my "funny feeling", but Diane resurrected it immediately. However, I wasn't ill at ease with the "feeling" so I yielded to its presence.

Shortly after, the symptoms which had, for the most part, lay quiet the last couple of years, emerged with a force that was breath-taking. Just when my life was beginning to get organized the damn symptoms appeared and threw me into disorder.

Every Sunday night I would sob into my pillow, terrified of going to work, when the inability to breathe and the feeling of faintness and dream-like existence waited to attack. Furthermore, I couldn't stand the thought of my friends seeing these attacks. I hated myself for being so weak.

I went to work, forcing myself through the day. Some were worse than others; some hours of the day were better than others. More and more, though, I ran from the office to the safety of the bathroom where I could be alone and try to regroup myself. Many days I spent almost the entire afternoon in the bathroom, begging God for strength and some relief.

Fortunately my job required me to be out of the office a great deal so I always had a good excuse for leaving my desk and no one knew I was hiding in the bathroom. My workload was not terribly heavy so I managed to keep up with it.

I talked to no one about this problem. I already felt inferior by being a woman. If I told my friends of my illness or if I actually fainted in front of anybody I would be looked upon as another feeble female. I couldn't stand the thought. Sick as I was, desolate as I felt, I would open up to no one, lest I blacken the name of woman even more.

* * * * * * * * *

During the past year I became a member of one of my church's women's Bible Study group. Mom had been a member for years and I joined her group enthusiastically. It was something we could do together as adults and I loved the idea of relating to Mom on this level. Furthermore, I yearned for more knowledge of the Bible and this group provided an avenue.

Whenever the discussion turned to the subject of women, I'd disregard the biblical passages and voice my equalitarian opinion. The women in the group couldn't understand how I could believe in such opposition to God's Word. I couldn't stand myself for disobeying God's Laws either, but I couldn't stand living by a law that made me inferior merely because of my gender.

Even when the women in the group said they agreed that men and women were created equal, I would not be appeased for they always added, "But women are not the same and they are not to behave the same. The man is the "head" of the woman."

How could the man be the head if women were equal?

I'd tell the other women, "Why is one person, merely because of gender, deemed the "head"? Shouldn't the head of a household be the person who is the most qualified? What if a man is a dummy or a bum? Is a woman supposed to obey him? Shouldn't a relationship have co-heads if it is to be truly equal?"

They seemed not to hear. I fought with logic and they fought with blind faith. There was no way I could win.

Mom listened attentively to my words, but stayed quiet till we got home. There she told me she agreed with what I had said. She had always believed in God's given equality between the sexes and never doubted hers, despite the Biblical references. She thought that the Bible was being misinterpreted in this area, but couldn't defend her beliefs with any facts so she stayed silent during the discussion at Bible Study. Beside, she told me, I was doing such a good job of debating the issue there was no need for her to speak.

I understood her silence, but without facts I was doomed. Mom's belief was based on her personal feeling, not facts. She had a strong faith in God, His Word and herself. I wished I had her faith, but my mind dealt in factual evidence. I could accept nothing less.

The more I related with people the more convinced I became of the superiority of men. They were strong and logical. They didn't get overly emotional, losing control of themselves, crying shamelessly. They were dominant, aggressive and in control. I didn't perceive women as possessing these traits. Surely these facts proved the validity of the Bible.

"I can't exist like this," I prayed to God. "I have to be equal! Why did you create me a woman? It's Hell to be an inferior being. It's not fair and I hate it."

I couldn't hold these thought in anymore. I needed to talk with someone who could give me the answers I craved or I thought I would burst. I couldn't turn to a man, for each time I talked on the subject they'd turn away and I wanted men to like me. Talking to women was no better for they continually debased themselves. Mom's confidence could not change my feelings for she just believed. I needed facts.

The only person I could think of who would be different was Judy. So I opened up to her.

In Judy's opinion women were superior to men. She loved men, but thought they were all jerks. I listened, arguing with Biblical words, but she'd tear them down, stating that the Bible was a "crock of shit."

Judy's words didn't satisfy me, either. Like Mom, Judy couldn't give me facts. It was uplifting to hear her talk on women's superiority, but the facts were against women.

Coming to a dead end with Judy I turned to literature, but every book I read reinforced the validity of woman's inferior status. These books merely aped Biblical words, adding the title of "protector" to describe men. I felt more inferior with this new word. It was as if women were weak, helpless children, incapable of taking care of themselves. Men, on the other hand, needed no one to care for or protect them.

There seemed no way to escape the fact that women were, indeed, inferior. If they weren't they'd fight back. Instead, they yielded to male domination. Worse yet, they seemed to enjoy their demeaning status.

Chapter 20: 1966

Work was becoming more difficult to perform. Mornings went pretty well, but by afternoon my symptoms were brutal. Sometimes I'd spend the entire afternoon secluded in the bathroom. In addition, eating became problematic. With the difficulty in my breathing, coupled with a throat that seemed to close, I was terrified to eat lest I choke and make a fool out of myself or, worse yet, die.

I knew if I didn't improve I'd have to quit my job so I broke my vow of never seeing a psychiatrist and, after consulting with Mom, made an appointment with Dr. Falano. Mom suggested we keep my therapy secret from Dad to avoid his traumatic objection, not only because of Dad's disbelief in psychiatrists, but also his dislike for Dr. Falano. Once, at a local town meeting, Dr. Falano had the audacity to disagree with Dad and he'd never forgiven the man.

My first appointment with Dr. Falano was scheduled for nine o'clock, the 20th of March, 1966. At eight-thirty, playing my charade perfectly, I told Mom and Dad I was going downtown. Since this was not unusual behavior for me, no suspicion was aroused in Dad.

I went to my room, put on a dress and then put my pants and shirt over the dress. I could have made things easier by just wearing pants, but I thought a dress was proper feminine attire. I wanted to make a good impression on Dr. Falano.

I left the house, arrived at Dr. Falano's, rang his bell, entered and sat down in the waiting room. The minutes ticked by and I counted them, along with my rapid heartbeat. Suddenly the door opened and a short, stocky, Italian man, with receding gray hair, which made him appear older than his 43 years, called me into his office.

There was a couch in the room, but when I asked if that was for people to use during therapy, Dr. Falano smiled and said, "That's only in the movies. I keep it for decoration." He was so friendly I began to relax as I seated myself on the soft, comfortable chair across from his. My prejudice against psychiatrists began to disappear with the friendliness of Dr. Falano. His warm, happy brown eyes seemed to say "I care" and his gentle voice was quieting to the nerves. We spoke casually for a few minutes and then he broke our chain of amenities.

"Why do you feel you needed to see a psychiatrist?"

"I don't really know. I feel like I'm going to faint all the time and I can't breathe. Nothing I do controls it and it's almost impossible to go to work."

Dr. Falano proceeded to ask questions concerning my present activities. I told him about my job and the difficulty I was having with the growing symptoms. I told him of my living arrangements and my limited social life. He sat quietly while I rambled on and then he asked me how I felt about my parents. I had no trouble telling him that I adored my mother and less trouble telling him how much I hated my father, expanding on our tense and argumentative relationship.

The session progressed on a rather light note. I felt a little disappointed. I was impatient to get to the root of my problem. Dr. Falano seemed to be taking his time. I had this great hope that once we found the one traumatic childhood experience that I'd repressed, I'd be instantly cured.

Dr. Falano seemed to read my mind for he said, "Therapy is merely a process of relearning. Everyone begins to learn from the moment he is born and each bit of learning makes an impression. Some are positive and help a person grow strong, but some are negative and can distort perceptions of reality. Your discomfiture indicates that negative influences are dominating you because you have not learned how to deal with them. In therapy we will discuss these negative influences, relearn whatever you've learned incorrectly and help you to change what you can and handle what can't be changed. There is no miracle cure, such as one incident causing your entire problem. That's Hollywood. In actuality, your problem stems from learning many things incorrectly which causes stress."

It sounded easy. Like going back to school and since I'd been a good student I was sure I would do well in therapy. For the first time in months I was optimistic.

"How long will it take before you cure me?" I questioned, still somewhat impatient.

"I'm not going to cure you. You're going to cure yourself. I'm merely going to help you do that. Hopefully it will take about two years." Dr. Falano spoke with a gentle, reassuring voice.

I left his office and returned home to find Mom sitting on the couch, anxious to know how everything went. As usual, Dad had gone to bed.

I told her, word for word, the whole session and she began to feel as hopeful as I. We hugged each other and prayed our thankfulness to God. At midnight I went to bed and fell into the most restful sleep I'd had in months.

I returned to work and my ritualistic running to the bathroom, but I knew I could endure as long as help was on the way. I had to hang on to the hope of getting better or totally lose my mind.

Judy was the only person in whom I confided my therapy. I knew she'd understand and not think me crazy. She, too, had spent many hours in therapy, but I hoped mine would go better than hers for, in my opinion, she was still quite messed up. Nevertheless, Judy was a source of comfort and encouragement.

The week passed slowly, but soon it was time to secretly dress and go downtown.

In Dr. Falano's office I began to unwind and feel the surge of optimism he had instilled in me the week before; optimism that had faded during the difficult week at work. Surely something would happen tonight to give me more strength.

Dr. Falano immediately began to pick my brain, delving into my relationship with Mom and Dad, with emphasis on Dad.

Dr. Falano was a good listener and showed me much compassion. He smiled easily and was a comfort. I found myself thinking that this man was on my side. He affirmed my belief that Dad was a difficult man to live with, but stressed that he was also a man with many problems and I should try to understand that my Dad had not been premeditatively cruel. Dr. Falano explained that Dad couldn't help himself and since he wouldn't change, I had to, unfair as that seemed to me.

We discussed anger and my guilt over the hatred I felt for Dad.

"Anger is not necessarily wrong." Dr. Falano said confidently. "If it is harmful or unjustifiable then you'd have reason to feel guilty. Your biggest problem is that you don't know how to handle your hostility in a productive way. You feel it and, for the most part, I believe it is justifiable, but you haven't learned this yet. Furthermore, you haven't learned how to release your anger correctly and, more importantly, you haven't learned to forgive yourself for your hostile feelings. Therefore, it backs up and makes you feel sick. You actually end up taking your anger and hatred for your Dad out on yourself."

I explained that Dad was a very religious man who raised me to believe that anger was a sin and I'd always tried to control such feelings.

"Your father may be religious, but he, too, has learned a lot of things incorrectly. Let's look closer at anger. Your father states that becoming angry is a sin, but even Jesus lost his temper. Was that as sin?"

"No". I replied, "But Jesus is God".

"That may be true", Dr. Falano continued, "but the reason Jesus' anger was sinless was because it was justified and that's the whole issue."

It was becoming clearer to me. I remembered reading about the time Jesus got mad when the people had turned the temple into a sinful market place. They were blaspheming God and Jesus justifiably blew his stack and even overturned the market tables.

One hour in therapy went by too quickly. I wanted to stay longer, eager for more of this wonderful knowledge.

Again, Dr. Falano seemed to read my thoughts and cautioned, "I know you're impatient, but take it a little at a time. Later on you will find that your emotions will try to reject what you have learned tonight. They'll fight the truth and you must give time for the intellectual learning to digest into your emotions. We can't overload you."

I understood, but patience was not one of my strong points.

I was scheduled for the following week and left for home, anxious to tell Mom about my newfound understanding of hostility, hatred and true guilt.

When I walked into my house, Dad was in bed. I told Mom every word of my session. I wanted to teach her, but I also wanted to reiterate what I had learned so it would sink into my emotions faster. Mom was always willing to listen, even if it meant staying up passed midnight and forfeiting the good night's sleep she needed to perform her duties at work. But, that was Mom.

I returned to work on a high, confident that my symptoms would lesson. The first session with Dr. Falano had explained my symptoms and assured me I was not going to faint, but I hadn't felt confident until after the second session when he backed up the reasons for my symptoms with the reality of how harmful holding emotions inside could be. I still ran from the office, but less frequently. I was also trying to analyze, per Dr. Falano's instructions, what preceded an onset of an attack, but I couldn't pinpoint anything. One minute I was fine and the next I was besieged by the symptoms, panicking and running to the bathroom to be alone.

My third session hit me with a force that was to bring my awareness to a peak. Dr. Falano was pleased with my progress and continued to delve into my relationship with Dad. It had already been established that I worshipped my mother, so little time was spent on our stable relationship. However, Dr. Falano cautioned me against the unrealistic feelings I had towards Mom. Even though he admitted she was a wonderful, supportive woman, he advised that I also see her as human, having faults like everyone else. My anger over his admonition was soothed only by the fact that a psychiatrist thought so highly of the woman I adored.

I expanded on my father's attitudes towards women and Dr. Falano somehow turned my attention away from Dad towards my feelings on the subject. I was hesitant to say anything for fear that Dr. Falano, like everyone else, would substantiate the reality of woman's inferiority, but I had to try just once more.

"I feel women are inferior to men. I don't want to believe it, but everything points to the fact and I can't handle being a woman if it means being inferior." I poured out my feelings, terrified of his answer.

"What makes you feel this is true?" Dr. Falano prodded.

"The Bible says that women are to be submissive to men and that means men are superior. I can't escape the truth of the written Word of God." I said hopelessly.

Dr. Falano laughed loud and heartily. Then he replied, "Women are by no means inferior to men. If anything, they are superior." I sat dumbfounded.

"We live in a world which has given women the short end of the stick," he continued, "but that doesn't mean it's true. You're quite locked into the Bible and interpretation is a tricky business. You must consider the times, traditions, social systems, social problems and a number of other variables including the fact that the Bible was written by men."

"Wait a minute!" I interrupted, letting some anger surface. "The Bible was written by God, through men, so it's not the men speaking, but God."

Dr. Falano was gentle, "That's another area we'll have to get straight. The Bible is not a dictated letter, word for word, as you have been taught. Men, inspired by God, wrote the Bible, but that doesn't eliminate the human element. The Bible was written for humans and because of this it is subject to the human condition and human comprehension. Both your parents taught you about the Bible, but I doubt your mother has as rigid an interpretation as your Dad. Take a good look at your Dad. He's an insecure man who, by his own admission, is a woman hater. Hate stems from fear. It's the same with all types of prejudice. Your father fears women because he feels inferior to them. So, to justify his feelings of inadequacy, he projects them onto women backing it up with Biblical words, which people often misinterpret, to justify his feelings of inferiority. By doing this he maintains his self-esteem or thinks he does. Unfortunately, you have been the sounding board for his insecurity. You have listened to him tell you how inferior women are when he is saying it only to lift his own deflated self-esteem. He told you a story and you bought it."

"Within the next months," he continued, "you will relearn about women, hopefully do some relearning on interpreting the Bible and eventually you will see how misguided your father is and how truly equal women are."

I sat their astonished that I had found another human being, a man, a Roman Catholic, who not only believed what I wanted to believe, but who also would give me the facts I so desperately needed to believe I was an equal.

Suddenly my mouth opened and, out of nowhere, shocking myself, I asked, "Dr. Falano, am I a lesbian?"

He paused and then said, "No. You're merely scared to hell of men because you feel inferior to them. Once you come to accept your equality, your fear of men will vanish."

I left his office and returned home, relieved and eager to tell Mom. She was happy; telling me that she agreed with what Dr. Falano had said about the Bible and women's position, but could never put her feelings and beliefs into any logical words. We talked for hours about my newfound equality, but I never mentioned the word lesbian.

* * * * * * * * * *

I returned to work with a new zeal for life, but found that Dr. Falano had been right when he said it was hard for one's emotional side to accept intellectual data no matter how right the facts were. I tried to draw comfort from his words, hoping that, in time, my emotions would accept the facts. I could feel the battle raging within and, for now, the negative emotions were winning.

Nevertheless, I was able to perform my tasks at the office more adequately, running to the bathroom less frequently and for shorter periods of time. I still suffered from depression and though it was becoming spasmodic rather than continual the attacks were all too frequent and all too consuming.

There were times when I really felt equal to a man, but it would take only one word in opposition or the sight of a man acting in a domineering way to make my negative feelings surface, throwing me into reverse. Through my tears I wondered if I'd ever truly believe in a woman's equality, for it seemed a battle that led to a dead end. No matter how much Dr. Falano or Mom fought with facts in favor of women's God given equality, I couldn't believe. The positive facts that poured into my head couldn't kill the negative ones long engrained. Besides the incessant influence of Dad's opinions chaining my emotions, I could see the subjugation of women everywhere and their passivity made me fear that Dr.

Falano and Mom were wrong. My mind was sealed. There seemed no escape.

Chapter 21: 1966

The Women's Liberation Movement was gaining nationwide publicity and strength in 1966. The influence of Gloria Steinham, Bella Abzug and other staunch women in the movement helped me in a way no one else had. Here were women living the way I wanted to believe was natural. They talked about socialization and its effect of separating men and women into two different groups, each with definite behaviors to adhere which resulted in giving women an inferior position. Until the onset of the Women's Liberation Movement my feelings were obstructed because I saw no women fighting for equality.

Without a doubt these women not only believed in their equality, but also fought for it and their belief was based on fact. I knew I had to be a part of the movement so I became a member of a NOW chapter recently opened near my town.

The membership consisted of approximately twenty women of two types. One group consisted of the unfulfilled housewives, guilt ridden because they were dissatisfied with home and family. They were taught that a woman's place was in the home, but many found they wanted more and they hoped this organization could help them find what was missing in their lives and free them from guilt. The second group, the women I had always hoped existed, those who exemplified equality, were the hard core women "Libbers". They never questioned their innate equality and fought with every breath they took to insure it for other women.

I listened to both sides, identifying with each. Facts, which were mere repetitions of Dr. Falano's words, bombarded my ears, but now they were setting in, opening my eyes as never before.

I was not giving Dr. Falano a second place, for he had been right. Without his guidance there would have been no foundation for my feelings of equality to grow. I know that I could not have reached peace without the two working together.

In any case, my intellectual and emotional sides were now responding in a positive manner. I had a long way to travel before I would feel totally secure for, as I came to understand, an enslaved person cannot feel freed overnight. However, it took only one meeting with NOW for me to know that I would fight for women's equality, never subjecting myself to male domination.

I grew confident in the validity of my feelings. Outside of the fact that I would not hate men, as a small handful of women libbers did, I was becoming quite radical. I voiced my opinion, always basing it on facts, with a fervor brought about by my broadened understanding and knowledge on the subject.

I began to read books written by women involved in the movement and found them totally different from the so-called equalitarian books written by men. I began to understand how easily women could end up like me or even worse. The unhappy housewives who attended the NOW meetings showed me that I was not alone in my confusion, guilt and unhappiness. The time had come and I was eager to grab the hammer of equality and break the chains of oppression. No longer would I have to fight alone. In unity there is strength and encouragement. If I took a step back the support of NOW would get me back on my feet. It would be a long, hard fight, but I knew I would be victorious.

* * * * * * * * *

Needless to say, Dad wasn't at all pleased with my new interest and our fighting escalated. There was no escaping. It would never end.

In Dad's opinion it was bad enough that I disagreed with the Bible on male/female matters. Now I was in with an "atheistic, commie group" with only one goal in mind – to put men into slavery. Arguments grew fiercer especially when I told him the Bible had been misinterpreted on women's equality. Dad never won, though, for my knowledge and increased ability to use the facts struck with killing blows. Nevertheless, being the stubborn man that he was, he never gave in.

* * * * * * * * *

There remained one area in which I was making no headway in feeling comfortable with my equality and this lay in the area of sexual relations. I was bothered by what I read and observed concerning male sexual behavior, perceiving their more powerful sex drive, aggressiveness and easy arousal as superiority. I knew, from my own solitary sexual behavior, that I had a powerful sex drive and was easily aroused. Also, although I never fantasized about having sex with a man, I knew that my behavior in bed (when I was married) would not be passive. This made me feel I was an abnormal woman.

With the help of Dr. Falano and the NOW organization I realized that socialization played an important role in the sexual behavior of men and women. Aside from a few innate differences, men and women were basically the same. I lost my hatred for my gender, exchanging it for a hatred of an unfair, misguided set of societal rules and roles to a more realistic interpretation of the Biblical passages pertaining to a woman's place

I also learned that men have a feminine side to their nature as women have a masculine side. Androgyny was the word used to describe this phenomenon. This last piece of information made it easy for me to see that my tomboy nature was not abnormal. I had never been abnormal! I merely let my masculine side show while other girls had not.

Yet, with the acceptance of my equality, with the love and respect I now had for my gender, I remained confused as to my lack of sexual interest in the male of the species. With acceptance of my equality and fear of men gone, why did I still lack sexual desire for them? All the requirements had been met so why was I still disinterested? The questions would not stop haunting me.

* * * * * * * * *

Amid the forest of positively answered questions and happiness that had come into my life since therapy, the NOW group and my job security, a little rain had to fall.

Judy, my friend and confidant over the last year, was leaving St. Charles Hospital because her husband had received a career opportunity, in New Jersey, that he couldn't resist.

I was heartbroken at the thought of going to work without this ribald, sacrilegious woman, who lived for the moment, pursuing every sinful, hedonistic pleasure with insatiable passion. A woman who was the antithesis of everything I believed to be good and Godly. A woman I'd tried to convert, but had failed. A woman I dearly loved.

However, I wasn't going to let my sadness show the night the office girls and I swarmed to Judy's house for a farewell party.

The night was full of gaiety and our general craziness. I remember, with fondness, the blisters I had on my thumbs, the result of playing the morocco's half the night as we all danced, sang and cajoled.

The evening grew late and all, save me, had gone home. The sorrow Judy and I had put on hold now surfaced.

I couldn't bear losing her. Though twenty years my senior, she was not a mother figure. She was a friend, yet different than any I had ever had. Different in a way I couldn't define nor comprehend. I loved Selina, too and she was more like me in her beliefs. It was odd that I could feel such a deep love for Judy given our totally different sense of morals.

Judy asked me to stay over that night. It was very late, her husband was already in New Jersey and there was plenty of room in her bed.

Fear kept me from saying yes. Only tonight it was not just fear of being away from Mom. Tonight there was more. It was as if something or someone was telling me that to stay would be dangerous. Ridiculous, I kept telling myself. Judy would never hurt me, but the thought would not leave.

Finally, Judy walked me to my car where we stood for an hour saying our farewell, locked in an embrace, kissing each other on the mouth. I recalled the incident when, as a child, I had kissed Bonnie on the lips. I remembered the sense of guilt I'd felt then. Standing here with Judy, loving every minute of our closeness, not wanting to release her from my arms, rekindled that sense of guilt. In addition, fear surged through me because our kisses were more intense than those with Bonnie. Though Judy and I kissed with mouths closed, they lingered and were firm.

Judy kept asking me to stay, but in the end I drove off, never to forget this night of partying. Always to secretly cherish the closeness and beauty of the special, though perplexing, love I felt for Judy.

Chapter 22: 1966

The physical symptoms were fading and I became more outgoing, making more friends at work. One, the personnel director's secretary, became especially close to me easing the loneliness I felt when Judy left.

Harriet was a blonde haired, blue eyed woman of medium height. Though not what you'd call beautiful, she possessed a personality that made you feel comfortable and had a sense of humor that made her seem much younger than her forty-eight years.

As we grew closer I found that she had a 19 year old son in the Navy. He was stationed on an aircraft carrier off of Viet Nam. She talked of her son, Seth, with such love and devotion (he was her only child) I found myself growing curious, especially when she showed me a picture of him. Seth's lean, Arian and gentle appearance attracted me immediately.

I learned that Seth was coming home for R & R (rest and relaxation) at Christmas when Harriet timidly asked if I would mind going out with her son. I saw the lonely sailor angle, but accepted her matchmaker invitation. With such a good woman for a mother I figured Seth would be a nice young man. Besides, it was only one date so what could I lose? If I didn't like him, that would be the end.

A few days before Christmas, Seth called and nervously asked me if I'd like to go out with him. I accepted, feeling as if I'd known him a lifetime.

The next night Seth picked me up and, after Dad's usual third degree, we went to a local club.

Seth and I had a beautiful evening of talking, dancing and laughing. There was a naivety about him that charmed me immediately. Seth was a decent man, more innocent than I. He was sweet and gentle. Very different from the stereotypical male society had produced. He was so like me in thought and actions, it seemed we were one.

From his picture I hadn't thought him a handsome man, but seeing him in person changed my mind. He wasn't Clark Gable, but there was something appealing about him. His blue eyes captivated me. He was lean, but muscular and stood a couple of inches short of six feet. His full, sensual lips and beautiful straight teeth made him quite attractive, but the gentility of his personality was what drew me to him.

Seth was a good listener and I found myself telling him most everything about my life. Most men wouldn't have found my conversation interesting, especially on a first date, but Seth was eager to hear all about me. Never did he make me feel inadequate or handicapped. He understood and accepted. He didn't even blink an eye when I told him I was in therapy nor was he intimidated by my involvement with the women's movement.

Seth listened without interruption and then he told me his life story. His sensitive nature had caused him much heartache. I was deeply touched by his ability to reveal the feminine side of his nature.

Never once did he act domineering, nor did he seem preoccupied with sex. Seth was the epitome of virtue and my soul reached out to his. I trusted this virtual stranger and knew I wanted our relationship to continue. With this gentle and good man at my side I knew my sexual hang-ups would disappear so I felt no need to discuss this part of my life with him. I was confident that it was only a matter of time and the right man to spark my sleeping sexual desire.

The evening grew late. I didn't want it to end nor did I relish the idea of Seth returning to Viet Nam, even though he assured me he was miles from the fighting.

I had such good feelings for Seth and knew he felt the same when he said, "I enjoyed tonight very much. You're a wonderful woman. Next time I get leave would you go out with me again?"

"I'd like that very much." I replied sincerely.

Seth didn't know when he'd get home again, but he promised to write. I told him I would, too. Without trying to kiss me goodnight, he was gone.

At last I had a boyfriend. The kind of man I believed was nonexistent.

* * * * * * * * *

Carrie was home from college that Christmas, giving me the best present anyone could.

"Jan, I have a question to ask you," she sounded coy. Bob and I are getting married this August and I was wondering if you would be my maid of honor?"

I didn't care how Carrie took my reaction, as I took her in my arms, holding this beloved person, ecstatically answering, "I'd be proud."

I felt her arms close around me in an embrace filled with love. At that moment it didn't matter that she was going to marry Bob.

Chapter 23: 1966-67

Nineteen sixty-six had been such a good year. Therapy was helping me stabilize, the NOW group had given validity to all I had hoped about women's equality, Seth brought me joy and a sense of normality and Carrie had reaffirmed her love by asking me to be her maid of honor. However, as is always in life, all cannot be rose colored.

Paul was home for Christmas and our house reflected the usual yuletide spirit. We stood behind Dad while he played the organ, singing carols in praise to the newborn King. When all our presents were opened we prepared for church, where Dad was the organist. It was the most beautiful service of the entire year and we all loved it. Except this year Paul was not going to join us.

"You're not going to church?" Mom inquired puzzled.

"No." Paul's reply was short and firm.

"Why not?" Dad sounded self-righteous. "Don't you believe in God anymore?"

Paul hesitated and then replied, quite emphatically, "No!"

Mom and I were stunned. Dad went wild. Fortunately, he had to cut short his sermonizing lest he be late for church service.

In church I sat beside Mom, drowned in depression. My brother an atheist! How could he be? He had always been a faithful churchgoer and in college was President of the Lutheran Club on campus. What had gone wrong? For years I'd worried about the souls of other people. I never thought I'd have to worry about Paul's. I was desolate.

When Mom and I talked with Paul on our return from Church (Dad just went to bed), there was no long explanation as to his change in belief. Paul had never been much of a talker.

Mom's heart was broken, but she never turned away from Paul and, after the shock wore down some, I knew I couldn't turn from him either. More than ever he needed our love. There was nothing we could do but pray God would help Paul believe again.

* * * * * * * * *

Towards the end of March I received an unexpected call from Carrie.

"Hey Carrie, how are you?" I said joyfully, for we hadn't seen each other since Christmas. She ignored my question and replied, "I'm coming home Friday to spend the weekend." She sounded troubled.

"Great! Maybe we can catch a movie." I said, trying to get her out of this mood.

"We're not going to any movie, Jan." Her rough tone shocked me. "I need you to hold my hand." She paused then continued, "I think I'm pregnant."

I went mute.

"I tried going to the doctor at school, but chickened out. If you don't go with me to a doctor here I'm afraid I'll do the same thing." She sounded desperate.

"Don't worry, Carrie. I'll go with you."

"Thanks, Jan. I'll call you when I get in." She paused and then pleaded, "Please don't tell anyone."

"You have my word." I said over the lump in my throat.

I hung up the phone in despair. I knew the wedding was set for August, just a few short months away, but not few enough. My feelings were dichotomous. According to my religion and the morals of the day, premarital sex was a sin, but to get pregnant before marriage was an abomination. Intellectually I knew Carrie and Bob deeply loved each other and lovemaking was a beautiful act between two people in love, but their sinning upset me. I wished they could have waited. If Carrie had only been more like me she wouldn't have to bear this awful burden.

I returned to the living room with a forced smile on my face, happily telling Mom and Dad that Carrie would be home this weekend for a visit. Nothing more was said on my part, though I ached to release the torturous secret. It was only Wednesday and I was not good at keeping secrets from Mom, but I had given Carrie my word.

The next two days were agony. I prayed Carrie was wrong, but she was studying to be a nurse so who would know better? In addition my heart felt another pang. Our childhood was truly over. Our relationship would never be the same. I couldn't accept the situation. It was alien to me. I was confused, sure of nothing except that Carrie had turned to me in her time of need and I wouldn't let her down.

* * * * * * * * *

The phone rang Friday night at six. Carrie was scheduled for an eight o'clock appointment at the gynecologist and I quickly left, telling Mom I was eating out with Carrie and not to wait up for me.

"Have a good time, honey and give Carrie my love." She warmly replied and I felt a twinge of guilt for deceiving her.

I picked up Carrie and we rode, in silence, to the doctor's office a few miles from her house. The ride seemed an eternity.

I opened the door leading into the waiting room, but Carrie hesitated. I took hold of her arm and looked into her eyes, which stared back like a child in pain. A thin smile crossed my face, but no words were uttered. Carrie smiled weakly, took a deep breath and courageously entered.

Inside the sterile, pale blue waiting room sat six very pregnant women. Carrie walked to the receptionist and was told to be seated. I sat as uncomfortably as Carrie, knowing her thoughts. These women were all married and going to be legitimate mothers.

Then a thought hit me like a ton of bricks. "What difference did it make? Bob and Carrie loved each other just as much as these legitimate wives loved their husbands so what was the big deal?"

I looked at Carrie. She sat quietly, tense and near tears. I felt so helpless.

"Miss Caron, please step inside." The nurse's voice brought me out of my thoughts.

The walls in the waiting room seemed to close in and crush me. I kept looking at the other women, abdomens distended with the joy of new life and a pain shot through my guts.

"Oh God, please don't let Carrie be pregnant. I know she's sinned, but she's in love. God, please understand our human condition and help her face what she must."

The door opened and Carrie walked out, face blank. She paid the nurse in cash and we walked out into the clear, crisp, night air.

"I thought I'd die when she said "Miss" Caron. Everyone knew I was an unwed mother." She said angrily.

"You don't know that. Not all women go to the gynecologist just because they're pregnant. I didn't so you mustn't feel that way."

"I guess you're right. I just feel so guilty." She paused, then continued, "The doctor says I'm either pregnant or else I have a very large tumor growing inside me. We wont' know until the test comes back. I hope it's a tumor."

What could I say? I prayed for God to help me find words that would comfort her.

"It may make things less difficult if it's a tumor, but don't hope for that. If you are pregnant you shouldn't feel guilty because the baby was conceived out of love and there can be nothing wrong with that." I stated, firmly, shocking myself for going against everything I had ever believed.

"I guess." Carrie acquiesced, but I knew she wasn't convinced.

We remained quiet as I drove down the road to the local bowling alley. Carrie wanted to stop for something to drink, stalling for time before she went home. I ordered a cola, but when I asked Carrie if she wanted the same she said, rather sarcastically, "No, better make mine a malted shake. If I am pregnant I'd better feed it properly."

After we'd finished our drinks I drove Carrie home and we stood in her apartment building's parking lot, hesitant to leave each other.

"I should have known this would happen. Rhythm isn't foolproof, but I thought I'd be lucky." Carrie cried out and my heart embraced her.

"I know, but it's not the end of the world. At least you had planned to get married. It's not one of those flings. You'll just have to move the wedding day closer."

"Oh my God! I don't even have my wedding gown. Bob's still got two more years at law school and we have no money. What are we going to do?" Carrie was near hysteria.

Feeling helpless I said, "I know it's going to be rough, but you and Bob love each other and you have good parents. They'll help you. Everything is going to work out all right. Please believe that." I wondered whom I was trying to convince.

"God! What will your folks think, Jan? Your father won't want to play the organ for my wedding. God is surely punishing me."

"Carrie, don't do this to yourself. You and Bob are in love and God understands that. He wouldn't punish you." Again I deviated from my beliefs, but was not uncomfortable.

"Well, I guess I'd better get inside. I'll call you when I have the results of the test, but please don't say a word until I know for sure."

"I promise." I said, turning to leave.

"Jan?"

"Yes?"

Carrie paused and then nervously asked, "Do you still want to be my maid of honor?"

Tears burned my eyes and my throat almost closed. There was never any doubt in my mind. I took her in my arms and said, "Don't be dumb. I wouldn't miss this for the world. Nothing could ever change my feelings for you and don't you forget it!"

She held me tightly and said, "Thank you. You're the best friend I've ever had."

On the drive home tears I'd held back poured down my face as I prayed, "Dear God, help Carrie and Bob. Forgive them, if they have sinned, because they truly love each other. Help me to be strong for her."

When I returned home Mom and Dad were asleep. Though I was not feeling tired, I prepared for bed. I couldn't face another conscious moment with this despair. I climbed into bed and fell into a troubled sleep.

The weekend dragged. I walked through it in a daze, avoiding Mom as much as possible lest I say something that might give away my secret.

Monday, at work, I was a nervous wreck. I performed my duties like a robot. That night at supper I was so anxious for Carrie's call I didn't feel like eating, but forced myself in order to avoid any questions.

I was watching TV when the phone rang.

"I'll get it." I said, trying to be casual. My hands were sweating and my heart beat fast as I picked up the receiver.

"Hello."

"Hi Jan," Carrie sounded terrible. "The test was positive. I'm pregnant."

"Oh Carrie," I cried, "Have you talked to Bob?"

"Yes. We've moved the wedding to April 15th. Can you be ready by then?"

"No problem."

"Ok, tell your parents. I still want them to come and tell your Dad that I still want him to play the organ for me, but I'll understand if he doesn't want to."

"All right Carrie. How are your parents taking it?"

"Not as bad as I expected. They're upset, but they're not angry with me or Bob."

"I'm so glad. I knew they'd understand."

"I'd better go now. There's so much to do. Call me tomorrow?" Carrie was calmer now.

"First thing," I replied.

The phone went dead. I took a deep breath, bracing myself for the scene I was sure Dad would create. I walked into the living room and, not seeing Mom, walked to her bedroom where she was reading a book. I breathed a sigh of relief for it would be easier to break the news to Mom first.

"Mom, I've got some bad news. Carrie is pregnant." I quickly got to the point.

She looked at me with shock on her face. Quickly the shock turned to softness.

"Are you sure?"

I proceeded to explain the last few days, telling her of Carrie's suffering and the new wedding plans. Mom listened quietly and when I'd finished she said, "You know I love Carrie, honey, and this hasn't changed the fact. I'll do anything to help and I want you to let Carrie know that."

Mom never changed. She remained compassionate and nonjudgmental. Though she had her religious beliefs and they didn't include approval of premarital sex, she understood and wasn't going to judge another human being.

"Mom, how am I going to break this to Dad? I'm terrified. Carrie still wants him to play at her wedding and if he says no I'll hate him!"

"Just relax, dear. You tell Dad and I'll handle any scene he may create. However, I think you have nothing to worry about."

Back in the living room I hesitantly told Dad. He sat quietly as I explained Carrie's predicament.

Then, quickly, before he could start preaching, I asked, "Carrie still wants you to play at her wedding. Will you?" I pleaded.

To my surprise he gently said, "Of course I will. People make mistakes."

I was amazed. For the first time in years I saw my father through the eyes of love.

Chapter 24: 1967

I called Carrie the next day and told her the good news. She was relieved and grateful. The wedding was scheduled for Saturday, April 15th. Carrie would make her own wedding gown, to conserve on money and she asked if I would mind shopping for mine without her because she just didn't have the time. This posed no problem.

Mom and I found a beautiful peach, satin gown with an empire waist and a straight skirt. I hoped it would be to Carrie's liking since I didn't know what her dress would look like and I wanted to complement her style.

The Friday before the wedding, Carrie and Bob took Joe, Bob's best man and me out for dinner in lieu of any costly bachelor parties or bridal showers.

Joe was tall, dark and handsome. However, as the evening progressed, dining in a lovely, yet inexpensive restaurant, I began to dislike him immensely because he was a domineering, insecure man. The table conversation was totally directed at Joe, by Joe. He was the most conceited man I'd ever met and I decided he needed to be brought down a peg so I began talking about the women's movement, its validity and my dedication to it, hoping to aggravate him. Apparently it worked, for he began a speech on the virtues of our traditional system and the idiocy of the women's movement. Never, except for Dad, had I heard any man speak so vehemently against the issue.

I fought back with expertise and we had a fiery discussion, each one verbally knocking down the other only to get up and throw another verbal punch. I was having a ball, for Joe couldn't take my punches and his barely touched me. I was practicing all I had learned in the last year and it felt good. No longer was I threatened just because someone believed that women were inferior. Instead of feeling insecure and intimidated, I fought back and Joe felt the sting of my attack.

As the fighting continued, I realized how foolish Joe was. His old, obsolete beliefs showed his ignorance and fear. My anger turned to indifference. I didn't want to continue wasting my time with such an idiot.

"What a shame," I thought, "such a nice looking man, but so ignorant and afraid." Thoughts of Seth came into my mind and I knew that he was one in a million.

* * * * * * * * *

I arrived at Carrie's apartment early Saturday morning to assist with the forest of last minute tasks. I helped ready the apartment for the reception while Carrie finished sewing her gown. Miraculously, Carrie's gown was the exact style as the one I had bought. Carrie adored the dress and the peach color was exactly what she had wanted.

The wedding took place in our church in Rocky Point. Carrie dressed in white for she was not going to think herself soiled. The service was simple, lasting only fifteen minutes, but it was beautiful and I felt proud standing beside Carrie, showing everyone how much I loved her.

As she said her vows I felt that twinge of pain again. I knew life had changed for us and I would have to accept the back seat, so to speak. Carrie's first loyalty would be to Bob and her family and I couldn't change that fact. I knew I had to accept her new status without feeling rejected and it wasn't going to be easy.

Carrie and Bob moved to Queens after they married. Bob worked at a bank during the day and went to school four nights a week to complete his law degree.

Little Bobby was born in September; a healthy, big boy with blonde hair, like his Dad's and brown eyes, like Carrie's. She seemed happy in her role of mother, working part time, doing private duty nursing to help with the expenses.

I wanted things to be the way they had been when we were kids, but knew I was being foolish and selfish. How could I deny Carrie the happiness Bob brought her even if I didn't understand it?

Carrie seemed somewhat cool towards me the first time I visited after the birth of Bobby, but maybe she sensed my discomfiture. Also, life wasn't easy for Bob and her. His job, school and little Bobby left them little time for each other. Perhaps it wasn't coolness I felt from Carrie, but fatigue or loneliness.

I left shortly after Bob came home from school, feeling empty and frustrated.

Chapter 25: 1967

A week after Carrie's wedding I turned twenty-one. For the auspicious occasion, Mom and Dad took me to Manhattan where we met Paul, who was attending college on Staten Island.

Dad was still not comfortable with Paul, but he kept his hostility to himself. A tense atmosphere existed between them, but it was better than before.

I was still crushed by Paul's atheism, but loved him so much I couldn't feel differently towards him. I kept on praying and had faith that God would have mercy on this wonderful man, who had always been the best brother anyone could have. Mom, too, could not stop loving her son. She hurt for him, but never withdrew her love and devotion to him.

I was high that night with the realization that I was legally an adult.

We had reservations at the American Hotel and spent the first part of the evening walking down 42nd Street looking in all the fascinating shops. We had dinner at Toot Shor's restaurant and afterwards went to a nightclub. Attired in an above the knee, pink dress, with a set of shocking pink, dangling earrings, which Paul had given me as a present, hanging from my lobes, I felt totally female.

The band began to play a fast song and Paul and I got on the busy dance floor and began dancing. Suddenly I heard a man say, "Look at that girl dance!" His words made me dance wilder. Paul took my cue and we danced like maniacs. One by one the other dancer's left the floor and stood around us clapping. Paul and I began to ham it up, loving the exposure and attention. The crowd went wild and the men in the band shouted their approval, too.

When the dance was over, breathless and sweating, Paul and I turned to our captive audience and bowed to their applause.

It was a night I would remember forever. I was twenty-one, a knowledgeable adult, uninhibited and feeling free. God, life was wonderful!

* * * * * * * * *

Early in May, Seth's letter arrived. Anxiously I opened it, noting the "SWAK" printed on the front of the envelope.
"Dear Jan,
I'm sorry it took so long for me to write, but things have been hectic on board. I think of you all the time and I don't want you to worry about me. I'm working in the print shop so I'm not in any danger. I hear the fighting, but its miles away."

His letter continued with sweet nothings and I couldn't have been happier. Grabbing a pen I barricaded myself in my room, eager to return Seth's affections.

The weeks flew by as my life became more organized. By day I worked and by night I wrote Seth. Our relationship strengthened, via the mail and I got to know Seth's innermost thoughts, which only reinforced my initial opinion of him. He was a wonderful, sincere, sensitive man. I was falling for him, but this time I didn't feel the need to stop myself. With Seth by my side, I could not fail.

Chapter 26: 1967

In June Seth wrote that he would be home in September for a month's R & R. I was in Heaven. It had been nine months since our first and only date, followed by almost daily letters, continuing our postal romance. I couldn't wait to hold him in my arms again.

When he returned home we went to the bar we had visited on our first date, dancing and talking the entire evening. Seth was as sweet as ever. War seemed not to have changed his sensitivity.

He told me that he had some family obligations that would take about a week to finish, but after that the rest of his R & R belonged to me. It was a lonely week, but when it was over, Seth kept his promise. Outside of my working hours, we spent every waking moment with each other. I was burning the candle at both ends, but never tired. My symptoms were almost gone and my energy level was high.

We went to the bar almost every night and those we didn't we spent at my house shooting darts, talking and kissing in my secluded basement. My feelings grew stronger.

When we went dancing it seemed as if our bodies became one. Never did Seth want anything more than kissing, for he thought petting and lovemaking should be reserved for marriage.

Seth never actually proposed marriage, but we both knew we were heading in that direction. One night he put a gold band on my wedding ring finger. I loved the idea, except I felt we were rushing it a bit (actually, I was scared; I didn't pursue why), so I gently told him that we must slow down some. I put the ring on my right hand ring finger and Seth agreed to the more comfortable compromise.

One Saturday night, as we talked and dance at the now familiar bar we called ours, a disturbing event occurred. Much to both our surprise, an exotic dancer was on the headline.

The music sounded, the drum pounded and out came a beautiful dark haired woman, scantily dressed in an Egyptian harem dress. I was in shock because I wanted to watch the woman, but felt terribly guilty for my curiosity. I should have only been interested in Seth, as he was in me. During the entire show he held on to both my hands and gazed, without once looking in the dancer's direction, directly into my eyes, singing softly, making up his own words of love to the background music. I felt so guilty for occasionally gazing from Seth's eyes to look at the dancer. At the same time I felt wonderful knowing that Seth only had eyes for me. He was truly a decent man, uninterested in seeing an almost naked woman dance. But what did that make of me?

The evening left me drained and in a state of confusion that I, with the finesse I'd unconsciously learned over the years, pushed out of my mind.

* * * * * * * * *

When I showed Mom and Dad the ring Seth had given me I was delighted at their response. Mom was thrilled, for she loved Seth very much and she loved the idea of having him for a son-in-law. However, Dad astonished me. Though not overly demonstrative, he was very happy. Seth was the first boyfriend Dad liked. More so, he was the first boy Dad trusted with his daughter's virtue. To add to my pleasure, both Seth's and my parents got along wonderfully. We were one big, happy family and I was overjoyed.

* * * * * * * * *

The month with Seth passed all too quickly and soon it was our last night together. I cared not that there was work in the morning and set out to spend the entire night with Seth.

We went to our usual hangout and sat rather silently, listening to the music, dancing and singing our favorite songs to each other. "The Shadow of Your Smile" became our song and it brought tears to our eyes as we sang it to each other, realizing that another long separation was only hours away. No one else existed that night, save us.

"Jan, I don't want to scare you, but I think I'm falling in love with you." Seth said, sincerely.

"I think I am, too." I said, hesitantly, for I was still afraid. Yet, I knew that no other man had touched my soul as Seth had and felt that my fear would dissipate with his love.

We left the bar and Seth drove me home. Outside my house we said good-bye till dawn, kissing passionately, without tongues (even tongue kissing was too permissive for Seth).

"God bring you safely back to me." I prayed as he slowly drove away, back to a world so foreign to him -- a world of war.

* * * * * * * * *

I fervently threw myself into work, trying to fill the void left when Seth returned to Viet Nam and was rewarded with a promotion and a healthy salary increase. I was in complete charge of the hospital's medical rehabilitation program (state aid for children born with birth defects). There was an overabundance of paperwork, but the exhausting pace kept my mind off the miles and months that separated Seth from me.

With my new job came new friends. One, in particular, became very close because her boyfriend was also in Nam. We spent many hours comparing our love lives, bragging about our brave soldier boys.

Genie had known Fred no longer than I had known Seth, but their relationship was more advance in the area of sex. This aroused my curiosity and intensified my worry over my lack of sexual desire.

I loved Seth, but could not get aroused by thoughts of any sexual activity except kissing. Beyond this, sex seemed such a rip off to me. After all, I had a soft, beautifully rounded body to offer. To me the female of the species possessed the more desirable body. I couldn't understand why women got physically turned on by men.

I felt cheated. Men had so many advantages and I could deal with them because most were the result of society and could be changed or ignored. But gender was not something that could, nor did I want to change mine. God created men and women to enjoy each other. It was His plan. I wanted to love and be loved, but I couldn't feel part of God's plan. Sometimes I thought I was destined to be a bachelorette, despite my feelings for Seth.

Furthermore, my negative feelings were reinforced when I became involved in the hospitals after hours club. I was in constant turmoil. We'd meet after work every Friday, all the single girls and all the married men and go to dinner and then to a local pub, where we'd talk, drink and dance till closing time. I never felt I belonged in this group. I didn't drink and, although I danced with the married men, I remained platonic, staying loyal to Seth, not that there was any danger in my being anything other. However, some of the girls and married men became quite involved. I abhorred their behavior, their inability to control their sexual appetites. Kissing and petting with a married man disgusted me.

Fear tormented me, though. Even with my rigid religious convictions, which are supposed to give one the strength to control our behaviors, should not I, at least, have feelings? Had I become so rigid that my natural sexual urges had grown cold?

I clung to the hope that with the love of Seth, my "Mr. Right", I would be released from this terrifying prison of apathy.

Chapter 27: 1968

Late in April I received a letter from Seth telling me that he'd be in Seattle, Washington early in June for R & R. Enclosed was a money order for plane tickets and $300 worth of traveler's checks. He hoped I would come spend the week with him, emphasizing his good intentions.

I wanted to go, but my fear of separation from Mom made my decision a difficult one. I trusted Seth's intentions so that was not a problem. After a week of pondering I decided it was time to grow up. The physical symptoms had almost totally disappeared so they were no excuse. I decided to go, provided my parents approved.

Mom was thrilled and encouraging and Dad, though anxious about my virtue, trusted me enough to agree.

At eight a.m., on a hot June morning, trembling with fear, but excited about seeing my beloved, I boarded the DC 10 headed for Seattle. Outside of my parents and Seth's, no one at work believed I would return as I had left; a virgin. Though intently proud of my status, part of me liked the thought that the others viewed my rendezvous with Seth as my rites of passage.

As the plane circled Olympia Airport, I forgot my worries. Seth would be waiting and our lips would touch. I was a happy woman.

The airport lobby was crowded as I stepped into it searching for Seth. Suddenly I heard his voice yelling my name. It was as if no one else was there as we ran towards each other. The long overdue embrace and kiss was a reality.

Seth went for my luggage and we set out for the motel where he'd made reservations. As we walked down the street a strange thought quickly flashed through my mind, making me feel uneasy.

"I don't love this man."

After so many months of writing and falling in love, why should a thought like that occur? I dismissed it as nervousness and being far from home and Mom.

We took the ferry across Puget Sound because Seth's ship was anchored in Bremerton, which is directly across from Seattle. He explained that he hadn't made reservations at the luxurious Olympia Hotel, in Seattle, because he wanted me close to him. I further learned that for the first 3 days of our time together Seth would have to work on the ship from 7 a.m. to 5 p.m. I was perturbed that he hadn't mentioned this before, but thought he probably hadn't known till the last minute. I trusted his judgment and let my anger disappear.

We landed on the shore of Bremerton an hour later and set out for our destination. I was feeling quite tired and weak from being too nervous to eat breakfast or the lunch served on the plane. However, I did salvage the splitz bottle of champagne that came with lunch so that Seth and I could toast each other once we were alone.

Bremerton was shocking. Dirty, run down and desolate. Yet, Seth wanted me close, needed me there so I went along with his plan, even when we reached the motel that was to be our home for the next week.

The motel was indescribably horrendous. It looked as if the most pitiful dregs of humanity would inhabit it and my first impression was not far from the truth. Still, I kept quiet. I was too tired to argue the matter and Seth was so happy I just couldn't burst his bubble.

Our room was on the third floor. Seth unlocked the door, which I could have opened with one swift kick, so flimsy was it constructed, swooped me up into his arms and carried me across the corroded threshold, making no apologies for what lay before my eyes.

The room was no larger than fifteen square feet of bare, dirty, wood floor, surrounded by paper thin walls so cracked they looked like a road map. One lone, naked light bulb hung directly over a dilapidated, metal-framed bed with a full size mattress that was about as clean as a stack of dirty laundry.

I wanted to run. Scream! Cry! The thought of spending five days in this room, much less this isolated town, while Seth was on his ship working was devastating. Yet, I still said nothing.

I took out the bottle of champagne and we sat on the bed toasting our togetherness and love. Within minutes I felt violently nauseous. I didn't want to spoil Seth's happiness so I excused myself to go to the bathroom, which, I found, was a communal one, twenty feet down the hall. I left our room composed, but once outside I took off like a shot and proceeded dry heaving in a room so filthy I decided to avoid bathing, urinating and all other bathroom functions for the length of my stay.

Feeling better I returned to Seth, smile on my face. We talked more, but the nausea returned. Even if I'd wanted to use the bathroom I wouldn't have made it, this time, so I told Seth to find something for me to vomit in. He was baffled and nervous, but found a waste paper basket, the only other item in our room and ran to bring it to me. For the next hour I was sick.

I felt guilty for messing up Seth's R & R, but he was understanding and tender. He even ran down the block and brought me some tea and toast which, after I'd eaten, made me feel better.

The remainder of the evening we talked and kissed as was our usual routine, only now, lying in a bed, we took turns lying on top of one another. I saw nothing immoral with this for our hands never roamed each other's bodies. We were just kissing horizontally instead of vertically.

Around eleven Seth fell asleep. I lay awake terrified by the sounds of undignified people in the surrounding rooms. Towards dawn I fell into a light sleep only to be wakened by Seth's goodbye kiss. He was off to his ship, but he'd be back soon after five that night. I could no longer hold back my feelings and told him how terrified I was staying in this rat hole. He assured me I'd be safe and that he was only ten minutes away if I should need him. All I had to do was call the operator and she'd connect me with his ship. Since the phone was in the lobby, three flights down, I felt little consolation, but there was no time to argue. Seth had to be on time.

After he had gone I lay in bed, frozen with fear, praying for the strength to get my emotions together. Feeling terribly guilty with the decision I had made, I slowly got dressed, packed my suitcase and, feeling weak and faint, dragged myself down to the lobby where I asked the beer bellied receptionist, dressed in faded jeans and a dirty T-shirt full of holes, to order me a taxi.

My taxi arrived, but we missed the ferry to Seattle by minutes. I was feeling so ill I didn't want to wait another hour till the next one arrived. The symptoms that had faded over the past year were in full bloom and all I wanted was to get to the Olympia Hotel and barricade myself in a clean, safe room.

Per my driver's suggestion we drove around the Sound and forty minutes later I was securely in my room at the Olympia Hotel, clean, comfortable and with my own bathroom. Relief was short lived, though. What was I going to do about Seth? I had thought little about him during my escape, but realized how heartbroken and angry he was going to be.

With shaking hands I picked up the phone and called his ship. After a half an hour wait, I finally got through and told him what I had done. Seth was quiet, but when he finally spoke I could tell he was crying.

"I only wanted you to be near me so you'd be safe and we could have more time together. Now I'll waste two hours each day traveling on the ferry." He couldn't see that I was not safe in Bremerton. All he could see were his needs.

We talked only a few minutes, for he was busy. He said he'd see me later and hung up the phone. I waited, not eating because my stomach was one big knot. I just prayed.

When Seth arrived the scene was far worse than I had imagined. I thought he would understand, but all he kept saying was, "If you loved me you would have hacked it."

We argued for hours, neither one of us yielding our position. Then it stopped and we began kissing and hugging as if nothing had happened.

I made Seth sleep on the floor beside my bed, for it was only a twin and too intimate for my morals. At five in the morning Seth left for his ship. I spent the day watching TV, roaming around the hotel lobby buying gifts for my parents and Seth's and drinking cola, the only thing that would stay in my stomach and give me some strength.

Our third night was a repeat of the second with the same arguing; neither of us admitting error. The arguing stopped after a couple of hours, followed by hugging and kissing; then sleep and a fourth day, Seth's last to work on the ship.

I'd been existing on cola and one turkey sandwich for the passed three days and felt I could go on no longer. I needed to calm down so I could eat. I needed peace, so I left the hotel seeking a church.

Within three blocks of the hotel I found an enormous, beautifully adorned church where I sat for hours reading scripture from the books on the back of the pew. God's Words of peace and comfort reached out as I meditated and prayed. My tension began to abate. Before I knew it the afternoon was gone and I returned to my hotel hoping that Seth had found some peace, too.

God heard my prayers, for Seth's attitude had changed and from that night on we were once again. No arguing; only loving behavior and our usual joyful antics.

The last two days of our time together were spent dining in the hotel restaurant, for my appetite had miraculously returned, visiting some of Seth's relatives who lived just north of Seattle and loving each other in our pure, chaste manner. We made our commitment that June and planned a September engagement, when Seth would be discharged.

I returned to New York sharing the happiness of my engagement. Yet, part of me could not forget the dark side of the week with Seth.

I told Mom about the arguments. She didn't think I was wrong in my actions, but told me that Seth mustn't be blamed either for he'd been to war and his taste, at this point, was not like ours. She warned me not to judge him and to be patient. When he came home from the war everything would fall into place.

I tried to be patient, forgiving and understanding, but still felt angry and wronged. Each week Seth called from Bremerton, where he was still based, confined to his ship, preparing for its journey back to Nam and our arguing resurrected. I felt myself pulling away and three weeks after my return home, during one of our tedious, nerve-wracking telephone arguments, I told Seth I was breaking our engagement.

He pleaded and cried, but I wouldn't change my mind. The thought that had so quickly gone through my mind the first day in Seattle would not leave me and I realized now why it had occurred. I loved Seth dearly, but not the way I should to marry him. I'd brushed it aside in Seattle, but couldn't avoid it now. I realized I wasn't and had never been in love with him. I'd been in love with being like other women. In our year and one half relationship we'd been together, physically, less than two months. When it got down to marriage I just couldn't handle it, as usual. I thought this time was going to be different for Seth was such a wonderful man, despite what happened in Seattle. It was me. I just had no desire to be married.

Mom was heartbroken when I told her, but it was my life and she would not interfere. Dad seemed unaffected.

In September, when Seth was discharged from the service, he dropped by to return all the gifts I had sent him while in Nam, but I knew he wanted to start over again when he apologized for the wrong he had done me. I forgave, but nothing could change my mind about marriage. I loved Seth too much to marry him. Somehow I knew that marriage to Seth, or any man, would end in disaster.

As he drove off I thought, "Dear, sweet Seth. God bless and be kind to you. I'm sorry I couldn't be what you wanted and needed."

Chapter 28: 1968-1970

With Seth gone from my life and after explaining my actions to his mother, who seemed to understand and continued to be my friend, I buried myself in work, avoiding anything but casual relationships with men.

Three men had wanted to marry me in the last five years and each time, finding one reason or another, I'd ended the relationship. I kept hurting men for whom I cared deeply. I didn't want to continue this habit. Sometimes I wished I'd been born Roman Catholic so I could join a convent and devote my life to the only man with whom I had a good and lasting relationship.

My emotional distress began to affect my work, together with the reappearance of the plaguing physical symptoms and shortly after I broke up with Seth I was fired from St. Charles Hospital. It was a devastating blow, but lately I had given much thought to going to college. I wanted to study psychology. In fact, I felt led by God to do so. Between the religious education I'd received all my life and an education in psychology I felt I would be more capable of helping people with their problems, thereby have more success in bringing them to the Lord. I had lost sight of this priority when Seth entered my life. Lost sight of my devotion to Christ and saving souls. Now I wanted to return to my prior commitment, wholeheartedly, without the complications of relationships with men.

That September I began taking two classes at a local community college, working my way back to school slowly after five years away from formal education. Furthermore, fighting the physical symptoms, that were always mildly present and spasmodically acute, I didn't want to overload myself.

One week into the school year tragedy hit our family. Nana Adickes, who had suffered a severe stroke four years earlier, leaving her an invalid, died.

Mom mourned her passing bravely. I never saw her shed a tear, but Mom always saved her tears for when she was alone. I knew she was happy that her mother's suffering was over. Beneath Mom's grief was the joy of knowing that Nana was with her Maker, healthy and at peace.

Not since Sara's untimely death had I thought much about death. Now I wondered and worried if I would be as calm as Mom if she were to die. The thought was unbearable so, in my familiar way, I pushed it to the back of my mind, avoiding the inevitable reality, repressing the thought, foolishly thinking that this would eliminate the problem.

A few months later, Grandpa Adickes suggested that when I finished my first year at the community college, I move in with him. He had plenty of room and Hofstra University was only four miles from his house. The thought of attending Hofstra tempted me to try my independent wings again, so I applied and was accepted.

I moved to Grandpa's in May 1969, to give myself time, before college, to get accustomed to living life away from Mom.

The first week was a complete horror. I missed Mom so much I couldn't eat. After four days of starvation I went to a stomach specialist and he gave me some medicine to ease the spasm that was creating my problem and within two days of treatment I was eating normally. Within the next few weeks I grew accustomed to being away from Mom, although I went home to visit almost every weekend.

A month after I moved in with Grandpa I sensed he was ill at ease with our living arrangement. I approached him on the subject. Humbly and apologetically he said he wished he could have me stay, but his nerves just couldn't take living with a young person. I told him I understood and would find another place to live as soon as possible.

Mom stood behind me all the way and two weeks later I rented an apartment in Hempstead. An elderly woman and her third husband lived downstairs. I and another woman, disable at the age of 57 by hip arthritis, occupied the top of the house.

My room was beautiful and large. It had a bedroom area and a living room/dining area. The bathroom was in between the two upstairs rooms and there was a small refrigerator, a hot plate and a toaster oven for cooking. Everything was perfect, including the price which Mom and Dad could afford to pay, along with my college tuition. I'm sure it was difficult for them. I was twenty-three years old and should not have been totally financially dependent on them, but Mom wanted me to have my education. She had paid for Paul's and would do nothing less for me.

Living alone was strange and scary, but soon I grew to love it. The feeling of independence was exhilarating. My high spirits helped battle the baffling physical ills. They had subsided a great deal, of late and I was growing accustomed to functioning fairly well, in spite of their presence.

Shortly after I moved to Hempstead I got involved in the Lutheran Church two blocks from my apartment. I joined because I couldn't feel fulfilled unless I was part of a Christian Church. I needed it for a more intimate relationship with God and for the Christian fellowship it brought.

This church offered a new realm of human relationships. I had grown up in an almost completely white world, but Hempstead was very integrated and so was our church. I had never been a prejudiced person, despite my father's bigoted influence and within this church I got caught up in the reality of the black experience. Martin Luther King Jr. had been assassinated the year before and on Sunday nights, when "rock service" was held, the building shook as our voices sang, "We Shall Overcome."

Overcome meant more than racial prejudice; it meant overcoming all injustice, all prejudice and all inequalities. The church and what it stood for was exactly what I needed. I cherished the feeling of unity and was deeply inspired.

* * * * * * * * *

September came and college was underway. It was a strenuous time. Six years had passed since I'd gone to school full time and the adjustment was difficult, despite the year of part-time college I'd taken in preparation.

I'd call my brother once a week, pouring out my frustrations. He listened patiently and told me the hysteria over the deluge of homework and assignment deadlines would fade and, as usual, he was right. Within two months I was in full swing, adjusted and maintaining a 3.3 grade point average.

I got to see more of Carrie, now, for she lived only twenty minutes from me. She was pregnant with her second child and this time I was happy for her. I suppose getting out on my own made it possible for me to accept her as an adult because I now felt like one. Though I would never have a life like hers, I no longer begrudged her the happiness she derived.

* * * * * * * * *

College introduced me to many diversified people from whom I learned much, but I grew close to no one, preferring to remain casual in my relationships. There was no Christian organization on campus; had there been I would have gotten more involved. Though my symptoms were under a certain amount of control, I still preferred the confines of my apartment rather than the crowded campus. I wanted no one to know about my weakness. Also, the strain of going to class (though I had to skip many on my symptom-filled days) left little energy for me to become involved in too many activities. The energy I had after a few hours at school was reserved for homework and church, which remained my only social outlet, in addition to bi-weekly visits to Mom.

Yet I rarely, if ever, felt lonely; content with my present life and my future aspirations. I was committed toward serving the Lord.

My hard work and reclusive live style paid off for I completed my first year, in May 1970, with a 3.3 grade point average.

Chapter 29: 1970

The summer after completing my first year at Hofstra a dream I'd thought impossible to actualize came true.

Evangelist Billy Graham was holding his crusade at Shea Stadium a mere half an hour drive from my house. It was at Billy's crusade, fourteen years earlier, when he came to our community, that I'd felt so sincerely inspired. Though a Christian at the time, I wanted to go before his stage to publicly commit my life to Christ, but Mom forbade me because I had such a terrible cold that evening. She told me I could dedicate my life, just as genuinely, from where I sat and I did.

Through an acquaintance at college, whose father was the minister at a Baptist Church in New Hyde Park, I found that the crusade was looking for counselors and the church in New Hyde Park was giving the month long study course to prepare anyone who wanted to become a counselor. I jumped at the chance and for the next four weeks spent Wednesday nights at the church, studying the Bible, memorizing scripture, praising the Lord and growing in His Spirit.

I put every ounce of energy into the last stage of qualifying as a counselor, which was writing a one thousand word description of my faith and the reason for wanting to be a counselor. It took me days to put my commitment into words, but I was happy with the final results.

Within two weeks my letter of acceptance came, together with all the materials needed (prayer books to hand to people who came down at Billy's invitation and other helpful pamphlets) and dates and times I should be at each crusade.

The crusade began on Wednesday night and would last till Sunday afternoon. I was thrilled and so were my parents, but I was also scared to death because it meant being in large crowds. I continually prayed for God's power to control the symptoms that had inhibited me so and, also, for the wisdom to counsel with the people who would come down from their seats to give their lives to Christ.

The first night my symptoms were severe. I felt faint, couldn't breathe and thought I would, literally, die. But God's power held me strong and I was able to defeat the powerful attack, becoming more relaxed as the crusade continued.

Anita Bryant gave witness that first night. I simply adored her and thought she was a model Christian. The choir singing and the packed Stadium singing filled my soul. I rededicated myself to Christ with each person I counseled.

On the second night, Ethel Waters, a Hollywood and stage character actress, who had led a wild life till well into her forties, was there to sing and testify to the power of God in her life and witness as to how He had transformed her from her sinful lifestyle.

Ethel was near eighty with a bad heart condition so they had her seated in the entranceway to the stadium field. That night I was seated there, too and when she walked to her chair, ten feet to my left, I thought I would faint. Ever since I'd seen her in the movie, "Member of the Wedding" I'd been a devoted fan.

It took all the energy I had to stand on my jelly legs, with my body feeling as if I would keel over at any second, but I got up and walked over to her.

"Miss Waters," I coyly said, "I've been a fan of yours for years. Your songs and witness to God have been an inspiration to me."

She took my hand in hers, looked me in the eyes and said, warmly, "Thank you, sweetheart." Her beautiful brown eyes and warm smile told me she cared. Her love, coming through to a total stranger was what Christianity was all about and I praised God for people like her.

The third night we heard witness from the infamous gang leader Nicky Cruz. His transformation from barbaric street fighter to gentle follower of Christ had been miraculous. His story brought tears to my eyes and filled me with hope that even the hardest people could be changed through Jesus.

   The crusade was soon over. I had counseled about twenty people. Some had come to rededicate their lives to Christ. However, the people who made me feel the most joy were the atheists with whom I counseled. When I saw the tears of joy and repentance in their eyes I remembered what the Bible said about what happens in Heaven when one sinner repents – "there is celebration." With this understanding, my commitment to save souls, by the power of God working in me, soared to new heights. I knew this was God's plan for me and I was ready to follow His lead, wherever it took me.

Chapter 30: 1970

After the Crusade my symptoms reappeared so acutely that I decided to take only two courses when school opened in September, hoping to relieve some pressure. I was becoming more reclusive because of the symptoms. I kept going to the Lutheran Church's nighttime rock service, but discontinued my involvement with the Baptist Church. It was difficult to go anywhere during the day so I locked myself in my room, reading, watching TV, worrying and praying for an end to this prison of ill feelings.

Campus life had settle some since the trauma of Kent State the previous May, when walking on campus, whether male or female, was dangerous. Longhaired hippies with their radical ideas and militant behavior continued to fight against the government's Viet Nam policy and for personal freedom. However, it was difficult for me to understand just what they truly wanted.

I had such dichotomous feelings. These dedicated radicals were fighting for principles that were, theoretically, good. They preached love and peace, freedom for the oppressed and a better environment. Yet, the way they went about trying to create a better world tainted their original intent. They preached of changing the present government, but seemed to have nothing to replace the existing one.

Not all, but many, displayed their justifiable anger with harmful hostility. Throwing Molotov cocktails into the school buildings, in addition to other vandalistic displays just didn't coincide with their speeches on peace and love.

Drugs became a way of life for many. I couldn't understand how drugs, basically pot and LSD, would help the situation, yet, according to those involved, drugs expanded their minds and senses so they could deal more adequately with the unjust system. I could see drugs only as an escape from a situation these confused, undirected and lost young people just couldn't handle.

Though they preached of love, they discarded God. I could see no hope of attaining success without the Almighty. "God is dead" became their theme and, unbeknownst to them, so were their hopes. They had given up on God because they felt He'd turned His back on the world He created. I didn't believe this, but, even if they were right, could anyone really blame God?

Of course I continued preaching that God had not turned from us, but they did not listen. God was dead for them, otherwise why would the world be in such bad shape? They blamed God instead of accepting our human responsibility for this cruel world.

My soul cried out to these lost young people, to the world that had gotten so destructive. It seemed a losing battle. Yet, I couldn't stop my way of believing and kept on praying for the fate of mankind, especially the present generation.

* * * * * * * * *

Each day at school was like a day in Hell. In addition to the battle I fought for love, freedom and a better world, I also had to fight against the hostile physical symptoms that rarely gave me rest. Home at night, secluded, trying to do homework, but watching TV and listening to country music instead, I slept little.

My friend, Sandy, had an attitude towards the rebelliousness compatible with mine. The Sunday before Thanksgiving she came over to visit and we spent the entire evening discussing the problems on campus and in the world.

The evening grew late. I walked Sandy to the door to say goodnight and wish her a happy Thanksgiving. At the door I wanted to embrace this young woman whom I had come to care for, but was afraid to show my affection. She looked at me warmly and the next moment our arms were around each other and we kissed on the cheek. A strange sensation shot through me.

Was it guilt? Shame? Fear? I couldn't tell, but it bothered me long after she'd gone.

There were only three days of school before the Thanksgiving break, but I knew I would not make it to class. I was completely barricaded in my room, which now offered little relief from my symptoms.

I called my brother, but this time he could not help, although his usual sensitivity and support was present. Nothing could rid the mysterious illness that overwhelmed me.

I searched and found Judy's number and called her. Why I thought of her, after so many years, baffled me. I really hadn't thought much about her since she'd left St. Charles Hospital, but now I had a desperate need to hear her voice.

We talked casually for a while and then she asked me what was wrong. I told her "nothing." Guess I knew she couldn't help, either. That was the last time I talked with Judy, but I would remember her the rest of my days.

I prayed and roamed aimlessly around my room, unable to feel calm. I felt weak and faint all the time. My lungs felt like they would collapse. I sounded like a steam train racing down the track, so fast and laborious was my breathing. I was afraid I was dying, but, deep inside I knew there must be more. What mental problem could be causing this illness? I'd gone through three years of therapy with Dr. Falano and had been helped much. Helped enough to be discharged and return to college. It had been more than a year since I'd spoken with him. What new problem could have risen in that time? There had to be something! My mind probed, but every avenue lead to a dead end.

That Sunday before Thanksgiving I lay awake, fearful, trembling, gasping for air till two in the morning. Finally I could take no more of the suffering. I had to go home. Home to Mom, where my symptoms would disappear.

Silently I walked downstairs, got into my car, feeling like I was in a dream world on the edge of reality and drove towards home, an hour and one half away.

Driving on the parkway I tried breathing into a small paper bag I had brought along, hoping it would ease the hyperventilating, but it seemed to make it worse. I was so giddy and starved for air I pulled to the side of the parkway three times to gain the strength needed to get home. Reaching Mom was the only thing on my mind. I prayed for the strength to get home safely, never fearing death from a car accident, which I surely could have caused, but fearing death from within.

After more than two hours of driving I pulled into Mom's driveway, thanking God for getting me home safely. I knocked on the door for a while, but no one answered. Small wonder, it was past four in the morning.

When no one came to the door I dragged myself, now doubled over, to my parent's bedroom window and began tapping lightly. They rose scared and when they took a look at me, as I entered the now lighted house, they turned ashen with worry.

I quickly told Mom what was happening, Dad busying himself in the bathroom to avoid what he couldn't face and after I had finished my story, Mom took me to my bed. Within seconds, safe and secure from whatever tormented me, I fell into a deep sleep, the first I'd had in weeks.

I awoke at two the next afternoon. Mom and Dad were at work and I felt tired, but calmer. All would be fine now, but just in case, I put in a call to Dr. Falano. He advised that I try to relax and get plenty of rest.

On that first day, shortly before my father came home from work, I began feeling sick again, but it stayed under control. By Tuesday, after sleeping again till two in the afternoon and feeling better, I became more optimistic. Then, shortly before Mom came home, I began hyperventilating so badly I could barely speak.

Mom was worried and called Dr. Falano who insisted I be brought in to his office immediately. He wanted Dad to be there, too, which was a shocking way for him to find out that I had secretly been seeing a psychiatrist for the past three years. I'm sure Dad was mad about this and more so, disappointed at my weak faith, but the sorry sight of his daughter curbed his anger. I was down to ninety-five pounds, some fifteen pounds lighter than my usual weight and looked like death. I was pale, shaky and in need of an arm to lean on as I walked.

Dr. Falano wanted to put me into one of the finest psychiatric facilities on Long Island, but seeing my father's distress at the cost of such a hospital, Dr. Falano suggested I be admitted to the State Hospital, actually the units which were not attached to the main hospital and cared for the less severe cases. I think this eased Dad some because, years before, when his brother was in the same hospital, it had been in the main section where patients were under maximum security. The fact that I was being placed in a minimum security unit eased Dad.

The drive to the hospital was horrifying. Dad drove with Mom beside him, while I lay in the back seat, in the fetal position, fighting for breath. I kept thinking I was going to die and prayed constantly for my soul's salvation, if that were my fate, asking God to forgive me for my weak faith. Dad must have been right all these years. He'd always preached that all things were possible through faith in God. I cried out for God to have mercy on my soul, help me get better and give me the faith I needed to be His servant. I asked God to release me from Satan's grip. I had tried to live for the Lord, but my faith must have been too weak; otherwise, I wouldn't be so sickly and vulnerable to the power of Satan.

Our new Pastor at church worked part-time, as a psychologist, at the State Hospital and met us at the door. There were commitment papers to be signed by me, which I barely could do, so ferociously was I trembling. The thought of this kind of hospital and being away from Mom terrified me.

My room was two flights up and I begged for a wheelchair and an elevator, but there were no such conveniences in the "L" wings, as they were called. With Mom on my left and Pastor on my right, giving each of my arms support, I made the two flights without my heart and lungs exploding, as I feared they surely would.

At the nurse's station they asked questions, took my pulse and blood pressure, which were 120 and 100/60, respectively. I was ushered into a room containing six beds, five occupied, counting mine. Mom tucked me in, smiling reassuringly. She kissed me and told me all would be fine.

After she left a nurse came in with a tranquilizer of great strength and a sleeping pill. I was shaking so violently I thought I would project into outer space.

With my parents gone, pills in my system and a very sweet nurse, who gave me a second sleeping pill an hour after the first had failed, I fell into a deep sleep.

Six o'clock in the morning was wake up time for the patients. We lined up in a single file before the nurse's station, like a herd of cattle, awaiting our medication. In the light of day, feeling a little better than the night before, the environment I was in began to sink into my brain. I felt sick to my stomach. Sick at the thought of being put in a mental institution, even though Dr. Falano had assured me that it was just that I needed to get away from my father and a regular hospital would not have taken me. Dr. Falano was almost apologetic for sending me to a mental hospital and that made me feel a little better.

Regardless, I was sick to death of the atrocities before my eyes. "L-4" was barren, dimly lighted, devoid of adequate nursing staff, full of people trying to dry out or sicker people who roamed around peering suspiciously over their shoulders, looking at everyone with their dead, yet piercing eyes that forbade danger if you moved too fast or said the wrong word.

After pill time came breakfast in a communal dining room that I successfully avoided because I couldn't eat in a crowd. The nurses were sweet and let me eat in my room, which was a disaster because nothing solid would go past my throat. My stomach was in such a knot I could do little but drink some milk.

Bedrooms were off limits until bedtime. All were to congregate in the TV room or the occupational therapy rooms downstairs. Still feeling weak, disoriented and faint, I'd sneak into my room and lie on my bed, avoiding all people. No one made an issue of this. Perhaps Dr. Falano had spoken to the staff and told them to let me rest as much as possible since my diagnosis was "physical exhaustion due to hyperventilation."

I felt like I was in the twilight zone. Nothing was real to me. It was like looking through a foggy tunnel. The medication only served to make me feel more like a zombie. I was on three hundred milligrams of Melleril and forty milligrams of Valium, daily, plus Compozine to ease the spasm in my stomach.

Each morning we had group therapy. The group consisted of about thirty people and the therapist would go around to each of us asking if we were comfortable and how they could help us.

When they got to me I asked that they cut my medication so I wouldn't feel half dead. That day my Melliril was cut in half and I began to feel more life-like. The symptoms I'd had the first night had calmed some and I got used to walking around in my foggy, gasping, dreamlike state.

By the second day I grew more accustomed to the environment and my separation anxiety from Mom abated. No other world existed except this Hell-hole. I was alone, except for God and sometimes I wondered if He'd gone away. He hadn't, though, for it was by His strength that I was able to journey from my bed trying to fight this sickness. Hopeless as I felt, I would not quit.

As I walked up and down the hall I contemplated taking a shower, but thought against it. As I found out, the bathroom had no door and anyone could enter. I used the bathroom to quickly exercise my daily excretory functions and no more. Attempted rape was not uncommon since both sexes occupied my floor; not that that mattered for one or two women made advances.

The evening before Thanksgiving, the first I would spend away from my family, I hit bottom. Here I was, twenty-four years old and going nowhere. There seemed no way for me to escape this nightmare. I prayed, but God was not responding as I would have liked. However, I kept on praying no matter how hopeless I felt.

That night, around eleven, a young woman was admitted and assigned the only remaining bed in my room, diagonally across from mine, next to the wall. We didn't speak that night for two reasons. First, it was after lights out and second, the woman was heavily sedated due to an epileptic seizure.

The next day, Thanksgiving, as I lay in bed praying for something to be thankful, the young woman opened her eyes and smiled at me, introducing herself in a cheerful and warm manner. Her name was Molly and she said she'd been admitted because her seizures had gotten so out of control the doctors wanted to observe her and try new medications. It never occurred to me that a regular hospital would be the place for that kind of treatment. Other than her seizures, she appeared to be sane, like me.

Molly had a happy attitude even though her seizures were a constant source of worry. Her sense of humor made me smile for the first time in many months. Our friendship grew quickly, each of us gaining strength from the other.

Accompanied by Molly I showered off two days of filth. I felt like I was coming out of my depression and when Mom, Dad and Paul came to visit that evening, they saw the change, too.

Mom thanked Molly for helping me and Molly was thrilled at the love she felt coming from Mom. Love, as I learned, that Molly had been deprived of all her life.

Chapter 31: 1970

   Molly's arrival was the beginning of my long climb back to health. With her cheerful support and loving friendship the horror and loneliness of the institution abated. Each day became an unforgettable education. God had heard my prayers and answered them, His way. He had allowed me to hit bottom for a good reason. Like Olivia DeHavilland in the movie, "The Snake Pit," I knew I didn't belong in a mental institution and this inspired me to prove I was well enough, sane if you will, to deal with reality. I knew it wouldn't happen overnight, but I was ready to return to the living, always to remember my eight days in a mental institution with a range of emotions.

   I would remember the first night I was admitted, listening to a woman in another room screaming while two nurses and a male orderly yelled obscenities at her and put her in a straight jacket. I wanted to get out of my bed and yell at these so called professional "angels of mercy" for their inhumanity. I wanted to tell them that this woman was already scared to death and didn't need them cursing and screaming at her. But I remained silent lest my fate be the same as hers.

   I would remember the time Molly walked into my room, just in time, for one of the male patients was taking off his clothing preparing to have sex with me. As Molly entered our room, fully aware of what was about to happen, I gave her a sign with my eyes. She grinned, left the room and brought an orderly to take the patient away. Though I'd be afraid, I felt more pity for this pathetic man.

   I would remember sitting next to a white woman in the TV room, quietly watching the set when a black woman came and stood in front of us threatening to kill the white woman next to me with the full can of soda she held back ready to hurl. I was frozen with fear, not knowing whether to run or stay. Either way I knew I could get hit. God was watching for soon the black woman cooled off and walked away as if nothing had happened.

I would remember feeling angry every time Molly went walking outside with one of the men in our ward with whom she had become friends. She was my friend and I wanted her all for myself. The strange fear that haunted me all my life laughed at me for not recognizing it.

I would remember waking up in the middle of the night hearing choking sounds, realizing that Molly was having a seizure. I ran to my room's door, which was ten feet from the nurse's station, but no one was there. By this time Molly had convulsed herself on to the floor and was wedged between her bed and the wall, banging and choking. I thought she'd die. Frantically, I ran down the hallway, this time not caring about being restrained for my behavior, yelling loudly for the nurses, waking everyone from their sleep. Finally, two nurses came running out of the staff lunchroom, mouths full of food.

It took them thirty minutes to get Molly out of her seizure. I'll never forget how infuriated I felt at their lack of concern.

I would remember the day I went to see Pastor Roy to tell him that I had to get out of this place because I didn't belong. I had problems, but I was sane.

He asked me what I'd learned at the hospital and I replied, "I've learned that I have to stand on my own feet and not be dependent on anyone for my life and the care of it."

Pastor Roy replied, "Those are the magic words. You had to learn this. I'll sign your release papers and you can go home tomorrow."

The next morning I told Molly I was going home. Shortly after, she had a seizure, the first in two days. She slept while I packed.

When Mom came to pick me up Molly woke. I went to her bedside, sat down and took her hand in mine, telling her how much I would miss her. That I wouldn't have gotten well without her friendship. I told her how very much I cared for her and hoped she would soon be well, too. Then I leaned over and kissed her cheek and the "funny feeling" shot through me. At that moment I realized I'd had the "feeling" for her the first day we'd met.

Molly looked in my eyes and said, "I'll miss you, too. That's what brought on this seizure."

Then she smiled warmly and said, "Good luck to you, breather."

As I rode home to the peace and solitude of sane life, despite my father, I prayed, "God, take care of Molly and make her well; my dear, dear, Molly."

Chapter 32: 1970-1972

Christmas and a new year were upon us. I hoped and prayed it would be the beginning of a better life despite my having to quit college.

Though my health had improved I was still restricted to my house, unable to walk to the mailbox because my symptoms of hyperventilation, unreality and faintness became so severe. Even within the walls of my home the symptoms were mildly to moderately present. I wasn't too ill during the day, but then most of it I spent sleeping. I was into a routine of rising at two in the afternoon and going to bed at six in the morning. During the day I watched soap operas, escaping into their world and problems. My "funny feeling" and the frustration it brought soared as I watched the actresses portraying their roles.

At four o'clock the soaps were over and Mom came home from work. Dad followed at five thirty and by that time the symptoms had dramatically increased, especially the hyperventilating, although nothing like before I was hospitalized. I don't know how my parents put up with the noise that came from me in my attempt to breathe.

After my parents went to bed I'd begin to relax by escaping into the TV. During the night hours I felt my best. I could relax and enjoy life a little. Only then did I laugh.

Paul was home for Christmas and the house reflected the usual gaiety of the Christ Child's birth. I was happy with Paul by my side, finding strength in his never-ending love and humor.

As per our tradition, we gathered round Dad, singing carols, as he played the organ, me gasping for air as I tried to sing. Paul's presence was healing, for his loving teasing of my infirmity made it possible for me to laugh at myself.

Afterwards we opened our presents and prepared for candlelight service at church. This was to be my first time in public since my illness and I was scared to death.

My symptoms were terrible during the first half of the service, but praising God in song and pray and the fellowship and compassion of my Christian friends brought me a peace that miraculously lessened the symptoms.

Jessica was home from Boston where she was an elementary school teacher. With all her handicaps she had made something of herself. Seeing her, hearing her words of encouragement, gave me strength. I wished she were not so far away for I needed her to fuel my weak faith. However, the prayers and friendship the congregation gave helped enormously.

From that night on I returned to weekly Sunday services, fighting my illness, hoping in the goodness of God, knowing that someday I would understand why this horror had happened.

I was seeing Dr. Falano once a week now, but therapy was slow, tedious and seemed not to lead to any solution to my problem, but I kept trying.

* * * * * * * * *

The months progressed in slow recuperation. I was getting out more now, spending time at the local drugstore where my old friend from Luther League now worked.

Debbie never changed. Cute, pert and happy go lucky, she brought me much joy. The "funny feeling" I'd felt for her years ago persisted. Though it continued to puzzle me, I was beginning to enjoy it.

Sometimes I'd go across the street from the drugstore to the Laundromat where Lucy worked. I had known Lucy, a member of our church, since I was a child. She had a son, three years younger than me, whom I had helped, a few years before, come out of his shell. He was afflicted with very bad asthma and it had inhibited his social skills. We'd play pool in his basement and through our relationship he grew more confident. Lucy and I had grown close then and we grew even closer now.

I'd visit her at least once a week, till closing time, telling her my woes and horsing around. She was a good therapist, understanding my problems, guiding me, yet never judging. She gave me strength and wisdom and I loved her dearly. Lucy would always hold a special place in my heart.

I'd visit other women in my church, attempting to get out as much as possible to rid myself of the fear of leaving my house, per Dr. Falano's instructions.

Nancy had been my "idol" since I was ten years old. I'd met her when she was a member of our church's choir. Since our family lived so close to the beach and my Dad was choir director and Mom was a choir member, they'd invite the entire choir and their families to our house for a beach party. It was one of the highlights of the year.

Nancy was twenty-four then, full of life and laughter. It was infectious and emerged often. She'd since married, given birth to four children and become very nervous. In that respect we shared a common bond. With her it was not a one way therapy session. She told me her problems, too. With Nancy I felt needed and could return the help given me by so many others, Nancy included.

Nancy taught me, perhaps the most valuable lesson one could learn. She taught me how to laugh through the tears.

A black family joined our church that year; the first we'd ever had in our congregation and some tension grew, causing a couple of members to leave. However, I liked Vanessa and her family and through her I began my return to the reality of racial cruelty in our world.

Vanessa was involved in social equality for black people and it reminded me of the way I had been when I lived in Hempstead; committed to those oppressed. Through Vanessa's first hand experience I learned more than any sociology book could have taught.

Another family I became involved with during this period consisted of Toni and her two children, June and Tara.

Toni was a nervous woman, but she had a great sense of humor. Sarcastic and sometimes a bit crude, she told it like she saw it and could make me laugh with ease. Yet, she was a tender, caring woman and I cherished her.

June, her thirteen-year-old daughter formed an immediate attachment to me. I loved her attention. It reminded me of my idolization of Nancy. I was twenty-five, an adult, but didn't feel much like one until June attached herself to me. We spent many hours together, playing and talking about all the problems that beset a thirteen year old.

During one of my visits with June I met her older sister, Tara. She was a beautiful fourteen year old girl with blonde hair and crystal clear green eyes, but she was the antithesis of June. Tara was trapped in a shell of shyness.

The minute I met Tara the "funny feeling" hit and from that day on I went over to June's hoping to see Tara, who had also formed an attachment to me. With these teenagers looking up to me a fire rekindled. I was sure God wanted to use my rapport with young people to help them, as so many adults had helped me. I also knew I wanted to return to college and get a degree in psychology specializing in teenagers.

Because of my ability to get along with young people I returned to my church's Luther League, not as a member, but as a sponsor. Involvement with these young people was good for my health, for it improved with each day. I felt I was being called for this type of work and prayed for more guidance and inspiration.

During one of our League parties I re-met fifteen year old Ann Sounder. She hadn't been a regular at League, but showed up for the party.

I'd known Ann since she was a child of five and remembered how she used to idolize me. She had been an adorable child and I dearly loved her. The years passed and we'd lost contact till the evening of the Luther League party.

Ann still adored me and followed me around all night. Sensing her lost attitude, I tried to give her as much love as I could. However, ten years had changed this child. Ann looked tired and depressed. I knew she didn't have a happy home life. Her father was an alcoholic and her mother was a tough woman. Both parents were nice people, but when I began to spend time with Ann, at her house, I could see her parent's emotional problems and the negative influence they had on Ann. It was little wonder she had gotten so bent out of shape and was so unhappy. She felt totally unloved by the parents whom she, for some odd reason, adored.

I tried to help Ann, but she was troubled unlike the other teenage girls who looked to me for guidance. Ann had a boyfriend, some ten years older than her. I disapproved of their relationship for they were sexually intimate (from Ann's own admission). She further explained that the only reason she had sex with this young man was because it meant he loved her. I tried to explain to her that having sex did not always mean you were loved.

One afternoon as we wrestled on her bedroom floor, she told me she was pregnant. Quickly I jumped off her for I had pinned her to the floor and was sitting on her stomach. I scolded her for engaging in such activity when she was pregnant. She told me she was only two months along and had not told her parents. Ann wanted to know if I thought she should get an abortion. Then her parents need never know.

Feminism had been my middle name for many years, but I didn't morally believe in abortion.

I told Ann that I didn't think abortion was the answer, but it was her decision. We talked about her options and, also, the spiritual side of the issue, at her request. She thought abortion a sin and didn't want to go against God's Will.

Shortly after, Ann told her parents the news. They were upset, but, to my surprise, stood by her. They even wanted to keep the child. Now this didn't sit well with me. The Sounders were a dysfunctional family of five, soon to be six and lived in a rundown, shoebox sized house. Given these circumstances and the fact that two of their three children had turned out delinquent (Ann's younger sister, at age fourteen, was more rebellious than Ann), I told Ann I thought the child would be better off if she gave it up for adoption.

A few days later Ann ran away from home. I was overwrought. Several nights a week I'd take my car and go looking for her. She had a secret hideaway down by the beach where we'd often gone to engage in lengthy discussions. Late at night I'd stand below our hideaway yelling her name, hoping she'd return because she loved and trusted me, but no answer came.

I went to Pastor Roy asking how I could help this girl when she returned. He had no answers, seeming more concerned with my well-being. He saw how worried I was and the sixteen pounds of weight I had lost (after I got out of the State Hospital my weight, with all the tranquilizers and inactivity had soared to 126 pounds). I, too, was concerned about my extreme subjectivity in this matter. I continued to pray for Ann's safe return and stopped looking for her.

Two months went by and one day Ann reappeared. I went over to see her to find out what had possessed her to run. She had no explanations, but begged my forgiveness. What was there to forgive?

Ann decided to keep Melissa when she was born, although with little confidence. I stood by her and went to the baptism, along with her older sister, the only child in the family who had turned out with a stable head on her shoulders.

One afternoon over Ann's house, I told her of my concern for Melissa. I still thought she'd be better off with another family, at least for a while. Ann's mother overhead our conversation and came into the room telling me that I had some nerve butting in.

Before I knew it I replied, angrily, "Do you want Ann to keep Melissa in this house with you around? Look how your own kids have turned out. Do you really want your grandchild exposed to the same unhealthy environment? A home where nothing grows? Well, I don't!"

Mrs. Sounder became irate and told me to leave, which I did. Ann and I continued to see each other outside the confines of her house which made our time together less frequent.

After this Ann's attitude towards me changed. I thought maybe she was mad at me because of what I said to her mother, but that was not the case.

Ann and I had always been physically affectionate with each other, but now she wanted none of it. When I'd go to kiss her goodnight she'd stiffen up and gave me her cheek to kiss. We had always kissed, platonically, on the mouth prior to her change. I went along with Ann's coldness for a while, not wanting to pressure her, but I was curious.

A few weeks later I asked what had happened to change her behavior towards me. Hesitantly, Ann asked me if I remembered the lady that had driven her mother to and from church many years ago. I did. She was a heavyset, dark haired woman who looked more like a man. My friends and I used to kid about the woman being one of those lesbians; a real sicko.

Ann continued and told me that, a month before, the woman had passionately kissed her on the mouth and it scared her to death. She explained that it wasn't like the way we had kissed, but it made her scared of my affection for her; scared enough to ask me if I was a lesbian.

I told Ann that I had never been sexually attracted to her or any other female. I loved her like a kid sister. Ann trusted me and relaxed.

Shortly after Ann gave her baby up for adoption and married the first man who came along. Fortunately, he was a nice young man and loved Ann very much, but Ann never seemed truly happy. Sadness just would not leave her. But there was nothing more I could do, except pray.

My life was changing, too. I was feeling much better physically and contemplating a return to college. Not away from home, but to the community college I had attended a couple of years ago. I needed one year to complete an associate's degree. Then I would apply to the State University to complete my BA in psychology. I was just in the thinking stage that spring, the year I turned twenty-six, but I knew I had to get on with my life.

I also knew I had to move out on my own. Not too far, maybe a half an hour from Mom, but far enough to feel independent.

So much was happening in my head. I knew I couldn't stay at home the rest of my life. Therapy was at an impasse. Maybe a change of residence would help. Furthermore, since I had been feeling better the fights with Dad had resurrected and I couldn't take them any longer.

The question Ann had asked me about my sexuality stayed with me. Was I a lesbian? How could that be? I'd had never been sexually attracted to females.

Then, one evening when Mom was out and Dad had gone to bed I was glued to the TV watching a movie about two homosexual men. The movie touched me deeply for they were men in every sense. Only their sexual relationship made them different. But they did love each other, faithfully, sensitively and beautifully.

When Mom returned home, shortly after the movie ended, she found me in tears. She asked what was wrong and I told her about the movie and how touched I had been. I told her I could see nothing wrong with this kind of love. She agreed.

My mind was a mass of confusion. How had my life gotten so messed up? When would God show me how to get control? When would I find peace?

Run, that's all I could think to do. But run from what and to where?

BOOK TWO: Wild Gay Years: 1972-1976

Chapter 1: August 1972

Debbie wasn't working when I reached the drugstore, but it didn't matter. Just to get away from Dad and our pointless argument was a relief.

I knew more than ever that I had to move out. Get away from my father. There was no future as long as I lived under his influence. I had my own mind, my own thoughts and my own needs. I couldn't be what he wanted. I had to go even if it meant leaving Mom. It was time to grow up; time to find myself; time to stand on my own feet and be responsible for my successes and failures.

I found myself thumbing through the phone book looking for old high school friends. Why, I didn't know.

Dora, one of my best friends, was not listed. Neither was Dotty. Suddenly, Lauren came to mind and I raced through the pages praying she'd be listed. Then I saw her name. Quickly I wrote the number and address, promising myself I'd give her a call.

After a week of working up the courage, I finally dialed the number. A woman's voice answered.

"Lauren?" I asked, sweating, trembling, my heart racing.

"Yes." The voice answered.

"This is Jan Liebegott, from High School. I don't know if you remember me. We shared gym class." I stammered.

"Sure I remember. How have you been?" She asked warmly.

"Fine", I hesitated. "I was wondering if maybe we could get together, sometime."

"Well," now she hesitated, "I just moved into a new apartment. Give me a week or two and I'll call you."

What could I say? I gave her my phone number and said goodbye. A week or two she had said. I'll go nuts waiting! She probably was just being polite and I'd never hear from her. After all, we had never been close so why would she want to get together with me?

The days drifted by slowly. All I could think of was Lauren. I was obsessed. Too obsessed to realize how strangely I was behaving.

Ten days passed with no call from Lauren. I could take the waiting no longer so I drove to her apartment. My heart raced as I approached her door and, with much guilt, knocked.

A woman opened the door, her appearance different than I'd remembered; no longer a tomboyish child on the athletic field, but a mature, more feminine looking woman.

"Lauren?" I questioned, not really sure I had the right apartment.

"Yes." She answered with a smile, recognizing me.

She invited me in, not angry or disturbed at my sudden intrusion. She told me to have a seat. As I did I noticed another woman, a few years older than Lauren, shorter, stockier and somewhat mannish looking, go from one room to the other. Lauren turned quickly and introduced Donna, her roommate.

Well, you could have knocked me over with a feather. Lauren could have dropped the "room" on her introduction of Donna because I had a feeling Donna was her lover. It was hard to believe, but obvious. Lauren had turned out to be a lesbian. With all the intellectual facts I'd acquired that homosexuals were not the perverted people I had once believed, I still couldn't erase the feeling that they were immoral people. Struck with the very real possibility that Lauren was a lesbian I was sick at heart. Lauren was a beautiful woman and, as we sat chatting, Donna off in another room, I could not define Lauren as an immoral person.

I stayed briefly, feeling guilty and apologizing for bursting in unannounced. Lauren was considerate and forgiving. She told me she worked at a doctor's office around the block and said I should drop by on Tuesday afternoon, when the office was closed to patients. Then we could talk more.

A week later I took Lauren up on her offer and spent a wonderful two hours with her. We talked and got to know one another as never before.

During this time I moved to Port Jefferson, only twenty minutes from Mom, into a small twelve square foot room with an adjoining bath. It was not accommodations I was used to, but the feeling of being on my own, independent and away from Dad, made up for the squalor of my living arrangements.

I could afford my room and living expenses because I'd applied, a few months earlier, for social services and they had put me on disability because of my physical condition and past medical history. I received a month check for $240 and my rent was only $110 per month. I barely existed, but Mom sent me care packages of food and an occasional few bucks. She continued to pay for my education, but at least I was taking some of the financial burden off of her.

I was taking twelve credits at the local community college, resurrecting my dream of becoming a psychologist. School was difficult because the symptoms were ever present. Some days were good and others so severe it was impossible to leave my room. Consequently, I missed many classes. However, I managed to maintain a 3.0 grade point average.

Every two or three weeks I'd visit Lauren at work. I wanted to affirm my initial thought that she and Donna were lovers and one day Lauren, nonchalantly, told me she was gay. I was in shock. I'd wanted to know, but didn't want Lauren to be a lesbian because that would mean her soul was in jeopardy. The Church's condemnation just would not leave my head.

Lauren was a devout Catholic and the issue bothered her, too. At one time, when she had been hospitalized, she told me that she'd asked to see the priest so she could take communion. Being a wonderfully honest person, she told the priest she was a lesbian and he refused to give her communion unless she promised to turn from her homosexuality. Lauren was happy with her life and told the priest she couldn't, nor wouldn't change. The priest left without giving her communion and from that time on Lauren stopped going to church. She couldn't be part of a Christian Church that didn't accept her for who she was. Her belief in God remained, but she told me that many gay people had given up on God after experiencing similar treatment from the Church.

I understood her plight and was troubled for her and all gays. What a shame to turn a wonderful, good woman, like Lauren, away from God's house, here on earth, just because she loved another woman in a carnal way. Lauren was not into immorality. She and Donna had been together almost three years. They were monogamous and their love was pure. Yet, I still could not rid myself of the Biblical message of damnation for homosexuals. I prayed constantly for Lauren's soul, without praying that she change. That would have meant unhappiness for her. It was extremely confusing and unfair. I couldn't understand God's Word.

The days passed swiftly. School took up much of my time so I didn't see Lauren as much. Also, I didn't want to intrude on her relationship with Donna. Though I didn't care for her lover, I didn't want to make trouble.

To fill my hours I began frequenting the bowling alley a few miles from my house. After eleven p.m. league play was over and the lanes were open to the public. The emptiness of the alley eased my symptoms so I could concentrate on perfecting my game.

I'd loved bowling since I was a kid, had joined a league when I was nineteen, but only stayed two years because the symptoms got so bad I couldn't continue. Now, with few people around I felt better and became obsessed with the game.

Sometimes I'd get to the alley before eleven so I could watch the other bowlers, hoping to pick up tips to better my game. I became attached to one of the women's team, first in the league. The best bowler on this team was a tough looking woman who had a husband and five kids. Instantly I was hit by my "funny feeling" and became friendly with the team in hopes of getting to know this tough looking woman. However, she remained aloof so I stayed passive, content to watch her.

Occasionally I'd give up after hours bowling and follow this team into the alley's bar. I got friendly with the bartender and a waitress, both of whom had a wonderful sense of humor. Talking with them made it less obvious that my thoughts and glances were in the direction of the tough woman on the team.

One night, while I bowled alone, I noticed an attractive blonde haired, blue-eyed young man, a few years younger than me, with a fantastic muscular body, watching me. After a while he came over and offered some advice. He saw my bowling talent and wanted to help me improve. I was a bit taken back because I didn't like him coming on to me as a superior bowler. However, he was nice about it and I found out that he was, indeed, a better bowler than I.

From that night on we met and bowled, helping each other with our bowling problems. Around four in the morning we'd hit the local diner and have breakfast, talking like we'd been friends forever.

Jeff had just gotten out of a local, minimum security prison. He'd gotten into a fight at a bar and hit a man, killing him. After three years in prison he was ready to restore his life. I couldn't imagine Jeff killing anyone for he was such a gentle man.
Jeff was engaged to a woman, but didn't seem too thrilled with the arrangement. He was more interested in spending time with me, as friends and bowling partners.

Chapter 2: 1972

    Weeks swept into months with me loving every minute of my newfound independence. I lived mainly at nights when the debilitating physical symptoms mysteriously lightened their attacks. School classes were strategically arranged in the afternoons so I could sleep most of the difficult daylight hours.

    Though Mom lived close by and I'd visit her almost every weekend, our relationship was changing. I'd tell her everything about my life, relationships and problems, but now she was becoming a sounding board rather than an answer machine. The apron string was finally breaking and an adult relationship between mother and child began to burgeon. It was wonderful for both of us.

    I continued living in the manner in which Mom had raised me, my own mind telling me it was the only way to happiness, presenting myself as a Christian, primarily through example rather than fanatically preaching God's Word as I had in the past. I preached when asked, but in a more subdued manner. I hoped my more gentle way of getting God's message across would lead to more success in saving souls, but I was wrong and almost always failed.

    There was a band that frequently played at the bowling alley's bar, consisting of four very talented young men whose lives reeked with sin. One member, an extremely handsome recently divorced man, who took pride in the fact that he was a womanizer, tried to change me. Naturally I retaliated, but our debates on sinful sex and other debaucheries ended in impasse.

    A nineteen year old boy, who worked at the alley and had dozens of girlfriends couldn't understand why I didn't swoon over him. I talked with him with a special interest because he was so young and I'd always had a way with teenagers. However, he would not be swayed either. God was surely dead to these people.

In my philosophy course at college we discussed the issue of sin for two weeks. I argued from a theological point of view, as did one or two others in the class, but most of the students talked in direct opposition to any Biblical answers, believing the concept of sin to be a man-made plot to take the fun out of life.

It was discouraging. Why had people hardened their hearts and minds? I didn't have the answers, but kept praying for wisdom so I'd be more successful for my Lord.

* * ** * * * * * *

One crowded Saturday night, dancing at the bar with a young man who had joined the group that was forming around Jeff and me, I spotted a familiar face across the room, seated at a table with a women. I guess he felt my stare because he turned suddenly, looked at me, got up from his seat and walked towards me. I stopped dancing as he neared, returning his sheepish smile.

It had been four years, but Seth was unchanged. Still shy and awkward, he asked me to join him and his wife. Hesitantly, I accepted.

Barbara was a sweet woman, not beautiful by any means, but with a warmth that, under different circumstances, would have made me feel comfortable. I felt guilty for intruding, especially since Seth was giving more of his attention to me.

At closing time Seth asked me to come back to their apartment for something to eat. I accepted and we stayed up till dawn, reminiscing. Barbara suggested I sleep over since it was so late and after breakfast we'd go visit Seth's mother.

A few hours later, Harriet was hugging me, the hurt of the past forgiven. Shortly after, I returned home feeling depressed and empty, despite the wonderful time I'd had with Seth, his wife and the warmth of my reunion with Seth's mother.

I couldn't believe Seth was married, but was happy he had found a woman who gave him the love I never could. However, seeing Seth stirred my questioning mind. Why was I, the only one of my childhood friends, still unmarried? I wanted the love my friends and ex-loves had found, but marriage was alien to me. My attitude remained a mystery, bothering me more than I cared to admit.

About this time a young man, whom I'd known in high school, entered my life. Naturally, I met him at the bar in the bowling alley and we hit it off right away.

Jess was divorced and had five children, all in the custody of his ex-wife, although he remained close to them. He was a gentle man of stocky physique and had a wonderful sense of humor and a great outlook on life. Within three weeks of dating he was getting serious. I was very fond of him and decided to give love one more try. I wanted and needed love. Despite my inability to succeed in the past, I felt abnormal so I went with the tide. At least I tried. Hidden deep, my subconscious knew I was playing a charade as I had done with men all my life.

* * * * * * * * *

April, with its promise of new birth, dawned and Jess asked me to marry him. Since he was in no rush, I accepted. Our physical intimacy hadn't advanced beyond kissing and this frustrated Jess immensely, enough for him to ask if I was a lesbian.

I was stunned, but negated any such thoughts, backing it up with my religious convictions on chastity. Frustrated, but understanding, Jess remained my obedient courtier.

* * * * * * * * *

One day while visiting Lauren she told me that she and Donna were going to Florida the middle of April, assuring me, per my request, that she'd drop a postcard.

I didn't like the idea of her leaving, quite baffled by my attitude. She'd only be gone a week and I didn't see her every week now, anyway. What was the big deal?

I turned to the diary I'd been keeping the past eight months, hoping that by writing my thoughts on paper I might solve the puzzle of my messed up, jig-saw mind. By this time, though, I needed a second opinion so I called Paul and made plans to visit, hoping he'd be able to decode my written thoughts.

I sat quietly as he read. When he finished I asked him if he thought I was a lesbian. I had asked Dr. Falano, the only other person to whom I'd confided, but he wouldn't give me an answer. I'd been angry with him. He was my therapist and was supposed to help me. I knew Paul would give me an honest answer.

Paul thought for a brief time and then said he saw nothing in my writings that indicated I was a lesbian. No matter how much he read about my feelings for Lauren, he felt I just admired her which was the explanation he gave for my "funny feeling" all these years.

It felt good for someone to give me a straight answer, but I was not appeased. I left Paul, thankful for his patience and love, but as confused as when I'd come. The restlessness would just not leave.

* * * * * * * * *

By the middle of April, three days into Lauren's trip to Florida, I was running to the mailbox each day, hoping for her post card. The days slowly passed, but no card came. I blamed it on the mail system, trusting in Lauren's promise.

Jess was there to console me, though he had no idea of his role or what was going on in my head.

On my birthday we spent a lovely evening dancing and innocently romancing. He drove me home and we spent our usual hour, in his truck, kissing and hugging. That night he tried to French kiss me, but when I resisted he got angry. Not being a man prone to anger, I was disturbed, but really couldn't blame him. I realized I turned him on, but again couldn't understand his lack of control. He told me he loved me and wanted to make love to me. Then he confessed that the last time we'd been together he'd been so turned on that after he left he sought out another woman to release his passion. She meant nothing to him and he felt awful about it. He was telling me this because he wanted me to know how much he needed me. I was beginning to see that, once again, I had started something I had no intention of seeing through to the end. I had hurt another man. There was just no way I could love a man the way he needed to be loved. God only knew why.

Gently I told Jess we should stop seeing each other. I just wasn't ready for a serious relationship, let alone marriage. He looked hurt, but relieved. We kissed each other tenderly and I left.

I returned to my room overwrought. Why couldn't I fall in love? No matter how much I cared for a man the special magic escaped me. Jess had been my last hope. Something was missing in me and I couldn't explain or change the horrible fact.

The next day I ran to the mailbox to see if Lauren's post card had arrived. Till April 27th I ran, fruitlessly. She had forgotten her promise.

I went back to my room feeling betrayed, angry, depressed and obsessed with Lauren. What was this loyalty I felt for her? Why couldn't I stop wanting tenderness and closeness with her? Why did I desire to be with her all the time?

"Oh, God! No, God! Please, no! Make these thoughts go away." I prayed, but the dam was breaking. "Dear God in Heaven! No!" I screamed out loud, realizing what was happening. Love, the love I should feel for a man was what I felt for Lauren.

Slowly I walked over to the mirror hanging on my wall and looked at my image, avoiding my eyes for a long time, lost in misery, deep in prayer. Then I looked up and the green eyes that stared back begged for release.

"God in Heaven," I said, calmer now, "I am a homosexual."

The polluted water behind twenty years of dammed up feelings poured down my face as I sobbed with relief. The specter that had haunted me finally revealed itself, answering all my questions, freeing me from the bondage of a life of torment, fear and loneliness. Yes, I was free and it felt wonderful.

But what about God?

Chapter 3: 1973

With the exception of Lauren, Paul and Dr. Falano I told no one I was homosexual. A new struggle raged within. Now I struggled with the relief it brought by putting the pieces of my tortured, questioning mind to rest and the pain it brought because of the Christian Church's beliefs. As long as I didn't practice my sexual desires I knew I was safe from God's condemnation. It was no sin to be gay, only to practice it.

I wasn't sorry I'd come out of the closet. I felt complete. Never in my life had I felt so normal, so at ease with my sexuality. In addition, coming out taught me a lesson in humility. Only now did I understand why people had trouble controlling their sexual appetites and I was humbled, recalling all the years of my self-righteous attitude towards such weak people. Of course I had been strong; I'd had no sexual desire for men. Now that I'd come to recognize the gender I sexually desired, I was sorry for passing judgment. This lesson was invaluable.

I didn't want to be anything but gay. I knew I should try to be straight, but I'd done that all my life and it had brought nothing but frustration, pain and sorrow to all the men who had loved me as well as to myself. Yet, I had to control my desires lest I spend eternity in Hell. It didn't seem fair. Why was my love for a woman a sin? I needed theological answers.

The summer after I graduated from Junior College I began attending a Baptist Church. My long time affiliation with Billy Graham drew me there. I hoped that through this church I would find solace. Actually I wanted and needed to be assured that God wouldn't damn me if I loved another woman.

Previously, Dr. Falano had tried to relieve my guilt and fear by telling me that the Biblical references about homosexuality were obsolete. Back in those days procreation was the number one priority. Naturally, strong rules and harsh measures had to be preached so the race would continue. Dr. Falano was logical and I could intellectually understand his theory, but my spirit needed a minister to say it was all right.

After listening to my story, Pastor Green told me, "Jan, you have two choices. You can go to our white prayer room and ask God to heal you of your homosexuality or you can leave and go to Hell."

I didn't know what to do so stunned was I that a man of God could be so cruel. Nevertheless, I found myself in the white prayer room. I didn't ask God to "heal" me or make me straight. I couldn't ask to be something I wasn't. Nor could I ask God to give me the strength to live without that special love. All I could do was ask for His guidance and forgiveness. I left the church and never returned.

Regardless of my not praying to be straight, I found myself going to straight bars. I just went there to think, drink a few colas and smoke, a habit I'd picked up along with coming out.

At first I continued frequenting the bar at the bowling ally, hanging around the women's bowling team with whom I'd attached myself. Naively I told one of the women that I was a lesbian. She seemed trustworthy. However, I was betrayed. Shortly after, my sexual orientation became the talk of the bar. The men, whom had been my friends, drew away from me as if I had the plague. They ridiculed me and told me I just needed to be "fucked" by the right man and each one tried to persuade me that he was "Mr. Right."

One night I went to the bar and my request for a cola was denied because "my type" was not welcome. I stood my ground while the bartender, once a good friend, got the assistant manager, also once a good friend, who told me they would not serve me. I pressed as to why and was told that two women at the bar said I had made a physical pass at them.

The accusation was totally false. Though gay I didn't flaunt it and would, in no way act in such an indecent, unchristian manner.

When I didn't leave the bar, the assistant manager tried to physically remove me, at which time I told him to get his hands off me or I'd yell "rape" so loud they'd hear me in California. Quickly he released my arm and said he was calling the police. I told him to go right ahead and returned to my seat at the bar.

Shortly after, two policemen arrived and we all went into the assistant manager's office. The police were baffled at being called for they saw no problem. Since the assistant manager couldn't get the word "homosexual" out of his mouth, I told the police what the problem was and the lies that had been told about me. The bowling alley, according to the police, could not refuse me on such circumstantial evidence and was told to serve me.

As I walked back to the bar, one of the policemen gently cautioned me not to fool around with the owner of this place. He warned I could get hurt. I appreciated his words, but ordered my drink and was served. I sat for half an hour, sipping my cola, just to prove my point. Then I left, never to return for I did digest the warning the police officer had given. From that time on I spent my evenings at other straight bars in the area.

One night at a new bar a young man came over to me and we began talking. He was quite intelligent and I enjoyed his conversation. After an hour he asked me if I was into girls. I was shocked, but felt comfortable with him and told him everything, unloading all the fears and guilt that haunted me. He seemed sensitive and understanding until he added that if I slept with him I would become straight. I wanted to puke. Why did men think they were the magic cure? I politely excused myself and left.

I returned to the bar a few night later and met another man, who, after an hour of conversation asked me if I was a lesbian. God in Heaven! Did I have a neon sign on my forehead?

I ended up trusting this man, too, telling him my story. He asked me back to his apartment, assuring me that if he were to make love to me I would not be gay anymore. All I needed was the right man. Hell, I thought, this was the umpteenth man who had said this to me in less than a month. Maybe there was something to it.

We lie on his living room floor (he had just left his wife and had no furniture), tongue kissing and hugging. He was not pushy and made no attempt to fondle me and I made no moves, either. After a few minutes of this behavior, which was doing nothing for me except making me sick, I told him it wasn't going to work. I appreciated what he was trying to do. It wasn't his fault. I just couldn't bear the thought of making love with a man. He was upset, but made no effort to stop me from leaving, although he surely could have.

* * * * * * * * *

There was no way I could make myself straight. Many people believe that homosexuals are merely afraid of having sex with the opposite gender. Get rid of the fear and gays will find out they are straight, that there is no such thing as homosexuality. My mind told me the same theory held for heterosexuals and is absolutely ludicrous.

Fear of the opposite gender is not the reason for a gay person's desire for his or her own gender. Apathy, disinterest, even disgust are more apt terms. Is sexual orientation even a choice? That's the bottom line. You can't change your nature despite what psychologists or clergy say. You can change your "behavior" and live a lie, but down deep you are what you are – gay, straight or bi.

I was gay and nothing could change the fact. I would never be complete married to a man. With these thoughts organized in my mind I stopped trying to be what I wasn't and headed for the nearest gay bar.

Chapter 4: 1973

It was a Thursday night in mid July and the gay bar Lauren had given me directions to was empty, save a handful of women. I had planned my first trip to such a bar on an off night so as not to intensify the nervousness ripping through me.

I ordered a ginger-ale, found a table near the empty dance floor and sat observing. To the right and up one step stood a recreational area containing some pinball machines and a small pool table where three women played. I sat quietly, keeping a low profile, not wanting anyone to notice me lest I become more involved than I cared to, at the moment.

Suddenly I noticed a red haired woman, in a dress, dancing alone and quite seductively. She didn't look like a lesbian, but I wasn't taking any chances. I tried not to look at her. I didn't want her to think I wanted to start something. I was at the bar to observe, not to participate.

The young woman danced for an hour, trying to entice me (I wasn't totally naïve), but I didn't budge. She wasn't my type. I laughed at myself. How did I know what my type was?

I went to the bar for another ginger-ale and when I returned the red haired woman was sitting at my table. Well, I decided to put my feet nearer the water. I sat down and she introduced herself and told me she'd wanted to meet me the minute I'd walked through the door. She was quite forward and I didn't know how to react so I listened to her politely, offering little response.

After an hour or so I told her I had to leave. She said she did, too, but didn't have a ride. Feeling scared to death, but sorry for her, I offered to give her a lift. I let her off at her destination and drove away, feeling mad at myself for giving in to going to a gay bar, but angrier because, deep inside, despite my fear and guilt, I had not met the woman of my dreams.

Nothing magical had happened, but I liked the bar, the gay atmosphere. I liked being in a place where I could be totally me.

Where gay was not only accepted, but encouraged. I knew that no matter how much I prayed I would return. God have mercy!

* * * * * * * * *

Return I did; four and five nights a week. I began making friends. Gay friends, but they were men. I was still scared to get close to women. Afraid I'd yield to the strong temptation knocking at my door.

Hank was a big, blonde-haired man on the feminine side and Josh was a muscular, dark-haired, extremely good-looking man, not at all feminine. I would have never guessed him gay.

It was through these men that I became familiar with the words "butch" and "femme". Butch gay men and femme gay women were luckier than their counterparts, for they were not identifiable. No one would guess, by their appearance or body language, that they were gay. Since so many people, both men and women, had asked me if I was gay, I knew I must be butch. I guess I'd always known that and the reality made me laugh because, all my life, Dad's pet name for me had been "butch."

Through Hank and Josh I began my gay education. They told me about the life and coached me on how to approach a woman. For now, though, I kept away from temptation and hung with them.

* * * * * * * * *

I had told Mom in May that I was gay and she took it well. She didn't mind as long as I never practiced it and I promised her I wouldn't. Now I felt guilty because I hadn't told her about my frequenting a gay bar. I'd spoken to her of Hank and Josh, but never let on that they were anything but straight men I'd met at the bowling alley. This was the first time I'd blatantly lied to Mom and I was sick at heart. But, if I were to be honest, it would break hers.

Soon, though, I could no longer live with the lies. One night, while visiting, after Dad had gone to bed, I brought up the subject.

"Mom", I said, tears stuck in my throat, "I know I promised not to practice my homosexuality, but I've been going to a gay bar for the past month."

She sat quietly, as if in a trance. Then she said, angrily, "Are Hank and Josh, Harriet and Josephine?"

Oh God, how I was hurting her!

"No, Mom. They are men, but they're gay. I haven't had any contact with gay women. I'm trying not to, but it's hard. I want a relationship. I want to love and be loved."

We talked and cried till dawn. I hated myself for the lies and hated myself for telling Mom that her daughter was gay. Mom wanted to understand, wanted me to love and be loved, wanted me to be happy, but not this way. She tried to understand, but it seemed impossible.

The night ended in agony for both of us. We hugged and spoke of our love for each other, but I had broken my mother's heart. Nonetheless, I knew I could do nothing to stop hurting her because I couldn't stop my need for a woman to share my life.

In the weeks to come Mom and I continued to talk, in a calmer, more logical manner. I answered as many questions as I could, but tried to keep details to myself. There really was nothing to tell in detail because I hadn't become intimate with a woman, yet. I'd danced with a few, but that was all.

Through the next few months Mom's love for me did not change. I knew her thoughts and feeling were torturing her, but she never showed any ill feelings towards me. Yet, our relationship was changing. I wanted her to understand and accept me, but knew she couldn't. A wall was growing between us. A wall I had erected and could do nothing to destroy.

Chapter 5: 1973

It was in August that I met Eve, a tall, blonde with captivating brown eyes. She was nineteen and very cute. We hit if off immediately, talking and dancing till closing time. Since she didn't have a ride home, I offered.

Outside her house we parked, held hands and talked more. I wanted to kiss this sweet girl whom I'd grown fond of and whom had turned me on the entire evening. She had given new meaning to the "funny feeling" and I now knew what I had experienced all my life. The "funny feeling" was desire; sexual and emotional. Feelings and desires I had repressed.

Now I sat alone with a young woman who had wakened my senses as never before. I was on fire. I now recognized the ache within me, the ache I'd felt years ago at Cindy's pajama party, when she had done her infamous strip act. The ache that had terrified me then, now filled me with ecstasy.

Eve was so young and I was green at the age of twenty-seven. I didn't want to be clumsy or frighten her. I didn't want to come on to her like so many men do, for that surely wasn't what she'd want.

Finally I worked up the courage to gently put my arm around Eve's shoulder. She didn't pull away. I looked into her eyes and she returned my longing gaze. I moved closer to her and our parted lips touched gently and briefly. We kissed again, more passionately, consuming each other's tongues. I was burning with passion I had never known.

We spent an hour kissing each other, not touching intimate regions. I didn't want to rush things and, more importantly, I wanted to remain chaste.

It was nearly dawn when we said our final goodnight. I drove home happier than I had ever felt before. Never had I known how beautiful and exciting a kiss could be. Never had I felt such fulfillment. Never had I felt so free from sexual apathy. Never had I felt so normal, so wonderfully alive.

However, in the light of day, the beauty, ecstasy and wonder of the night before were tainted by guilt. I had stepped over into sin. I had practiced homosexuality and, worse yet, loved it. I knew I could not stop. I wanted to see Eve again; wanted a relationship with her.

I was torn between my feelings for Eve and my love of God. I couldn't see sin in what had taken place between us, but the Bible condemned such activity. I was in a frenzy.

Then I thought of Pastor Andy, the minister whom had confirmed me and had been my inspiration even after he moved to a parish in Dearborn, Michigan, ten years earlier. I wrote a letter to him and his wife telling them of my dilemma, asking if I could come out to visit them and talk. I thought that through him I would find solace.

Andy wrote back quickly and invited me to stay with them the first two weeks of September. I was free till the end of the month, when school opened again, so I called them and made plans.

That night I went to the bar to see Eve. I told her I would be going away for two weeks and hoped she'd be here when I returned. I didn't notice her nonchalant manner for my mind was already out in Michigan with Andy and his wife.

At five a.m., September 1st, I boarded the Greyhound bus that would take me to Detroit, Michigan. It was a grueling twenty-five hour ride, full of anxiety. I stayed to myself, despite the crowded bus, slept little and prayed much, hoping Pastor Andy would assure me that I was not going to Hell if I continued my gay life.

Andy met me at the Detroit bus terminal and drove me to their home in Dearborn. Corinne greeted me with open arms and, after ten years of separation, reintroduced me to Danielle and Preston, whom I had babysat many years ago and introduced me to three year old Sara, their new addition.

Andy had to get back to work at the church so Corinne showed me to my room. I unpacked, showered and changed, then went down to their backyard where Corinne had made me a cool drink and set up a lounge chair. It was hot and I was exhausted. We talked casually for a few minutes and then she excused herself to fix lunch. The next thing I remember was Corinne waking me for dinner.

Feeling cool and refreshed from my long nap, I went in to dinner. Conversation was light and happy. Ten years of catching up took all of dinner and halfway into the night. Andy and Corinne retired around two in the morning. I'd wanted to bring up the subject of homosexuality, but didn't know how. Andy and Corinne probably felt the same. Regardless, I could feel their love and knew they felt no differently towards me, despite my shocking news.

Each morning Andy went to the church and I hung around the house reacquainting myself with Danielle and Preston, who were thirteen and eleven, respectively. Danielle and I hit it off right away. She had grown into quite a bright and cheerful teenager. With the aid of bicycles, she showed me around the town.

On the third day I rode my bike over to the church determined to talk to Andy. He wasn't busy and welcomed me into his office. I had trouble beginning, but the words finally emerged. I asked him why love between two women (or two men) was a sin in God's eyes, explaining how beautiful it had been with Eve. He gently said, "God created man in His own image, male and female; they fit," he explained by putting the fingers of both his hands together. I understood he meant intercourse, but didn't agree that that was the only way two people could "fit". There had to be a better explanation as to why I would lose my soul by loving another woman. We talked for an hour, but Andy couldn't tell me homosexuality was not a sin, although he was compassionate.

Returning home I found Corinne in the kitchen. Wonderfully brazen as ever, she opened up the conversation of homosexuality.

I pointed out the Biblical references on the subject, all of which are negative. She read along with me and then nonchalantly said, "I really don't see how these words could mean that wanting to love a woman like I love my husband will send you to Hell. Personally I don't see what's wrong with being gay. Love is love."

Then she left to go back to her cooking. I sat at the table, tears stuck in my throat. Good 'ole' Corrine. She saw what I saw. She had never been the most popular minister's wife at our parish in New York. She wasn't passive. Corinne spoke her mind even if it hurt. Yet, I always thought she knew more about the love of God than the stuffy, pragmatic Christians who disagreed with her. Whatever, I loved Corinne for her words of encouragement. They meant more to me than I could express and they stayed with me, helping me find God's truth. I would never forget that day nor would I forget the trust Corinne had in me. Never did she fear I would take advantage of Danielle. Corinne was a special woman, one whom I would forever love.

Andy got time off so the remainder of my visit with the Hintman's was spent sightseeing and having conversations on every subject except homosexuality.

The day before I left for home Andy drove me to Canada where we had lunch at a small café. I had to question him one more time. Would I lose my soul to Hell if I decided to love another woman? Andy wasn't as sure as he had been ten days ago when I'd first talked with him. Now he could only say he didn't know and his confusion on the subject gave me hope.

Our last night together was a sad one. I'd had such a wonderful reunion with all of the Hintman's. I'd felt safe with them because I was a stranger in town, unaware of the location of any gay bars or gay people. The real world waiting for me back in New York was all to full of temptation and sin.

The next morning Andy drove me to the bus terminal. We embraced for a long times, tears rolling down my face. Andy stood back from our embrace, holding my shoulders. With eyes of love piercing through to my soul he said, "Jan, we want you to know that whatever road you choose, we'll always love you and stand by you."

His words stayed with me on the lonely trip back to New York. I sat in the back of the bus, praying and thinking.

"Why God? Why is it wrong to feel the way I've felt for women like Lauren, Eve or any other woman I may meet down the road? Why is my love and my expression of it a sin?"

Loneliness had not vanished with the freedom I'd felt by coming out of the closet. It had merely changed arenas. Now it was coming, not only from the separation I felt from society because of my difference, but also from the fact that if I chose to follow my feelings and desires I was taking a chance on separating myself from God for eternity. This reality, supported by people of God, tormented me more than I could endure. I loved the Lord and didn't want Him to turn His back on me just because I was gay. According to the Church I was giving in to the sins of the flesh, letting Satan control me instead of God. Otherwise, my homosexuality would not be so difficult to abandon.

Over and over these thoughts bombarded my mind. I had failed God and feared my soul would be lost. The choice was simple. Be straight or be damned. God have mercy was all I could pray for I could not and would not change. I had lived a life of hell trying to get out of my "closet". I would not return to that hell again, despite the phenomenal risk the Church taught. I had to be me and, somehow, something deep inside told me my soul would not be lost. I would find the answer. God would show me the way.

Chapter 6: 1973

Shortly after my return to New York I heard about a group of Christians located in Brooklyn, who had built a home where drug and alcohol addicts could stay to dry out and learn a new life through Jesus. Although their main purpose was to help drug addicts, they also worked with homosexuals, claiming they could, through the power of Jesus Christ, transform them.

Despite my strong feelings about living and loving gay, Church Doctrine of eternal Hell pushed me to make a date with them to see if they could change me or even make me want to change. I had to try.

I called Teen Challenge and spoke with a woman and briefly told her my story. She told me they were having a revival meeting the first Friday in October and I should come because there was a converted lesbian she wanted me to meet. The woman added that I could sleep over in her apartment, which she shared with four other women who counseled at Teen Challenge, since I lived so far.

A couple of days later I went to the bar anxious to see Eve. Still green to the gay scene I had no idea how fast beautifully romantic evenings could be forgotten.

I found Eve sitting at a table with another woman and sat down, expecting Eve to welcome me with some show of affection, but she barely said hello. My naïveté began its fast paced journey towards maturity as I realized that the night spent with Eve, which I had perceived as tender and with the promise of commitment, meant nothing to her. In two short weeks she'd forgotten me and taken up with another woman.

I was devastated, especially since the woman she was with was a tough one, defined as a "dyke" because of her domineering and mannish manner. Eve was an obedient "femme" and I couldn't understand why she had chosen this woman, who treated her like an inferior, over me.

I observed many gay relationships that completely baffled me; relationships that spoke of love, but acted the opposite; relationships based on sex and competition, like some sport; relationships ruined by the overabundance of drinking; relationships devoid of God.

I got in with a group of about ten women, most of them coupled, but a few singles. I liked them and we had good times together, playing pool, dancing and horsing around. They ranged in age from nineteen to twenty-three and all of them were flirting with alcoholism.

The sinfulness I saw horrified me and served to reinforce every Biblical condemnation of homosexuality. There seemed nothing Godly in the gay world. Drinking, sexual promiscuity, fighting by word and fist, were common. No one seemed happy, at least not for long. None of them cared about God. They wouldn't admit any sin in being gay and if God (i.e. the church) said it was wrong, then they had no interest in Him.

I tried to change their minds, but felt inadequate since I was feeling insecure, too. However, they had given up on God and I wasn't going to do that. Some middle ground, where homosexuality would not be an automatic ticket to Hell must exist. I could not rid my soul of this feeling.

* * * * * * * * *

I took Friday off from school the day of my sojourn to Teen Challenge. The train ride to Brooklyn seemed endless, for I knew that when I returned home the decision as to my future life would have to be finalized. I thought my trip to see Pastor Andy would have been the deciding factor. It hadn't been, despite the peace I felt from loving, devoted friends. Teen Challenge was the last door I could open and the thought of what I'd find on the other side terrified me. Yet, they claimed they could transform me even though I didn't want to be straight.

I was desperately confused; wanting to be God's servant and wanting to be me, a lesbian. According to the teaching of the Church I could not be both. Unless some miraculous healing happened tonight at this revival meeting I would find no peace here or in the next life. Had I jumped from the frying pan into the fire? This is what church doctrine told me, but something would not let me believe this. The torment raged within and seemed Hell itself.

My train came to a stop, the end of the line, leaving a hick like me lost in the busy city of Brooklyn. Quickly I looked at the directions given me, took a deep, unfulfilling breath and made my way to Teen Challenge. The walk was not a long one, but it seemed an eternity before the old building came into view.

Inside, people were setting up for the meeting, a mere hour away. I inquired for Terry, the woman with whom I had talked and shortly she appeared. She was pleasant and told me briefly about the upcoming evening events. She advised me to find a seat and she'd join me when the service began.

I sat, lost in the dichotomous emotions running through my mind. The hall was slowly filling and I observed everyone, especially the women. I seemed to have a one-track mind and cringed at my helpless state. Here I was, in God's house, with non-platonic thoughts of women in my head.

One woman, who had walked in about a half an hour after I, struck me as especially attractive. I stared at her, watching her every graceful and seductive move, although I don't think that was her intent, trying to rid myself of the amorous feelings shooting through my mind and body.

She was young, tall and slender. Her brown hair was long and beautifully waved. I couldn't see the color of her eyes from where I sat, but her face was beautiful.

"Enough of this!" I said to myself and got up from my seat to go outside for a cigarette, hoping it would calm my libido.

When I returned I nearly bumped into the very woman whom had captivated me moments before. Now I could see her blue eyes looking at me with warmth and affection. We began to talk and she said I looked troubled. I told her that was the reason I'd come to this service. Then she asked me if I was a lesbian. I almost fell to the floor. The young woman introduced herself as Ruth and gently told me that Terry had mentioned that a new woman, who was having trouble with her lesbianism, was coming tonight. When she saw me go out to have my cigarette she thought it was me Terry had spoken. At that moment I knew this young woman was the transformed lesbian Terry had wanted me to meet.

Ruth told me she was twenty-three and had been a practicing lesbian until last year when Teen Challenge had changed her life through Jesus. She was now heterosexual and felt free from the chains of Satan. She assured me the same would happen to me if I let Jesus heal me.

I listened half-heartedly. All I could think was, "What a waste of such a beautiful woman. Too bad she'd been transformed. She was the type of woman I was looking for as a life's mate." I went back to my seat beating myself for my sinful thoughts.

The service was nothing like I'd ever experienced. It was very emotional with people yelling, "Yes, Jesus", "Praise Jesus", "Amen" and "Hallelujah", every minute. A young man, seated next to me kept repeating these expressions with eyes closed and one hand raised to the heavens, throughout the entire service. I wondered how much he actually absorbed while making such a racket. I knew I couldn't get into whatever message was being preached, finding the whole service annoying and useless.

When it was finally over, Terry took me back to her apartment and introduced me to her four roommates. She made coffee and tea and we all sat in the kitchen talking about my problem.

Biblical Scripture was read, every word that I had known since I was a teenager, but could never relate to what I was feeling.

Genesis 1: 27-28 "So God created man in His own image, in the image of God He created them, male and female He created them and God blessed them and said to them 'be fruitful and multiply'".

Leviticus 18:22: "If a man lies with a man, as with a woman, it is an abomination."

Leviticus 20:13 "If a man lies with a male as with a women, both of them have committed an abomination, they shall be put to death, their blood is upon them.

I Corinthians 6: 9-10 "Do you not know that the unrighteous will not inherit the Kingdom of God? Do not be deceived: neither the immoral, nor idolaters, nor adulterers, nor homosexuals, nor thieves, nor the greedy, nor drunkards, nor evildoers, nor robbers will inherit the Kingdom of God."

I Timothy 1: 8-10: "Now we know that the law is good, if any one uses it lawfully, understanding this, that the law is not laid down for the just but for the lawless and disobedient, for the ungodly and sinners, for the unholy and profane, for murderers of fathers and murderers of mothers, for manslayers, immoral persons, "sodomites", kidnapers, liars, perjurers and whatever else is contrary to sound doctrine."

Roman 1: 18-27 "For the wrath of God is revealed from Heaven against all ungodliness and wickedness of men who by their wickedness suppress the truth. For what can be known about God is plain to them because God has shown it to them. Ever since the creation of the world His invisible nature, namely, His eternal power and deity has been clearly perceived in the things that have been made. So they are without excuse, for although they knew God they did not honor Him as God or give thanks to Him, but they became futile in their thinking and their senseless minds were darkened. Claiming to be wise they became fools and exchanged the glory of the immortal God for images resembling mortal man or birds or animals or reptiles. Therefore, God gave them up in the lusts of their hearts to impurity, to the dishonoring of their bodies among themselves, because they exchanged the truth about God for a lie and worshiped and served the creature rather than the Creator, who is and shall be forever. Amen. For this reason God gave them up to dishonorable passions. Their women exchanged natural relations for unnatural and the men likewise gave up natural relations with women and were consumed with passion for one another, men committing shameless acts with men and receiving in their own persons the due penalty for their error."

    Added to these, of course, was the Biblical account of Sodom in Genesis 19. There was no in between. No gray area. Terry and her friends were inflexible. If I didn't ask God to change me, if I didn't, at the very least, admit homosexuality is a sin and abstain from all homosexual behavior, I would go to Hell. Despite my argument that what I felt for my own gender was not exclusively sexual, but desire for intimate love, just like heterosexual people, I was doomed to fire and brimstone. Terry and her roommates would not budge and after two hours of useless debate and their prayers for a miracle to occur within me, they went to bed. I tried, but sleep would not come.

    Despite the taboo on smoking in their apartment, when they fell asleep I got out of my bed, grabbed a pack of cigarettes and proceeded to chain smoke till dawn, rehashing their words, prayers and the Bible.

    Homosexuality, as I wanted to live it, in a monogamous, loving, marital way, just didn't fit my definition of sin or these Biblical passages. The homosexuality I had seen in the bars did, but not the way I felt. I had physical desire, but that is programmed into each human being from God. I felt no sin as long as that desire was not forced on another and as long as it was used in the act of unselfishly loving another woman. I didn't want to have sex just for the sake of pleasure. I wanted to love and be loved in an intimate sexual relationship, just like heterosexual marriage.

I wanted love. One may feel sexual desire first, but that is an innate response we should control until we find someone we want to share our life and love with and that is what I intended. I couldn't see anything wrong with this.

The passage of Romans 1: 18-27 convinced me more. I had always lived my life devoted to doing God's will. I was a sinner, for sure, but my love was for God. According to this passage, men and women turned toward lustful homosexual behavior because they had turned away from God first. It was as if God punished the unbeliever by letting them turn towards homosexuality. There was no way I could believe this was what God had done to me. I had felt my homosexuality before the age of seven, before the age of reason, according to most Christian faiths and these feelings intensified AFTER I'd dedicated my life to Christ at the Billy Graham Crusade when I was ten years old and had re-dedicated my life to Christ each day since. Was this the way God treated me for giving my life to Him? There was no way I could believe my God would do this.

On and on my mind began to organize its thoughts and feelings. I prayed for guidance from God and received it.

I was gay and gay was the way I was going to live and love. There would be no miraculous cure. I was gay and someday I would find fulfilling, pure love with another woman and I would NOT go to Hell for my behavior.

With the dawning of a new day came the dawning of a new me. I felt that, though Terry and her friends believed in the same God, our understanding and perception of His Word was different. God loved me, gay or straight, saint or sinner and as long as I kept Jesus as my Lord and Savior, God would NEVER turn His back on me or send me to Hell.

   I was free at last and for some reason (which I would understand in more detail later in life), blasphemous as many would call me, I was gay and I was going to live and love gay and I knew, when I died, I would see the smiling face of Jesus welcoming me into His Eternal Kingdom.

Chapter 7: 1973

   With my mind at peace I put all my energy into trying to help my gay friends and acquaintances understand what I had come to in the passed few months and, also, into finding a life partner. I spent five nights a week at the local gay bar, making new friends, listening to their problems, trying to help, hoping they would find peace with God, too.
   I kept myself chaste, refusing to engage in the sinfulness of drinking and sexual promiscuity. I earned the reputation of "Ginger Ale Jan, the goody-goody." I took the bantering good-naturedly for it was largely meant that way. I was proud of being different. I felt it showed that I was serving my Lord through example. One can't merely preach faith and dedication to Christ. You have to live it.
   Weeks passed with no sign of the arrival of my life partner or any change in the behavior of the many gay people whom I tried to help.
   The scene was a bad one, full of sin. Most everyone had a drinking problem. Drugs, basically pot, were a common practice. Cheating on one's lover was commonplace. Fighting, by word and fist (the latter we called "dyke fights"), a weekly event. Double standards, which I'd abhorred in straight life, existed in the gay world, too. My naiveté matured quickly through observation.
   Gay relationships, contrary to wide belief, do not consist of one partner playing the part of the man and the other the part of the woman. However, many gays identified themselves as either "butch" or "femme". With some couples it was easy to identify one from the other. However, with the majority of lesbians and gay men it was more difficult to distinguish. You had to get to know the individual to see the difference and, even then, it was very fine.
   Gay women are proud to be women. To be thought of as wanting to be a man is not only an insult, but erroneous. In the

vast minority, where role-playing prominently exits, butches are more aggressive and femmes are passive. As in the straight world, this role playing is misguided and harmful. Underlying insecurities in each individual, whether gay or straight, lead to such roles and serve to separate two people rather than join them.

Gay men are basically the same as lesbians, insofar as the butch/femme roles. However, butch or femme, men are men. They're more sexually active, more physical and more prone to violence.

I met a couple of men who were into S & M (sadomasochism). Yet, these gay men had their soft sides, but it showed little and when they were enraged or displayed their tough side, it was best to go elsewhere. Thank goodness the S & M gay population is an exception. Regardless, butch or femme, macho or effeminate, gay men consider themselves manly and, indeed, they are.

In the beginning I had a difficult time understanding the dyke female and the effeminate male, feeling that if you were a woman or a man you should be proud of it and not act the opposite of the gender to which you were born. In time, though, I found that most of the mannishness on the part of the women and the effeminacy on the part of the men was an act. However, for a few it was not. It was "natural" and made them no less of a man or a woman. You'll find effeminate men and masculine women among the heterosexual population, too.

The feminist movement brought to attention the fact that each gender is androgynous (having psychological characteristics of both male and female). Perhaps it is more difficult among heterosexuals to show their opposite side, although it seems easier since the birth of feminism. I'm not saying men should walk with a wiggle and women like truck drivers. I'm speaking on an emotional level. A level of a raised sense of esteem that isn't afraid to let the soft, feminine side show, if male or the aggressive, masculine side, if female. The homosexual world seemed less concerned with such stereotyping of acceptable gender behaviors. Perhaps the straight world should learn from us in this area.

The most difficult thing for me to accept was the unhappiness I observed and was a part of by virtue of my listening ear. Hidden beneath the laughter and merriment in the bars, beneath the very term "gay", was the devastating reality of the life I saw. Sadness, loneliness, confusion, anger, alienation, guilt, rejection and low self esteem were the bottom line. Many spoke of wanting a monogamous, lasting relationship, but couldn't make it a reality. With all the negative feelings which gays are subjected, low self esteem is an inevitable by-product. How could gays maintain a stable relationship?

My heart was saddened and discouraged by what I saw and heard. I knew that my desire for a monogamous, Godly relationship was relatively impossible.

* * * * * * * * * *

Mom was doing her share of soul searching during the time I was acquiring my informal education. Without actual observation, only what I told her of my world, she was forced to blindly deal with the situation.

I was still chaste and that brought Mom some solace, but she feared (probably knew before I) that my purity would not remain unaffected by the world I had entered.

At Christmas time, my first out of the closet, the usual festive atmosphere greeted my brother and me as we spent a few days with Mom and Dad. Beneath the outward joyous atmosphere, though, there loomed the grief I had added. Dad was unaware of my new life; to tell him would have killed him. He had enough trouble dealing with Paul's atheism, which he'd come to tolerate, if not accept. He greeted Paul in his usual inhibited style, but didn't preach to Paul anymore. The topic was ignored. Were Dad to learn that his daughter was a lesbian would be too much and I didn't want to hurt him anymore than he had been so it was kept a secret. When he questioned Mom about my single status, at the age of twenty-seven, she made up a story that my relationship with Seth, years ago, had been so painful, I'd turned against marriage. Dad seemed to accept this story.

Paul accepted my being lesbian without question. I never felt any difference in his attitude or his love for me.

Mom, Dad and I went to church service that Christmas Eve, but sadness pervaded. Mom and I still loved each other. I worshipped her and I knew she loved me, but the happiness that had been ours was dying. Mom didn't have to say anything. I could sense it in her and was tortured because I had brought such pain into her life, pain to the woman whom had given me nothing but joy throughout mine.

We sang praises and gave thanks to God for the Christ child, but, deep within, each of us ached. I desperately wanted Mom to accept me as I was and as I had learned to accept myself in relation to God. I wanted her to accept me without shame and without fear for my soul. I wanted my homosexuality to have no negative effect on her.

I asked monumentally. Some of my friends, whose families had found out they were gay, were disowned, a few literally thrown out of their homes. Other families tolerated the shame their child had brought upon the family. Only a few accepted their child. I was fortunate because Mom never withdrew her love. Yet, I could not help wanting more, feeling guilty for my selfishness. I shed many tears that night, during service, regretting what I'd done to the relationship Mom and I had cherished.

Over the past few months, between school and my gay life activities, I saw less of Mom. No longer did I pay her weekly visits. I was too wrapped up in my own world, a world that Mom didn't understand. One I couldn't force her to accept. A world that had come between us and seemed destined to destroy the love we'd shared in the past. However, God never left us, though many times He seemed far away, for in January 1974 I received a letter from Mom:

"My dearest Jan,

Forgive me for writing. I just have so many things to say, so much on my mind, I know I couldn't say it to your face. I'd forget half of what I wanted to say.
These past months have been a living Hell for me. I've been wrapped up in guilt, anger, shame and every negative emotion we frail humans have. I've had to take a good hard look at myself. I've had to deal with a heart that couldn't accept my daughter being homosexual, despite my liberal attitudes of the past. When it strikes your child, liberalism goes out the window.
I must now deal with being in a closet, just when you are out of yours and I don't like it. I've had to deal with feeling that I did something wrong to make you gay. I don't like the idea that I failed you.
I've had to deal with anger towards myself for being less of a Christian than I thought I was. I've been humbled in a way I never believed I'd have to face.
I live in fear that someone will find out. My friends would either pity me or turn from me. I could take their hatred, but not their pity.
I fear for you because of society's attitude towards gay people.
I've prayed for wisdom and strength all these months, but God seemed to have not heard my cry. Then I began to remember, years ago, when you were in the hospital with your heart racing so fast. I thought I would lose you then and prayed God would heal you.

On the third day you were hospitalized, your heart still racing so fast, I fell to my knees, helplessly praying to God, "Lord, I've been praying for three days that you make my little girl well and I still ask that, but if you want her, take her. Thy will be done."

Later that night when I visited you at the hospital, your heart had slowed down to almost normal. I asked the nurse what time your heart rate had returned to normal and she told me, "at three o'clock," which was the exact time I gave you up to God in prayer. It was a miracle. I stopped being selfish that day, fifteen years ago and remembering then, rescued me now.

I thought your being gay meant I would lose you to a world that would hurt you, perhaps destroy your faith in God. I never thought your soul was in jeopardy because you are homosexual, but I was afraid you might turn your back on God because the Church turns its back on gay people.

I focused on myself, not concentrating on the Hell you have been going through. I know it was the hardest thing in your life to come out and even harder to tell me. The risk you took. The courage it took. Yet, in my grief and despair, I couldn't see your side.

Now I see that nothing has changed. You are the same person I gave birth to and have loved, without ceasing, all my life. You are and will always be my precious daughter. I have made peace with God and know that He will watch over you and me as we take this new journey, together!

I hope and pray you will continue to find peace, whether it is homosexuality or any other problem that will hit you on your walk to eternity. But be patient, dear. After all, it's taken me fifty-five years and I'm still learning.

    God bless you.
    All my love,
        Mom"

I sat stunned, reading the letter over and over until it sank in. God had heard my prayers and given peace to Mom's soul, too.

The next time I visited Mom was the most beautiful day of our lives. The mountain had been removed; the barrier destroyed. Satan had tried to separate us and kill our love for each other, but Glory to God, Satan had failed. He would try again and again, but Mom and I knew, from that day on, that nothing could destroy our love, chain us or enslave us, as long as we relied on our Lord and Savior, Jesus Christ. Despite what the Church and the Bible, which are one and the same if it is a genuine Christian Church, said about homosexuality, despite the hopelessness and helplessness we had felt, peace with God and each other was ours. The love of God had saved us and carried us through the storm that had hit so ferociously and Jesus would carry us through whatever life had to offer.

Mom and I prayed our thankfulness to God for His strength, His never-ending love and for turning tragedy into joy, evil into good.

Chapter 8:   1974   Start

   Many times since I'd recognized my homosexuality I'd thought of Carrie and our eight-teen year friendship. Though I'd never consciously thought of Carrie in a sexual way, I knew she had been the first love of my life.
   As we grew older the "funny feeling", my homosexual love for Carrie, submerged, replaced by the love of friendship. However, I now understood why I had been so possessive and upset each time she had a boyfriend and especially when she married. A tiny part of my homosexual love had never died.
   Given our close friendship I had to tell Carrie I was gay. We'd been friends for so long, shared our joys and sorrows, I couldn't keep this from her. Yet, I was petrified to reveal the haunting secret which I'd only come to understand. I remembered the time we tried to slow dance. If I remembered, surely Carrie would. If I told her I was gay would she feel I was perverted to have asked her to dance? Would she think I had merely lusted for her all the years of our friendship? Would she ever believe that the love I felt for her was pure? Would she believe that any subconscious non-platonic feelings were gone?
   No matter what she thought or how terrified I was of telling her, I could put it off no longer. So after eight months of avoiding her, I called and made a date to visit.
   Carrie had two children now and a third on the way. Her boy was six and her little girl was three. They played outside as Carrie and I talked about everything except my love life.
   Towards late afternoon I could take the pressure no longer and, with little build up, told Carrie I was gay. Her facial expression changed not as she said it was probably just a phase I was going through that I'd outgrow. I tried to tell her it was no phase, that I had felt this way since I was five, but she wouldn't or couldn't believe me. I didn't tell her of the "funny feeling" I'd had for her. I didn't have to. Carrie wasn't dumb and she had a good memory.

Our conversation was cut short when Carrie's husband came home from work. He asked me to stay for dinner, which I did, but I left right after.

As Carrie walked me to the door I desperately wanted her to know that my love had never been dirty or perverted. I loved her like a sister, despite my past homosexual feelings, but, she'd never believe me.

I turned to say good-bye and in her eyes I saw disgust or fear or betrayal. I didn't know, but it upset me. When I went to hug her I could feel her body tighten. Maybe she thought our embrace was turning me on and nothing could have been farther from the truth. Maybe I was just imagining her negative response because of the turmoil inside me. I hoped that was the reason, but feared I'd lost the dearest friend I would ever have.

* * * * * * * * * *

That May I received a letter from Carrie. She and Bob had moved to Virginia where Bob had gotten a job as a commercial bank lawyer. Her letter was short. Actually it was merely an announcement of the birth of their third child. Because she had taken the time to write I felt I had misinterpreted her negative reaction to my shocking revelation.

From the return address I tracked down her telephone number and called.

"Carrie, it's Jan. Congratulations on your new son." I said joyfully and quickly, still not confident, afraid she'd hang up on me.

"Jan, it's good to hear from you. How are you?" She sounded friendly and my confidence grew.

After a few minutes of conversation I said, "Look, Carrie, school will be out next week. Maybe I could drive down and visit."

She was silent for a moment and then replied, "I don't think that would be such a good idea. It was another C-section." She sounded nervous and her voice was cold.

"I understand," I said, my heart broken with the realization that I had not read her wrong.

We both felt awkward after that and within a minute said goodbye.

I was hurt, angry and desolate. Carrie couldn't handle my being gay. After eighteen years of friendship she couldn't see that I was the same person she had once loved.

Then I shook myself and said, "Stop it! You're being overly sensitive. It happens to us gays, so stop the pity party."

I tried to obey myself and succeeded, for the most part, but I never heard from Carrie again and grieved my loss. It was the first and most painful experience with rejection because of my sexual orientation, but not the last. Sorrow that I thought would never fully heal.

* * * * * * * * * *

A week later I graduated from community college with a "B" average. I applied to the State University at Stony Brook and was accepted, much to my elation. Community college was nice, but the State University offered an alternative place to meet gay people because they had a feminist women's center, on campus, comprised mostly of gay women. I wanted to be part of it because of my involvement with feminism, but also to meet a different kind of gay woman. I hoped that within the atmosphere of a learning institution, among gay people fighting for justice, I would find a woman, with whom I shared more in common, to be my life partner.

Bar life was not neglected, though. That summer a new gay bar opened and I began dividing my time between the two bars, staying close with the women who had befriended me first at the Shore Club. They were family and the Club was home.

I'd been out of the closet almost a year and, except for that one romantic night with Eve, hadn't indulged in any sexual activity. I wanted to stay pure, obeying God's law against misusing sex. Unbeknownst to me, the debauchery of my world was influencing me in a covertly dangerous way.

Finding a life partner was high on my list of goals, but after a year of failure I'd become disenchanted. The forever love didn't seem to exist. So, despite my devotion to God, I began my journey into darkness. I needed to be close with a woman; feel the magic I had felt with Eve, even if it meant a one-night stand. I was changing direction, guilty about even considering the change, but unable to restrain myself. A lifetime partner was exchanged for my immediate needs, physical and emotional.

In a gay bar it isn't difficult to find a short-term lover, even one who was already attached, but the latter was a taboo for me. No matter, so many women were single and most of them were ready and willing. Commitment was not high on their list of priorities. Sexual satisfaction and someone to hold them through the long, lonely night was the bottom line. I, too, needed arms to hold me and, at this point in time, my morals were pushed aside.

At twenty-eight I was scared. I knew nothing about making love and wanted to be a good lover. So I began slowly, finding a willing woman, a dark corner in the bar and a gentle, but persuasive line.

At first I just necked with a woman in the bar and then progressed to heavy petting in my car. For weeks I behaved this way, practicing the fundamentals of foreplay on a forest of women, trying to gain confidence in my ability to please. Being a gentle, satisfying lover was all-important to me. I didn't want to come on like so many men; pushy and domineering, interested only in their pleasure. My first concern was for the pleasure of the woman in my arms. Mine was secondary. I'd let a woman know I wanted her, but from then on the speed and end result of our sexual activity was in her hands. When she said "enough", whether verbally or with body language, that's when we'd stop and just hold each other. I was content.

* * * * * * * * *

The middle of May I was picked up by a woman who was bisexual. She wasn't a beauty, but she was affectionate and overt about her desire for me. We saw each other at the bar and also had a few dates outside the bar, getting to know each other both intellectually and physically.

June was not the kind of woman I'd bring home to mother. She could be quite aggravating and slutty, but she did have a keen sense of humor which I enjoyed, she was femme, with a fairly nice shaped body and I was turned on by her. I thought she'd be the perfect woman to be the first to make love with because of her bisexual experiences.

Two weeks later June and I decided to go to the diner for some breakfast after an evening of dancing and petting at the Club, but as I parked the car, in a dark area outside the diner, I soon realized that June didn't have food on her mind.

We began making out as I had never done before. I was going crazy with excitement and so was June. She made it evident that she wanted to go 'all the way' and my system said 'go'.

A few days later I saw June at the bar and that night I took her home with me. Consummation in a car was one thing, but I wanted to make love in a bed, like an adult instead of an overheated adolescent, which, I suppose I was, given my retarded sexual experience.

Even with the knowledge that June had enjoyed our automotive lovemaking, I was nervous. Tonight was different. I felt modest. I'd never seen a woman nude before, nor had one seen me. Despite June's sexual experience, she, too, seemed ill at ease. The night outside the diner had been spontaneous. Being caught off guard made it easier. Less is expected in the small confines of a car. Now, in my full size bed, I felt inadequate. I didn't know how to begin and, to my surprise, neither did June.

We fumbled awkwardly through the entire act. June left before dawn. I felt so dirty I changed the sheets on my bed and took a long, hot shower. The thought of June disgusted me. I knew that my desire for June was gone. However, my desire for females had not abated. Rather, it had intensified because, disappointing as our lovemaking had been, I loved making love.

Despite the guilt I felt, my desires overpowered any logical or moral reasoning I held and I returned to the bar, continuing my search for female comfort. I saw June once or twice and she seemed not to feel the same as I, for she was still flirtatious and seductive with me, but I stayed cool towards her. She soon got the message and I never saw her again.

Shortly after I met a kooky nineteen year old and we hit it off immediately. I was always attracted to a person with a good sense of humor and Pam certainly had an abundance of it. She was less experienced than I (she was still a virgin) and since she had observed my sexual behavior at the bar she believed me to be worldly. Feeling insecure about my naïveté on sex, at the age of twenty-eight, I loved the thought of Pam or anybody thinking I was sexually experienced and did all I could to reinforce that reputation.

In a gay bar, if you're seen kissing a woman all night, no one believes that when you leave together you get into separate cars and go to your respective homes. They think you head for the nearest bed. Indeed, many did, but I usually ended up going home alone. I wasn't terribly choosey about with whom I made out, but I was when it came down to making love. My experience with June taught me to discriminate. Nonetheless, I developed a reputation for being an easy mark. My desire to build it had become a reality. Captivated by my new world, which was pulling me down to its sinful level, I reveled in it.

Anyway, Pam and I were together a lot at the bar and we went to a movie or two. I had no intention of making love with her, although we had made out a few times, for she was like a kid sister. However, one night, after an evening of dancing at the bar, I drove her to my house instead of going the extra twenty miles to the summer camp where she worked as a counselor because it was very late. Pam didn't object.

In my small apartment I fixed myself a sandwich, Pam declining my offer of something to eat. I had no idea what was on Pam's mind. At the time I was madly in love with another woman who had absolutely no interest in me, so any sexual thoughts I had were directed at my unrequited love.

I took the last bite of my sandwich and Pam asked if she could take a shower. I almost choked, finally realizing what she wanted. Pam looked at me with a nervous expression on her face. She didn't know how to begin, so I forgot my unrequited love, took Pam in my arms and gently kissed her.

Pam was green, following my every move, but our lovemaking was pleasurable. We never made love again, though. Both of us realized that we weren't what the other wanted. I think Pam just wanted the experience and I was ready to initiate a willing virgin.

We remained close friends, though. At the bar we'd dance and kid around, as we'd done before we'd made love, remembering with gratitude the special night we shared.

I felt less guilty about making love with Pam, skillfully learning the art of rationalizing. June had been wrong because I didn't really care for her. Pam was a good friend. I was beginning to believe that if you were friends with someone and you cared about that person, there was no reason why you couldn't extend that friendship with lovemaking, as long as the other woman felt the same.

With this reasoning almost all my guilt vanished and I continued to feel that I was still a good Christian.

Chapter 9: 1974

A third gay bar opened in the area and I began spending many nights at this spot. Most of my college friends didn't frequent this bar nor did my friends from the Club, so new barrages of women were there for the asking.

One sparse night I found myself in conversation with two women. Both were eighteen years old, blonde and blue eyed, but that was where their similarities ended.

Samantha, or Sam, was a boyish looking, immature girl, what we in the gay scene refer to as a baby butch (a young girl trying to establish her image by acting overly tough). Sam could be tough. She had stabbed a girl a few months earlier during a fight that was not started by her. However, underneath Sam's tough exterior there was a good heart and a girl with much insecurity.

The other woman, Lee, was a poised, feminine woman who appeared older than her eighteen years. She was tall, four inches taller than me, of stocky build, but with everything proportioned nicely. Her eyes were as blue as crystal water. Her lips were full and sensual. Dressed femininely, with beautifully applied make up, she was nothing short of stunning.

Despite Lee's attractive appearance and desirability, I turned towards Sam. She talked more and commanded more attention. Lee was quiet and she intimidated me. Quite out of character for me, but Lee was a lady, someone you'd be proud to bring home to mother. She was the kind of woman I'd wanted before I'd lost track of my original intent. Without realizing it, I had gone astray and was caught up in the very promiscuity I'd tried so diligently to change in others. Lee just didn't fit into the lifestyle I had come to embrace.

Shortly after that night, Lee became lovers with Dee, a woman I had met a few months before Lee. Dee was an alcoholic and though she was a nice woman when sober, she was dangerous when drunk. She was also very mannish. I don't know what Lee saw in her, but I felt that Lee's maturity and loving nature would change Dee.

I took up with Sam, who was about to marry another woman. Patty, her intended, had told Sam she had a brain tumor and was not going to live long. Marriage was her final request and Sam went along with it even though she wasn't in love with Patty. Like I said, Sam had a good, if not wise, heart.

Sam and I saw a lot of each other during the month before her wedding. Within a few nights we ended up in bed where I discovered that just because a woman looked butch didn't make her one. From that day on I never judged a woman by her outward appearance, perfecting my ability to tell if she was butch or femme simply by kissing her.

Anyway, Sam and I grew to love each other. Although I came to realize that the love we shared was like a mother to a child, at the time I felt as if I was in love and Sam felt the same. We both felt guilty for making love. After all, Sam was getting married, even if it was for the wrong reason. Nevertheless, sinful as I felt, I could not stop myself. I tried to persuade Sam to call off her marriage, but she couldn't back out, much as she wanted.

Her marriage took place and Sam and I never made love again, even after her marriage broke up two months later when Sam found out that Patty had lied about her brain tumor. By this time Sam and I realized that we had misinterpreted our feelings for each other. We'd mistaken need for love. However, we remained close friends.

I continued to see Lee at the bar with Dee. Our inhibited friendship continued. I avoided getting to close to Lee, especially since she had a lover. However, I thought it odd that Lee was the only friend whom I greeted with a kiss on the cheek. All my other friends, whether single or coupled, got a kiss on the mouth. It just seemed proper with a woman like Lee.

Chapter 10: 1974-1975

Gerry was a butch, almost dyke looking woman in her mid thirties. She was blonde, her hair cut short in a somewhat mannish manner, her eyes were blue and she had a feminine figure, despite the men's clothing she wore.

She'd come to the bar that night with a woman named Barbra, her lover until recently. Gerry still lived with Barbra and her family (a husband and five children), but their lover relationship of several years was finished. Finished as far as Barbra was concerned, but it was apparent that Gerry was still involved.

Barbra was an extroverted, fun loving woman, whom I remembered meeting, a few months earlier, at another gay bar. She remembered me from that night and asked me to join them. Fascinated with Gerry, I accepted.

Fortunately Barbra kept the conversation flowing, for Gerry wasn't much of a talker. I couldn't keep my eyes off this butch looking woman, despite Barbra's center stage performance. I had to find out if Gerry was really as butch as she appeared.

After a while Barbra left Gerry and me to go flirt with some friends who'd walked into the bar. Alone with Gerry I was nervous. Extroverted as I had become I could never be anything but shy with a person who was introverted. Awkward at first, talking about casual matters our conversation began to ease as the beer uninhibited Gerry.

I was very attracted, but hesitant to do or say anything to lead on this woman until I found out if she was as butch as she appeared. I had no intention of becoming involved with a dyke whom, I felt, was not comfortable being a woman. I could not tolerate a lesbian hiding her womanhood. However, the only way to find out was to kiss her, which I finally mustered the courage to do.

As the evening and the necking progressed, my hunch about Gerry's identity proved correct. She was a femme in butch clothing and I got more turned on to her. My kisses grew passionate and Gerry reciprocated.

I'd had many crushes, a few unrequited loves, but what I felt for Gerry was different. The special warmth that burned within me wasn't just sexual desire.

Gerry and I dated for three months, getting to know each other and growing fonder with each date. We never spoke of love, but I could feel myself falling in love. However, there were problems. I wanted Gerry exclusively, but she was strongly attached to Barbra and her family. Sometimes I wondered if Gerry and Barbra still, occasionally, made love. Barbra seemed devoted to her husband and children and her husband adored Gerry. I knew that Barbra still made love with her husband. She admitted it to me and Gerry backed up her story, explaining that was the reason she and Barbra had split.

It was a complicated situation. Gerry was still involved with Barbra and Barbra wanted to keep up the threesome. Gerry couldn't handle a threesome. I was falling in love with Gerry and unwilling to share her with Barbra and her family. I told Gerry I wanted her exclusively. It was her choice. With tears in her eyes she told me she couldn't leave. Barbra and the kids meant too much to her.

I wished Gerry happiness and we parted friends, never having consummated our love, as I would have liked, but couldn't under the circumstances.

* * * * * * * * *

I was heartbroken over the loss of Gerry. To ease my pain I frequented the bar every night of the week, playing pool, joking with my friends, dancing and romancing the many available, willing women.

One night I saw Lee at the bar without Dee. They had been lovers for almost a year now and I was surprised to see Lee by herself. I'd seen Dee alone at bars many times, talking with other women, leaving with them and drunk as ever. Seeing Lee alone was a complete oddity.

I walked over to her, greeting her in my usual fashion and before I knew it was sitting with her. The bar wasn't crowded, our table was away from the others and the music wasn't blasting so it was a good time to talk.

Lee seemed upset. Life with Dee, she explained, was a horror. This came as no shock to me, knowing what a disturbed person Dee was, but I had hoped Lee could change her. However, Lee was at her wits end, hoping that Dee's trip to a special hospital in Louisiana would help the hypoglycemia, brain allergies and drinking that cause Dee to go crazy and become physically violent.

Lee spoke of Dee with love, despite the hell she was going through with this messed up woman. I couldn't understand how such a loving, gentle woman like Lee could stay in this kind of relationship, but that was not for me to question. I listened supportively, growing fonder of this sensitive, lovely person, hoping life would treat her more kindly.

We talked for hours. I found Lee to be a good listener. I told her of my brief affair with Gerry. We talked about every issue under the sun. I discovered that Lee and I thought the same about almost everything. Lee believed in God, which was a rarity in the gay scene and she believed in monogamy and family life. My morals and values were coming out of her mouth and I knew this was the kind of woman I wanted.

Around one in the morning Lee had to leave. I sat alone at the table, the lingering smell of her perfume pleasing my senses, thinking of our evening together; how nice Lee was and how much I enjoyed being with her; how much I respected her; how lovely looking she was; how poised and mature; how she never said anything bad about Dee, though there was plenty to say on that subject. Lee's patience and love was far more than mine would have been. I would have told Dee to pack up and leave. Lee was certainly different from any other gay woman I'd met. Wonderfully different!

  I was totally wrapped up in my feelings for Lee. Feelings I didn't want to have. If pursued they could put me in the position of being a home wrecker and I certainly didn't want to be that. I still believed in monogamy too much to continue to see Lee on anything but an infrequent and casual basis.

  I left the bar shortly after Lee, uninterested in any comfort another woman could give me that night. Lee had brought me back to reality, at least for the moment. I realized that she was the kind of woman I'd hoped to meet when I'd first come out. But it was too late now. Lee was taken and even if she weren't, I had too much mileage on me. It was for the best. What would an angel like Lee want with a woman like me? I didn't consider myself a full fledged whore, but I was tarnished and Lee deserved better than me.

Chapter 11: 1975

School was going great. I enjoyed my classes in psychology and was maintaining a "B" average.

The women's center was always full of new faces, most of them gay and in January I met a woman who made my heart flutter. Every time she entered the room I'd melt and my broken heart over Gerry was instantly healed.

Dana was a twenty-three year old, blonde haired, blued eyed woman, on the butch looking side, but femme at heart. (By now I was getting proficient at telling a butch from a femme just by observation). Her humor was wild and her intelligence stimulating. I was totally captivated by this woman who was an avowed atheist, had a drinking problem and was sometimes vulgar and crude. Yet, I thought my love would transform her.

One night as she rode with me on the campus bus to the parking lot where my car awaited, she stared coming on to me by putting her head on my shoulder and cuddling in front of all the students on the bus; straight students.

I was nervous, never having been so publicly overt about my sexual orientation, but I enjoyed Dana's attentions so much I didn't care what people saw or thought. Yes, I was gay! What of it? The hell with what others thought!

Taking Dana's affections as a signal, I asked her for a date and she invited me to her suite on campus, which she shared with another woman, who was straight but totally accepting and one gay man. Jack was quite effeminate and extremely funny. He answered when I knocked on their door and the three of us went into his room to watch TV, all of us lying on his large bed.

I was a combination of nerves and sexual excitement. I guess Jack sensed that Dana and I wanted to be alone because he left for a while.

Dana and I lie on the bed, she stroking my forearm till I thought I'd have an orgasm. I wanted to kiss her badly, but was hesitant, despite her seductive caresses. I didn't want Dana to feel I was rushing her. I thought she might be unaware of the overpowering effect her touch was having on my body.

Finally, I could contain myself no longer and rolled on top of her, kissing her passionately. She returned my passion with a disappointing kiss for it was rough. However, this didn't stop me. I knew that Dana was new to the gay scene and her rough kiss was probably due to inexperience.

Not a moment too soon, for I was losing all control, Jack walked into the room with an effeminate scream. We laughed hysterically and it eased our libidos.

He suggested we go to the straight bar down the road and do some dancing. Dana loved to dance and dance we did, till two in the morning when I had to leave because I had an early class the next day.

They drove me to my car in the campus parking lot and I kissed Dana goodnight. Again, her kiss was rough, but I knew it would change with continued tenderness on my part.

I fell asleep with Dana and our wonderful evening on my mind, hopeful that I had found the woman I so needed.

I saw Dana at school a few days later, but she seemed cool towards me. After the closeness we'd shared only a few days earlier, after she'd come on to me, she was turning off.

I kept trying to be around her, skipping classes to spend more time in the women's center, hoping to see Dana so I could find out what had happened to change her. Finally I saw her and worked up the courage to ask her to go to a movie, but she made up some flimsy excuse. I couldn't accept this and pressed the issue, asking her what had happened. She calmly, but somewhat nervously, said she just wasn't into anything serious. I listened, not telling her she had pegged my intentions and acquiesced to her wish that we remain friends. Inside, though, I knew she would change her mind. After all, she had come on to me. There must be some, more than casual feelings on her part.

* * * * * * * * * *

Before entering the State University I'd thought I would find more suitable gay women within the college atmosphere. Not because college women were more stable, but because their strong commitment to social reform would more closely resemble mine, we'd communicate better and a more stable relationship would be possible. However, this was not the case.

There was as much insecurity and drinking among my college friends as my non-college friends. It seemed there was no escape from the torment gay people faced, for whatever reason. My torment had been caused by Church doctrine, but most of the gay people I met at college had little or no religion. Their problems with being homosexual stemmed from other sources, such as family dishonor and rejection, societal judgment and pressure and discomfiture with their sexual orientation. It's hard for gays to escape feeling guilty, outcast, unloved, misunderstood and rejected. Whatever the reason, the gay people I met were not happy, fulfilled or at peace with themselves. They may have denied this, but I knew they were lying to themselves. Their lost, unorganized behaviors belied their outward look of happiness.

I did find one woman who was an exception. Sarah Stein had her insecurities, but not like the others. Since she had been raised in a strict Jewish family, her religion negatively influenced her feelings about her homosexuality; however, for the most part she was more stable and comfortable with her self than anyone else (except for Lee) I'd met in the gay scene. Perhaps it was her relative stability and our common religious beliefs that brought us together. Our conversations were full of philosophy, religion, psychology and any other serious problems facing humanity.

This, coupled with her humor and warmth, made our friendship one that I cherished immeasurably.

Sarah, who was only twenty, had just broken off with her lover of three years. I felt secure telling her about Dana, whom Sarah knew fairly well. Many hours were spent counseling and comforting one another. She was my only true friend.

* * * * * * * * * *

Dana continued to frustrate me, only more so now, for when I'd see her she'd switch, often in the blink of an eye, from cool to affectionate. Sarah observed this and told me she thought Dana cared for me deeply, but was afraid.

Not into Dana's games, I chose to give my attention to women who wanted me and went back to my life of promiscuity. It seemed more fulfilling than games and better than being celibate.

I met a sixteen year old girl, one afternoon, as I stopped in at the bar to talk with another acquaintance.

Neva had recently broken off with her lover of many years and needed a shoulder to cry on. Sometimes she needed a bit more than my shoulder for comfort. We had a casual, brief and unconsummated affair, but it satisfied both of us.

Anyway, it was during one of our chats that little Cory sat by me, quietly glued to my every word. I knew she had a crush on me and found it both titillating and unsettling.

Cory was a troubled girl. Her parents were divorced, her family poverty stricken and there was little love in her home. Her mother was not much older than me, probably the reason Cory grew so attached to me. She was a good kid and we became friends. My feelings of empathy for troubled teenagers were still in me and I tried to help her. She'd listen to me like I was some kind of sage.

When I danced with her she'd shake in my arms. I knew she was physically attracted to me and had to watch myself. I was looking for sex, but not from a sixteen year old. What bothered me most was that I knew Cory wanted more than a casual relationship and I didn't want to hurt her. I was honest with her, telling her about Dana. I could tell that Cory felt Dana was out of reach, so I had to keep Cory at arms length by telling her that I was not into anything but casual relationships and that she was too young. I was no hypocrite on this issue, acting out the words I told Cory by continuing to see other, more mature women. No one had exclusive rights to me, except Dana, if she wanted.

Martha, a large framed, tall woman, in her mid twenties took a fancy to me and I found myself (God help me) using her. Despite my distaste for playing head games, I was doing the same thing as Dana, although my games were defensive so that justified them. Another rationalization I would recognize later in life.

I was up front with Martha, telling her all about my love for Dana and that there would never be a change in my feelings. If she wanted to be casual, I'd oblige. Martha accepted the no strings arrangement I demanded, probably feeling she would change my mind and make me forget Dana. I would have done the same thing.

As the weeks flew by, despite our lovemaking, Martha knew my heart was not hers. She was destined to be hurt, but continued to see me.

Dana was always at the bar and seemed disturbed by my behavior with other women, especially when it became obvious that Martha and I were lovers. Maybe it was wishful thinking on my part, but Dana flirted more than ever, now. I kept my distance, though, never letting her know how much I liked her teasing. I'd tease back, but kept her at emotional arms length just in case she was not sincere. I wasn't taking any chances of being hurt more.

Sarah was kept abreast of the situation with Dana by my words and by her own observation. She said Dana never took her eyes off me when I was with another woman and her eyes were full of envy. Hearing Sarah's words made my spirits rise in hopes that Dana would come back to me.

* * * * * * * * *

On my twenty-ninth birthday my friends kept prodding me to drink something alcoholic, just to see my reaction. To appease them I ordered a sloe gin fizz, feeling nothing after downing the first glass. Half-way through the second, though, I was definitely feeling different. I was feeling mischievous and sexually aroused (I knew liquor had this effect on me when I started taking communion in church. After downing the tiny glass of wine, offered at the holy sacrament, I'd return to my pew feeling anything but wholesome. God forgive me, it was just the way alcohol hit me.)

I began fooling around with Melanie, a girl from the woman's center, whom I had no sexual desire, but now was kissing and nibbling her neck in front of all the women from the center, including Dana. Melanie had a drinking problem and was very drunk at the time and as I playfully lunged for her neck, again, she lost her balance and fell to the floor taking me along with her.

Everyone was in stitches, laughing. Tea totaling Jan was bombed. Actually, I was just feeling amorous, but was astutely aware of everything I was doing.

Later that night, as I went to leave the bar, I saw Dana sitting alone in the small room made for intimate conversations and necking. I stopped by her and asked for a goodnight birthday kiss. After all the games I thought it was the least she could do and she hesitantly went along with it.

I was feeling cocky and a bit angry so I played a game with her. I leaned down and kissed her gently. After a few seconds Dana tried to pull away, but I held her head tightly in my hand and my kiss turned passionate. She resisted at first and then relaxed.

With our kiss over, I looked Dana directly into her eyes, trying to tell her, "Enough of your teasing, enough of your games. If you want to play, you're messing with the wrong woman."

Dana looked me in the eyes with shock and something else. I didn't know. I turned and left the bar, feeling a little guilty for forcing my kiss on her. It was terribly out of character. I had never forced my affections on any woman, but, in Dana's case felt good knowing I had succeeded in unsettling her for a change. Nevertheless, a few nights later, I apologized for my rude behavior and Dana quickly forgave me.

Shortly after my birthday, at the bar with Martha, dancing to a slow song, she pulled back for a moment and gazed longingly into my eyes.

"Jan, I know I promised, but I can't help it."

I got her drift. She had promised to stay casual, but had gotten serious. I'd seen it coming, but ignored it. I felt terrible for her, but she had been warned so I felt no guilt. Our relationship had been one of casual sex. No strings. Those were the terms and if Martha couldn't follow them, I'd have to end our relationship, which I did that night, as gently as possible.

My Christianity was becoming more deeply buried under the barrage of justifications, rationalizations, terms, definitions and codes of right and wrong that I created. However, I couldn't see this at the time. Since I still prayed every night and communicated with God during the day, I believed my faith was as good as ever.

Without realizing what was happening to my relationship with God I blindly led my life the way I ruled, feeling I was a good Christian, preaching whenever someone wanted to listen, but falling short of behaving like one. By comparison I felt I was a good Christian, but comparisons aren't what Christianity is about, something else I would learn later in life. At the time I felt I sinned less than everyone else in my gay world, thereby could hold onto my Christian identity, never realizing that sin is sin, whether you commit one or many. I didn't recognize the danger waiting to completely destroy me.

With Martha out of my life, or should I say out of my bed, I turned, once again, to the many available women. I engaged in necking and petting with a variety of women, but never did I see another woman, in a sexual way, if I became lovers with a woman. No matter how short term or casual my sexual relationships were I remained monogamous until the affair was over. This behavior reinforced the belief in my Christianity, for to be unfaithful was a deadly sin. More rationalizing, but it worked and, without knowing it my soul was headed for permanent residence in Hell.

Chapter 12: 1975

May brought the end of my first year at the State University. My "B" average had fallen to a "C", but any scholastic worries were pushed aside by my love of nighttime activities and Dana.

She continued to flirt and toy with my affections. I went along with it, enjoying the attention, feeling that her behavior proved she was still interested. I didn't let her know how I felt, though, remaining indifferent, seeing other women, hoping to force Dana's hand through jealousy.

Cory was still my ardent admirer. Since she was now seventeen, I gave her a little of what she craved. She knew I loved Dana, but was content with the small doses of sexual attention I gave her. I felt obligated to help Cory learn some of the art of love making, but not all. We never made love. To do so would have intensified the hurt I knew would be Cory's destiny. In my ever deepening rationalizing, it was her choice since I had been honest. My sense of guilt numbed under this reasoning.

In May I met a twenty-six year old bisexual woman and we became lovers. Cory didn't like it, but went along with my rules. She knew that Jenna would not last because of my love for Dana and, with wisdom more realistic than my own, at the time, Cory knew my hope of a relationship with Dana was futile. So, Cory waited for me for me as unwisely as I waited for Dana.

I was totally honest with Jenna, again justifying any hurt feelings that were inevitable for any woman who took up with me during this time. She seemed to accept the situation and we shared many pleasant times, in and out of bed.

I was heavy into a frame of mind where I felt that making love was sinless as long as both people felt the same way about each other and the relationship. With the exception of Dana I wanted only casual sex. If another woman wanted the same I'd make love with her. However, if she got serious, like Martha had, our sexual relationship would end. Being honest about my intentions kept my Christian identity in tact.

In June, Ally, a gay acquaintance from the women's center, had a party at her house. Her parents were away and the house, which was high class and gorgeous, turned into a gay women's weekend resort.

Dana was her flirtatious self the minute I entered the house. She vacillated from hot to cold, but tonight I enjoyed her antics more than ever because I had a plan to get even with her. A plan I felt sure would speed her return to me.

As the night grew late we all congregated in Ally's den to watch TV and talk. At one in the morning a classic three hour movie came on that fit into my plan perfectly, for not long after the movie began the girls became bored and tired so they went to bed; except for Dana. I was not surprised. I didn't think she'd go to bed until I did and that meant watching the movie with me, like it or not. All I wanted was to be alone with her so I could play my game to its fullest.

I sat on a recliner while Dana lay on the couch a few feet away. I sensed her waiting for me to make a move on her, but I intently watched the movie, talking infrequently, aware of Dana's every move or glance in my direction.

Dana waited up with me until the movie ended. Now she would expect me to find a piece of floor on which to sleep. Then she'd expect me to make love to her or at least try. However, I got out of the recliner and said I was going home. Dana seemed disappointed. My plan was working perfectly.

I started to leave and she was at my side saying she'd walk me to the door. I knew she expected a kiss goodnight, but she never got it. I just said goodbye and left her standing in the doorway, looking forlorn.

My plan had been a success. She wanted me, I was sure. It was only a matter of time.

A few nights later a good friend, whom I hadn't see in over a year, called and asked if I'd come down to the bar. He didn't have to twist my arm. I'd missed Keith and his crazy, effeminate nature. Though he could be a real "bitch", he'd always been a good friend to me and I loved him dearly.

As I entered the bar he came running towards me, arms outstretched. I ran to him and we embraced. Keith hadn't changed a bit. We talked for hours, catching up on lost months.

I'd seen Dana the minute I walked through the door and was aware of her eyes on Keith and me as we talked. Suddenly she was sitting next to me. I kept cool, despite the thrill I felt by her presence.

Keith left around two o'clock, but I stayed just to see what Dana's next move would be. She was different tonight. She was sober, mellow and not into games. We closed the bar, talking and getting to know each other better. It was a wonderful evening. I could tell that Dana cared and knew it wouldn't be long before she restarted our aborted romance.

A couple of days later I received a call from Dana. We talked for half an hour before I invited her over to my place. She had been coy, but it was obvious that she wanted me to ask.

When she arrived we talked more. The more we communicated the more I fell in love, but made no sexual advance. I felt that's what she wanted, but I wanted her to make the first move so I'd know if she was sincere. She didn't so we just went to sleep.

We woke late the next morning and began talking again. My back was sore from the two of us sleeping in my tiny twin bed and when I mentioned it, Dana told me to roll on my stomach and I did. The next thing I knew she was sitting on my behind massaging my back. It felt great, clinically and sexually. I was fighting for control and was doing a good job until she bent over and ran her lips across the back of my extremely sensitive neck. Within seconds I turned around and told her, with a smile on my face that mirrored hers, that she 'played dirty'. Then I took her head in my hand and pulled her mouth to mine, passionately kissing her. She reciprocated. We necked for a while, but I got control of myself and stopped. I wasn't going to make love to her till I knew what was going on in her head.

After questioning her strange behavior over the past few months, she replied, "I care for you very much, Jan, but I'm scared." She sounded so helpless.

As we lie in each other's arms, I told her I understood and would try to help her get over her fears. Shortly after, she left for I had to get to class.

I walked on a cloud all day. Dana cared. She wanted me. I had felt it in her kiss for it was no longer rough, but gentle and caring. My dream of a lasting relationship was coming true. Together we'd help each other.

The following week Dana and I were together every night, expanding on our emotional and sexual intimacy, but we never made love. I still didn't trust her. Were we to make love and she pull away again my hurt would be unbearable. I had to remain in control.

One Saturday Dana and I went out with another couple. Dana had a few too many drinks and I was worried. It was the first drink she'd had that week.

When we got back to her dormitory suite she had sobered up and we began to make out, heavier than usual. I knew she wanted to make love and so did I, but I didn't want to give myself to her all the way till I was sure she loved me as much as I loved her.

I pulled back and gently said, "I'm not going to make love to you."

"Why not?" She asked, naturally puzzled.

"Because I don't trust your feelings for me. When I'm sure you feel the same for me as I do for you, then I'll make love to you."

I thought she'd get mad, but she didn't. We gently kissed each other and I left.

For the next few days Dana didn't call nor was she in when I called. Finally I got through to her.

"Dana, I'm sorry about the other night."

"Don't be. You were right." She sounded sad.

A couple of days later she called me and asked me to come over to the dorm because she had to talk to me. I knew what was to happen. It was over.

I got to her suite and Dana sadly told me, "Jan, I care for you deeply. I want a relationship, but I'm too scared."

"Scared of what?" I was frantic, but didn't let her see my emotional state.

"I don't know. All I can say is that I'm poison for you." She looked unhappy and I knew she wasn't playing any game. She was hurting, too.

I held back my tears, not wanting her to see how hurt I was. There was nothing I could say or do to change her mind. I got up, kissed her gently, told her I loved her and left.

I drove home feeling crushed and heartbroken as never before. How could Dana say she was poison for me? I felt so good with her. Never before had I felt such a love.

Yet, I never shed a tear, for I held fast to the hope that she would return again.

Chapter 13: Late 1975

My depression over losing Dana a second time was devastating, but I let no one, except my dear friend Sarah, see my broken heart. Sarah was my rock during the time in which I helplessly pined for Dana. Sarah's love and support was a constant source of emotional energy that kept me from descending into a depression from which I feared I would never return.

We grew closer during those months. She was still having troubles with her ex-lover and we looked to each other for strength and comfort. At times our comforting became sexually intimate.

It was a time of soul searching. Except for the few intimate moments with Sarah, I put my sex life on hold. Doubt became my constant companion. Maybe God was telling me He didn't want me to be gay. My decision to be myself, gay, a decision that had brought peace of mind was now under scrutiny.

To reinforce my doubts was my growing friendship with a young man whom had moved into one of the downstairs apartments in the house in which I lived.

Roger was twenty-six years old and recently separated from his wife, by her request. He was heartbroken, still in love with her and desolate over the separation from his five year old daughter. We reached out to one another in our common heartache and became close friends.

At first I didn't tell Roger I was gay, but soon I was forced to tell him because he was growing fond of me. He wasn't shocked, merely disappointed that I would not become his lover. Regardless, as the weeks passed and as we shared our sorrow and joys a beautiful love burgeoned.

Soon Roger couldn't afford to pay his rent and he began living in my small room. Though his desire for me was evident by his word and by anatomical changes whenever I was near (when I'd come home from school he'd greet me at the door, dressed in my silk shorts, with an erection, saying "Junior is glad to see you"), he respected me, making his bed on my floor, though there was plenty of room in my newly acquired full size bed.

We talked incessantly, exposing our deepest feelings. Not since Seth had I felt so close to a heterosexual man. The thought that God wanted me to be straight hounded my heart and I decided to try, again.

Roger had a premature ejaculation problem. He said it was one of the reasons his marriage had failed. Being a psychology major and having spent hours in classes on sexuality, our relationship grew into a clinical sexual arrangement. I tried, by using techniques I'd learned in textbooks and class, to help him conquer his problem.

Though Roger wanted to make love to me, he respected my wishes and never forced the issue. However, we did kiss a couple of times. I wanted to see if a man could turn me on, but there was no feeling. However, I was happy to help him with his sexual dysfunction through manual and oral stimulation, but I never let him touch my body. I thought by engaging in some heterosexual activity I could learn to enjoy it and stop sinning against God. I knew what I was doing with Roger was a sin, but it seemed a good way to try to give up the more sinful life of homosexuality.

People always asked me, "How do you know you don't like something unless you try it?"

Having only kissed men, I'd answer, "You only have to put your foot in the water to know if it's too cold."

What I did for Roger was done out of love for a lonely, horny man and out of curiosity. I wanted to test my answer, put more than my foot in the water and see if it would make a difference. It didn't. There was no sexual feeling on my part. I gave it my best shot, but any kind of love making with a man held no excitement or pleasure. If God was trying to get a message across that I should go straight, it was no use. I was gay.

After a while Roger realized this, too and we went our separate ways. He tried to start his life over again and I took myself off the shelf and began to go to the gay bars again.

* * * * * * * * *

In September my senior year of college began. I saw Dana once in a while. She was now renting a house, off campus, with five other gay women. Sarah had gone with them and it was through her that I learned that Dana had becomes lovers with one of the girls renting there. This broke my heart even more. Only a few months earlier Dana had said she was scared of having a relationship and now she was in one. I felt totally rejected and used. My hope of ever having Dana for my life partner died and I buried myself in the newly formed Gay Student Union, consisting of both men and women.

We opened a telephone hotline for gay people and I became a phone counselor. We had to go through a month long training program that was fascinating and more educational than anything I'd learned in my textbooks.

During the training session I grew very close to a twenty-two year old young man. Billy was a mess of insecurities. Shy, withdrawn and vulnerable, I took to him like he was my child, though I was only seven years his senior. He was brilliant, carrying a double major. As if that wasn't enough pressure, his homosexuality caused him unbearable pain.

Brought up in a devout Jewish family, Billy was torn between following the wishes of his parents (both unaware he was gay) by being engaged to a young woman (also unaware he was gay) and his physical and emotional need to be with a man.

Though Billy wanted a monogamous relationship, he couldn't find one. He lacked esteem badly, believing no man could love him enough to want a long term relationship. So his sex life consisted of one night stands every weekend, when he'd go to Manhattan and cruise till he found a man or many men (in a gay bathhouse it is not uncommon to engage in sex with a dozen men in one night) to satisfy his need for love.

Billy was a good man, no matter what society would say. Indeed, his life was full of sin because of his promiscuity. Nonetheless, his true self, which I had come to know, was nothing like his behavior would indicate. He hated being gay; hated cruising; hated what he was doing to his family and his fiancée, who loved him dearly. Billy wanted to please everybody, not realizing he demanded too much of himself.

I loved this young man beyond words and tried to help, but was unsuccessful. This world was too cruel and insensitive for Billy. He couldn't handle the pain he felt inside himself or the pain he was causing his loved ones. On December 8, 1975 he put a plastic bag over his head and passed on to what he hoped would be a better life, although he did not believe in God.

Sarah broke the news to me and I sobbed like a baby as she held me. My Billy committed suicide. Dead through an act that Christians and Jews believed to be an automatic ticket to Hell. The thought of my beloved Billy in Hell was unbearable.

The entire Gay Student Union attended his funeral. We all sat in the back of the Temple, gay brothers and sisters holding on to each other's hand. When Tim, to my left, began to cry I squeezed his hand and when he was composed and I began to cry I felt the strong, comforting grip of his hand on mine.

Gay people; mourning the death of a brother driven to suicide by a world that doesn't understand, much less care. Driven, more so, by the religious community where all sinners are supposed to be welcome. Unless gays give up their sex life, they are turned away. In essence, being told that God loves all sinners except gay people. No wonder so many gays turn from God.

Through the funeral and the week long Shiva, I worried about Billy's soul, not able to see this vulnerable young man doomed to eternal separation from God because he was gay and took his life. Wasn't it bad enough Billy felt separated from God while he lived; separated by an uncaring, self-righteous Church. In death was Billy to live the same Hell he could not escape while on this earth? The thought tortured me night and day. All I could do was keep hoping that God would have mercy on Billy's tormented soul.

Chapter 14: 1976

Good comes from all evil, so the Bible teaches and I believe this with all my heart. Not just because the Bible says so, but also because I have experienced this seemingly ridiculous concept as truth. However, not until Billy's death, a needless death brought about by apathy, hatred and ignorance did I remember how many times in my life good came from evil. Again it was happening, for it was Billy's death that started me traveling back from my trip to Hell.

I still grieved over Dana, still loved her, but her loss seemed petty in light of Billy's death. Time would heal my grief over Dana. She would fade from my heart, but Billy would always have a room there.

My climb back wasn't fast, but neither was it slow. My sex life came to an end. I was back to my original intent of finding one woman for a lifetime partner. No more one-night stands and no more casual affairs. I began to see the error of my homosexual living and in my relationship with Roger. I felt guilt again. True guilt and through repentance, received the forgiveness of God and the ability to forgive myself for my sin. I clearly saw how I'd let Satan deceive me. How I'd begun with pure motives towards finding a life's mate and let discouragement and failure lead me down the path of self-destruction and separation from God. It was no one's fault but mine.

God had stayed with me as I journeyed to Hell, never letting me go, never taking His love or guidance from me. It wasn't surprising. He'd gone to Hell for all mankind two thousand years ago. Would He do less now?

* * * * * * * * *

On the eve of my thirtieth birthday I took Cory to the bar. There was a classmate of mine to whom I was attracted and she seemed like a nice young woman. I went to the bar that night hoping to see her and take her home with me, regardless of Cory. My trip back to purity wasn't fast nor was it without setbacks and mistakes.

Once again I was honest with Cory, telling her that I was going to the bar to bring Nan home with me. However, I promised Cory that if Nan didn't want to come home with me I would make love to her.

Cory went along with me hoping, I'm sure, that my evening plans with Nan would fail. And they did. And I took Cory home with me, but we just went to sleep. I'd lied to her, hurt her, as I must have done dozens of times in the past. However, there was a reason for my abominable behavior. I'm not justifying it, but that night was the last time I used another person for my own selfish desire.

You see, Nan never showed at the bar. I was disappointed, but consoled myself by playing pool with Sam, my one time lover and now good friend.

Sam took an instant liking to Cory and the feeling was reciprocated. My conscience was eased.

As I played pool I noticed Lee sitting at a table, alone. I went over, greeted her with my usual kiss on her cheek. She looked radiant, her blonde hair soft and styled to my liking, her crystal blue eyes captivating me as they always did.

I couldn't sit with her and talk because I had won the pool game and the table was mine. The line of challengers was long and I was on a roll and kept winning.

As I watched my opponent clear a few balls off the table, Sam came to my side.

"How would you like to go out with Lee?" She asked.

I looked at her, shocked and replied, "I don't know. She's still lovers with Dee and I'm no home wrecker."

"To tell you the truth, Dee and Lee haven't been lovers for six months. They live together, but it's been over for quite a while." She had an encouraging look on her face.

With this bit of knowledge I was glad that the woman opposing me cleared the table and sank the eight ball, beating me. Finally I was free to sit with Lee.

I approached her table feeling awkward, nervous and shy; totally out of character.

"Hi." I managed to speak. "Would you mind if I sit with you for a while? I'm waiting for someone, but until she gets here I'm all yours."

God! What a thing for me to say to Lee. I didn't mean it offensively, but tact had never been my forte. I guess Lee intimidated me and I was defensive. Forget the rationalizing; I was being a total ass.

Lee invited me to sit with her despite my pompous and demeaning proposal.

We hadn't seen much of each other since that night, over a year ago, when Dee was out of town and Lee was at the bar, but she hadn't changed. Still sweet, warm and kind, I forgot about my rendezvous with Nan and wished I could take back my opening words.

Things were as Sam had said; Dee had gone off the deep end, constantly drunk, taking woman and men home to have sex while Lee was made to sleep in the living room. She stayed only because she had no place else to go except back to her family and, after two years away from them, that was impossible.

Being the lovely person I had come to know, it was no surprise that there was no hatred in Lee for Dee. Lee was the most patient, loving woman I'd ever met.

All too soon it was my turn to play pool again, but I told Lee I'd lose real fast so we could continue our conversation. As I played, Lee and Sam came over to me. Sam had told Lee that the next day was my birthday and Lee wished me a happy birthday.

At that point, Lord knows what came over me, I said to Lee, this time humbly, "Do you think I could have a birthday kiss at midnight?"

God! What was I doing? Even though Lee had told me it was over with Dee that was her opinion. If Dee found out about this I'd be a dead duck. However, my control seemed to have disappeared. Only I wasn't thinking in my usual depraved way. Not with Lee. You didn't treat a lady like her with smart lines or lack of respect.

Suddenly her mouth opened and she said, in a voice so sensual my heart began to race, "You don't have to wait till midnight."

"Oh God!" I thought, panicking. "I can get a kiss now; on the mouth? How do I do it?" Smooth talking, casual, confident, cocky Jan was falling apart.

Slowly I put my face close to Lee's and our lips parted and met. It was not what one would define as a passionate kiss. It was gentle and warm, but I thought I'd burst. Not just from a physical aspect, as had been my experience with other women, but with a new dimension. Lee's kiss emotionally floored me. No woman had ever kissed me like Lee.

When our kiss was over my legs felt like jelly and I turned from Lee and walked to the pool table, leaving Lee puzzled, I'm sure, as to my unusual behavior. She probably thought I didn't like her kiss, but she couldn't have been further from the truth.

Well, I lost the pool game I was playing prior to Lee's kiss, but not because I tried, as I had told her. I just couldn't play for beans.

I went back to Lee and we talked more. As we talked our chairs moved closer to each other and soon we were locked in an embrace, kissing each other, taking cigarette breaks every few minutes to cool down.

I wasn't worried about Dee anymore, lost in my feelings for Lee and I emphasize, not just physical. I still hadn't fully gotten over Dana and I told Lee all about her. However, what I felt for Lee and what I felt for Dana was completely different, though I couldn't explain how.

Lee and I closed the bar that night and I drove her home. My usual self would have taken her to my house to make love, but Lee had changed me.

After I dropped Lee at her house I remembered little Cory sitting in the back seat. I took her home feeling sorry I'd ever promised to make love to her if I came home alone. But I think she sensed that I really hadn't come home alone. Thoughts of Lee were with me. Besides, Cory and Sam had hit it off well and she was high on her feelings so everything was working out nicely.

I couldn't get Lee off my mind and it wasn't the thought of getting her into my bed. Something was different. Lee's beauty, warmth, gentility, humor, intelligence, morality and wonderful kiss obsessed me. I'd been obsessed by women before, but not like this.

On Friday night there was a gay dance at school and I had asked Lee, before we left the bar, if she'd like to go. She'd accepted.

On Thursday Lee called, terribly upset because she had to break our date. She'd forgotten that she and Dee had made plans to go camping that weekend. I said I understood, but spent the rest of the day angry and depressed.

On Friday morning Lee called and said she had told Dee she wasn't going to go camping because she was going to a dance with me. Dee, whom I had known before Lee and who absolutely adored me, didn't seem to mind. I walked on cloud nine all day, happy that Lee had chosen to be with me.

Whenever I went to the bar I'd spruce up, but that Friday I spent three hours getting myself ready for Lee. I had to present her with the cleanest, dressiest woman in the world.

I took the longest shower of my life, not realizing what was happening. I was washing away the past two years of slime and dirt that had soiled me and almost taken my soul. Lee had resurrected my original purpose to love and be loved in a pure fashion and, if she'd have me, I wanted to share the rest of my life with her.

BOOK THREE: Gay Married Years: 1976-1994

Chapter 1: 1976-1978

During the school dance, Lee and I talked about her relationship with Dee. It had been over for a long time, but Lee could not return to her parents so she endured the verbal and physical abuse, witnessed by her friend's and by the left- over black eye Lee had covered with make-up. I asked if she wanted to stay with me and she said "yes". We left the dance, stopping at her apartment to gather her few possessions and leave a note for Dee and headed back to my place.

We lie in bed holding each other and talking till we fell asleep in each others arms. Emotions I thought dead had resurrected. My ability to love in the pure way I'd intended when I first came out, only three short years before, years packed with experiences which nearly ended in disaster, awakened and the emptiness I subconsciously denied was filled by Lee.

The living arrangements were tight, but we didn't mind. We talked about our pasts, being totally honest about everything, even ex-lovers. Through communicating our souls grew as one.

A woman and her three children occupied the remainder of the upper part of the house where we lived. Since only a door separated us from their apartment, sounds told our neighbors much about us and since they were Pentecostal Christians they weren't thrilled living so close to lesbians.

Some nights we'd hear them holding prayer meetings, shouting to God to save the perverted souls living in this house.

Shortly after, my landlord told me to do my socializing elsewhere. That night Lee and I packed my car with the few possessions we had and took off in search of a place to stay. We had little money. I still got my disability check, but Lee had to quit her part time job with our swift move.

Lee remembered her old landlord telling her that if she was ever in trouble she should contact him. We did and he told us we could stay, rent free, in the dilapidated building across from where Lee and Dee had lived. Dee was thrilled to have Lee close again. We weren't thrilled, but what other options were there?

Our apartment had no heat, but it was summer, no water and no cooking facilities, but there was electric and we had brought our hotplate and toaster oven. The accommodations were filthy and dangerous, but we never gave this a second thought. It was better than sleeping under the stars.

My disability check lasted the first half of the month, with two of us, so we ate well till the second half of the month. Then we'd mooch meals from Lee's family, whom I finally met in May of 1976. I kept in touch with Mom, but told her little of the squalor in which we lived, not wanting to upset her.

Mom had met Lee, but didn't know we were lovers. I was scared to death to tell her, despite the letter she'd written after I'd come out. I told Mom that Lee was gay, but just a friend living with me to help with expenses. Again I was lying to Mom and was profoundly guilt ridden.

When I finally worked up the courage to tell Mom that Lee and I were lovers, Mom was very happy. She had come to love Lee very much. From that day on Mom and Lee grew closer and soon Mom referred to Lee as her adopted daughter.

After a month of living in our dump Mom knew we were in need and gave us the money to afford a small apartment atop a bar that had once been gay, one I'd spent many a night philandering, but was now a straight bar. Shortly after we moved in Lee got a full time job and with my disability check we finally stopped eating ketchup and mayonnaise sandwiches. Life was looking up.

It was at this time that Dee finally realized that Lee was not coming back to her. She knew we'd become lovers, but was never mad. Now, one of our friends told her that Lee and I were very much in love and Dee went crazy. We found out, later on, that Dee followed us everywhere.

One evening she came to our new apartment, banging on the door, shouting that she wanted to talk and if we didn't open the door she'd break it down. Dee was drunk, as usual and extremely strong when she was in this state. Lee was upset and I was scared. Dee wasn't heavy, but she was about six inches taller than me and quite an adept brawler.

I tried to reason with her, through the safety of the door, but she wouldn't listen. By this time Lee was frantic and Dee was threatening me from the other side of the door. All of a sudden the whole incident became quite funny to me, so, in an effort to break the tension I responded to Dee's threats, in the toughest voice I could muster and yelled, "Oh yeah!" Dee stopped screaming and Lee and I started laughing. In the end, though, I had to call the cops and Dee left.

We saw Dee at the bar once or twice after, but she was controlled and very sorry. She knew she had lost Lee and felt no anger towards me, just sorrow for herself. After the hell she'd put Lee through, the cheating and the beatings, she still loved her and wanted her back, but she loved me, too and knew I would take good care of Lee.

Shortly after, Dee moved down South, but not a birthday or holiday went by without Lee getting a card and a long love letter from Dee.

In addition to the trouble we had with Dee, the first few months weren't easy on Lee for other reasons. My sordid reputation followed and she had to deal with a past we both wanted to bury. Much as I thought I'd found true, lasting love, I feared our relationship would end up like all the others I'd wanted. I wanted to fully commit myself to this lovely woman, but fear kept me from giving Lee the love she needed and deserved. Her patience, understanding and love slowly assured me that our relationship was different. Ours would be a lasting one. Lee's steadfast love tamed my restless, searching soul and the peace I'd found in the early months of coming out, peace soiled and almost lost along the way, blossomed and flourished in the light of Lee's love.

Three months after we became partners Lee and I got engaged and in October 1976, in the church where I'd been raised, we secretly committed ourselves to each other, using parts of the marriage ceremony in the hymnal. Before God we pledged our love and were joined. (A year later, when we could afford a public union, we renewed our vows before a Unitarian minister, our friends and our Lord. Mom stood by my side and her best friend, Mare, stood up for Lee as we vowed our love and loyalty.)

Our union, marriage, is comparable to any heterosexual one, complete with in-laws (since we were not legally married by state or church, we referred to them as our 'out of law in-laws'). Despite what the Church taught on the Biblical condemnation of homosexuality, we felt married in the eyes of God. We looked to Him as the Head of our house, tried to obey His laws, served Him and worshipped Him as our Creator and Savior.

Yet, our life was not a fairy tale. We didn't marry and ride into the sunset free of life's dark side. No one ever does and one must be prepared for life to do its best to destroy you.

One of our biggest problems was my persistent physical illness. I had learned to live with them, had told Lee about them, but living with me was asking a lot. Lee was patient and as understanding as anyone could be, especially at her tender age of twenty. However, she was upset and, at times, felt like an outsider, which in many ways she was. It was as if she lived with two people, the stranger and me.

Not only did this stranger affect out social life, causing us to be a rather homebound couple, it also interfered with our sex life, especially when I got a job the second year of our marriage. Until then the stranger was weak, but when I had to work it was difficult enough to get through the workday. I ran, as I'd done years before at jobs, although not nearly as frequently, trying to calm down so I could return to my desk and perform my duties. When I got home all I wanted to do was stay there, watch TV or read. Rest was all I craved and TV was my tranquilizer. Consequently, lovemaking was few and far between.

Since we had only one car, Lee stayed at home, lonely and bored. When I came home she wanted some excitement and I couldn't deliver enough. She became restless, but rarely complained.

Despite my infirmity and its limitations, I wasn't totally without energy. Lee and I pushed the problem to the background, concentrating on the happy times we had when I was able to function, socially and sexually. I don't know how she did it. It was like living with two people; one stable and healthy, the other lethargic and boring. With all my education in psychology I never thought how severe the effects were on Lee. I thought she had adapted, as I had.

* * * * * * * * *

After a year in the apartment above the bar, Lee and I left suddenly. Some of the male patrons at the bar below found out we were lesbians and began to harass us. They'd peak in our windows, turn on the bar's dishwasher whenever they heard us in the shower, leaving us with cold water that barely trickled out of the pipe and played the jukebox extra loud, till six in the morning. It became unbearable so we left fast and found a one room, roach infested place down the road, escaping the unpleasant situation before it got dangerous.

I was now thirty-one and feeling better so I tried a job. My job lasted only a couple of weeks due to my temper and acid mouth. I was fired because of a 'personality conflict' with the boss of the accounting office shortly after I told her, "change your condescending attitude or shove this job up your fat ass."

God I had a mouth! For years I'd kept my anger suppressed, but now I was having trouble controlling it. Dr. Falano did a good job un-inhibiting me, but I was over-compensating for all the years of keeping a lid on my anger. Whenever I felt unfairly treated I saw red and my mouth went into fifth gear. I had no diplomacy or tact. I'd never start a fight, but would always end one, even if it meant being fired.

Thanks to me, we were in financial trouble, again, back to living on ketchup sandwiches and mooching meals from our parents. As before, Mom came to our rescue by loaning us money so we could move out of our roach infested environs into a small, but beautiful cottage not far from where Mom lived. Shortly after, I got a good paying job at a nearby nursing home and, once again, we were financially making ends meet. With only one car Lee stayed home, happy to be a housewife.

It was in our tiny cottage on October 29th, 1977 that we renewed our marriage vows, a year after we'd secretly wed. We were very happy. Despite my physical symptoms and their limitations, it was the beginning of one of the happiest years of our marriage. Though I was tired from working and fighting the symptoms at work, Lee seemed to be adjusting and our home was full of love and joy.

A year later I was fired, but this time I collected unemployment. Lee got a part time job babysitting and Mare, the woman who had stood up for Lee at our wedding, moved in with us, helping our financial deficit, until she made a decision as to what to do with her life since she'd recently divorced. At the age of forty-five and with five children, three of whom were on their own, the younger two living with her mother, Mare had much to sort.

In June, 1978 Mare moved to Colorado, my unemployment check ran out in May, 1979 and we were financially struggling on Lee's part-time job. I tried getting work, but jobs were nil in the area where we lived. I had to travel twenty or more miles for a job and, with the symptoms, it was just too far away from home for me to hack it, although I tried.

We had to move west, away from our love cottage, back to the middle of Long Island where jobs were more plentiful. Again, Mom gave us the money to make the move and we found a house to rent. Mom had bought a new car and sold her old one to Lee for one dollar, so both of us could now get jobs. Lee found one in June 1979 and I got one in October 1979. Once again, life was looking good.

The first day of my job Lee had a terrible car accident, being hit and run off the road onto a neighboring lawn by some man who ran a stop sign, leaving us, once again, with one car, but worse yet, leaving Lee with a severe neck and back injury. Our expenses outweighed income, but our house was large and we decided to share it with a divorced woman and her two small children. With her financial help we broke even.

Chapter 2: 1980-1981

My new job was going well. I worked nine to six and was tired, but we managed to have some social and love life. We'd go to the bar every weekend and made some new friends. However, Lee's car accident left her with a painful spine.

Despite her pain she enrolled in beautician school and graduated, with honors, as a hairdresser. However, she could not take the needed state board exam because by the time she graduated, the neck and spinal injury made it impossible for her to elevate her arms for long, so there was no way she could do hairdressing, even part-time. She'd had such high hopes, but her growing infirmity killed her plans.

Depressed and in pain, Lee became withdrawn and in constant need of emotional attention. Attention I couldn't supply. I was working forty-six hours a week to keep us financially secure and Lee was neglected. This led to restlessness in Lee that our friends filled. A vicious cycle began. Lee had her gay girlfriends over our house on the two nights I worked till 9 PM. I tried to keep up with the three times a week trips to the bar, but couldn't take the pace. I kept catching one cold on top of another so I had to stop. Lee went out without me, knowing I disapproved.

Though I understood Lee's situation, I was enraged. Going to the bar with her friends, Lee could have the fun she craved and, with the help of a few glasses of wine, forget about her painful back.

One of our friends told me that she thought Lee and another one of our new friends were having an affair. I wanted to punch this so-called friend, but couldn't because I had the same fear.

Our marriage was falling apart. When I confronted Lee on the subject she denied having any affair and assured me she loved only me. But it was hard for me to believe. I'd let her down so much. I was all work and little play. Lee wanted all play. We were growing apart and there seemed no way to save our marriage.

I turned to God in prayer, asking for His help and healing and after a couple of months my boss sold his old car to me and Lee's back was feeling better and she got a job in January 1981. With the job, Lee realized her errant ways. She stopped seeing her gay friends and our marriage grew stronger.

With both Lee and I working and with a little more financial help from Mom, we decided to move again. Three women and two screaming kids in the same house, for a year, had gotten to us. We wanted to move and start over again; away from gay friends who wanted to hurt us. We just wanted to be together as we had in the past.

We found a lovely apartment in a complex and our wounds quickly healed. Overwork on my part, boredom and pain on Lee's and unstable friends had almost torn us apart, but our love wouldn't quit.

I had prayed to God to heal our marriage. I believe He did, but the Church would disagree. No matter, we were together, again, paying our bills and happier and more in love than ever.

During the next year Lee worked diligently at her job in a bank. Within six months she had been promoted three times and was holding a responsible position. Now she'd become a workaholic, but I didn't mind. She was growing up, learning about responsibility and loving every minute of her success.

With both of us working hard we had little time for each other, but what time we had was quality and that out-weighs quantity. It does in every area of life. Though apart more physically, our souls grew closer.

Chapter 3: 1982

    Christmas 1981 brought an additional joy to our celebration of the Christ Child's birth.
    Though my Dad no longer played the organ to our singing carols, due to his failing health (in the passed two years he'd had stomach surgery and had developed emphysema), he'd long ago accepted Lee as part of our family and loved her in his inimitable, inhibited way. I don't think he ever realized we were more than good friends. Lee brought more comfort to him than any woman since Mom. Even a confirmed woman hater, like Dad, couldn't help but love Lee.
    However, it was Paul who brought the added joy to our Christmas this year. Susan, his lover of three years and he announced their engagement and plans to marry on June 6, 1982. Even Dad was happy, despite the fact that Susan was of the Jewish faith. In Dad's eyes it was better than them living in sin.
    Susan came into Paul's life at one of his lowest times, bringing him a beautiful love that lifted him up and filled his emptiness. With the addition of Susan into our family a sense of completion filled all.

                       * * * * * * * * *

    The New Year began with high hopes. Lee's job was going well, along with mine and our financial situation was improving. My symptoms still plagued me, but weren't as inhibiting. We were very happy. We seemed the perfect couple, to others and to ourselves. Yet, a crucial test was coming that would change our lives and test our marriage, again.
    In the middle of February, Mom took Lee and me to see "On Golden Pond". We all cried at the lovely story, but it was just

fiction, till afterwards, when the three of us stopped for something to eat.

When we finished eating, Mom said, "I wanted you two to see this movie because I have bad news to tell you. Sometime before Christmas I began having some trouble. Once I went blind in one eye for a few minutes. Another time I couldn't speak for five minutes because my mouth went numb. My chiropractor told me I have practically no circulation to my feet, so I went to Dr. Seth and he found that my blood pressure was very high and my carotid arteries are clogged. I have to go for some tests, but it looks like I'm going to need surgery. I don't want to hide anything from you; it's dangerous."

I was frozen with fear. All my life I'd leaned on Mom. I'd lived on my own three years before I met Lee, solving my own problems, dealing with life independently, feeling the apron string break. With Mom's revelation I realized that my sense of independence was not complete; I hadn't fully broken the apron strings. I'd suppressed the thought of life without Mom; a fear I thought was gone, given the confidence I had in my ability to handle myself in life's challenges. Now, with the possibility of losing Mom, I felt alone, zapped of my strength and confidence. Could I live without her? The thought of losing Mom devastated me. I tried to be brave, but inside, I felt like a coward.

Lee gave me much comfort at this time. She and Mom had grown so close over the past six years. Mom had told her that except for the fact that she had given birth to me, her love for Lee was equal to her love for me. Lee loved Mom dearly and the news flattened her, too, but she never showed her fears. How could she? Lee was in a catch 22, not wanting her fears to show so she'd be able to give me strength.

Lee didn't have to say anything. Her presence and love gave me strength. Yet, I knew that I, alone, must come to grips with the possibility of Mom's death. A spouse can give you love and someone to lean on, friends can give you comfort, but in the final analysis, the individual must deal with the illness and possible death of a loved one, alone. Yet, I knew I wasn't alone. God was with me. I kept on praying for Mom's recovery and for strength for myself, Lee and Dad.

Mom went through test after test for the next few weeks. The CAT scan, given at the doctor's office, almost killed her because she was allergic to the iodine dye. A minute after the dye was injected Mom went into a severe asthma attack and had to be shot up with epinephrine to save her. Hearing her somewhat weak voice, on the phone, when she returned home from the test, upset me, but Mom was in good spirits. She even joked about the irony of dying before she got to the operating table. That was Mom. Despite the danger facing her, she was full of humor and faith.

Mom was admitted to the hospital on March 11th to prepare for the final test, an angiogram, on Friday and surgery on Monday.

I knew this test to be extremely dangerous. If a piece of plaque broke off Mom could have a stroke, possibly die. I was scared to death, but kept praying for God's healing touch.

With Lee steadfastly by my side we visited Mom the night before the test, walking into the lobby where Mom would smoke her last cigarettes. After surgery she'd have to stop. She was supposed to have stopped already, but hadn't. Foolish, maybe, but Mom joked that even a condemned prisoner is offered a last cigarette.

Mom knew the operation was dangerous. She knew she could die, but she accepted the fact without fear. Her only real fear was of paralysis. Having seen her own mother fail after her stroke, suffering four years before she died, Mom preferred death. Yet, her deep abiding faith in Jesus gave her the strength to face her illness and its options. I wished I'd had my mother's faith so I could be as calm as she.

Since hearing of Mom's illness I'd prayed for God to heal her. Prayed for my own selfish need probably more than for Mom. Yet, my fear subsided none. Outside I held an appearance of strength, as I was told, but my fear of losing Mom was overwhelming.

I went to work the Friday Mom had the angiogram, barely concentrating on my work. All I could do was pray. Pray she wouldn't die because Mom was allergic to the dye. However, this time the doctors doped her with plenty of antihistamines to reduce the risk of an allergic reaction.

By afternoon Dad called telling me that Mom had gotten through the angiogram perfectly. I held my tears back and gave thanks to our Lord for taking care of Mom.

Despite my feelings for Mom, I was not unaware of Dad's. Though his emphysema was a moderate case, he had lost much of his ability and had grown more dependent on Mom. His fear of losing her, though he never said a word to me, must have torn him apart. I tried to give him strength, but, the bottom line is you've got to find it alone, with God's help. I prayed much for Dad.

Monday, March 15th, 1982, the Ides of March, Dad, Paul, Susan, Lee and I sat in the waiting room of St. Charles Hospital. Sister Martha, whom I'd grown to love when I'd worked for the hospital, years before, said a pray with us. She was a beautiful nun with a quick sense of humor and a faith I've seen in few people. I came to love her even more when Jennifer's mother told me how much Sister Martha helped when Jennifer had polio in 1950. Sister Martha slept in the ward with the infected children, giving no thought to her own health. She was an inspiration to me and knowing she was praying was a great comfort. If there is such a thing as a 'hotline to God', Sister Martha had it.

Our family sat for hours, talking little. Dad uttered not a word, occasionally looking at me to smile weakly. I winked at him, knowing exactly how he was feeling.

Lee and I made a trip to the hospital Chapel where we prayed and on our return I saw Dad at the receptionist's desk, frantically waving his arms for me to come to the phone. It was the doctor with news of Mom and Dad was too upset to take the call. Trembling, I took the phone in my hands.

"Your mother is doing fine. The operation was a success. Go home and come back tonight when she'll be awake." The doctor was confident.

I hung up the phone and told all. Dad come over to me, put his arms around me and sobbed. I returned his embrace and whispered in his ear, "God has been good to us," feeling penitent for my shaky faith.

That night we all went to visit Mom in intensive care. My symptoms were bad enough under normal circumstances, but illness and hospitals were my nemesis. Had it not been my mother lying ill, I'd have run, but she was alive, though she barely looked it. When she was aware of our presence, she weakly uttered, "My beautiful, beautiful children," then lapsed into sleep. I welled up, but would not cry. I hadn't cried once since Mom told us. I had to be strong for her, but how I wanted to cry. Cry and scream for her not to be lying there so helpless. My rock was gone and my heart ached. Mom was alive, but would she ever be capable of being my rock again?

Mom was to be in intensive care for two days and out of the hospital in ten days, but there were complications. Mom was on her feet within two days, but her blood pressure remained sky high and she suffered excruciating headaches. The doctors said this sometimes happened. It would take time for the medication to regulate her system.

Lee and I went to the hospital daily. Paul and Susan left for Brooklyn the morning after the operation, but kept in touch, by phone, on a daily basis.

By Thursday night Mom's condition was not improving, but she was being transferred, the next day, out of intensive care.

On the ride home Lee and I had a fight. I don't remember what it was about, but I started it. Just something stupid, needed for me to finally break down.

Lee pulled the car over and held me as I sobbed and asked what I was going to do if Mom died. It had been four days since surgery and she wasn't improving. If her blood pressure didn't drop, she'd have a stroke.

The doctor had only cleared one carotid artery; the other, which was to be operated on next month was being pushed off and that artery was 60% blocked.

Lee told me I'd be all right, whatever was to happen. We held each other, Lee now crying, shedding her pain and fear. God, I loved her so!

Chapter 4: 1982

Mom's recuperation was not going well. She continued to suffer severe headaches and the doctors could not get her blood pressure under control. She was given aspirin to thin her blood, but that was not enough. Mom was beginning to have mini strokes. She'd go paralyzed on one side or lose her speech for a couple of hours, then be all right. The operation had not helped, for these mini strokes affected her right side and the operation had been on the left carotid. Since this artery was clear, I questioned the doctors as to why she was having these strokes. They kept telling me it was merely spasms in her brain and nothing to worry about.

I began to get angry at not being told the truth. I'd been a hypochondriac all my life and knew a lot about the body. These weren't spasms; they were strokes and my anger grew towards these doctors. I prayed to keep my temper under control and the Lord heard me for I never directed my anger at the doctors.

Mom was upset by all the evasion, too and became more agitated.

On Holy Thursday, April 8th, Mom's sixty-fourth birthday, two weeks passed the time she should have been sent home, she wanted to go to the Chapel for service. Her blood pressure was 220/120 and the nurse said no.

Mom finally had enough and lost her temper while Lee and I waited for an artery to burst as she fought with the nurse.

"You call my doctor!" Mom yelled. "I want to go to church! You think my blood pressure is high now? Well it will soar to the moon if I don't' go to church. Now, you get through to my doctor and get permission or I'll have my daughter take me anyway!"

God, she had a stubborn streak, but I was on her side. Let the woman go to church, even if it kills her.

The nurse returned saying she couldn't get through to the doctor, but acquiesced to Mom's demand. Smart nurse; one shouldn't argue with my mother.

The service was beautiful, inspiring and filled me with peace. It was two hours long, but Mom got through the service better than me (my symptoms were killing me), returning to her room without having a stroke.

Within the next two weeks Mom's condition improved. The doctors stopped giving her aspirin and prescribed a strong blood thinning medication that stopped the 'spasms', which I finally got one neurologist to admit were really minor strokes (today they call them TIA's). Mom was released from the hospital on April 18th, refusing Lee's offer to take off from work for a week so she could care for Mom.

After weeks of working everyday and going directly to the hospital, forty minutes away, seven days a week, it was good to have Mom home. I called everyday and she was doing pretty well. We made plans to celebrate my birthday, Dad's and Mom's on April 25th. Paul and Susan were coming out to celebrate, too.

When Lee and I got to the house, we found Mom with her head over the toilet, vomiting and complaining of severe abdominal pain. She kept saying she just had a virus and would be all right, but after an hour we all realized she had more than a virus.

Paul and Susan had not arrived yet. I was to pick them up at the train station at three o'clock. In the meantime, Lee and I followed as Dad drove Mom to the doctor's office. Lee went inside the examination room with Mom and the doctor. Dad, like me, had no stomach for sickness and Lee, who always wanted to be a doctor and whose grandmother was a nurse, tended Mom. I felt badly about my weakness. Lee was doing what I should, but I thanked God for Lee's selfless caring.

After an hour of waiting and praying the doctor came out and said he thought Mom had an aortic aneurysm and should be hospitalized immediately. It was getting close to the time I was to pick up Paul and Susan so Lee drove Mom and Dad to the hospital while I greeted Paul and Susan with the 'wonderful' birthday news.

The hospital was total confusion when we arrived. Lee told us Mom was in bad shape, almost unconscious. When we got to her room Mom acknowledged all of us then fell into unconsciousness. There was a tube up her nose going to her stomach and blood was coming out of it. She was pale and it looked bad.

There was nothing to do but go home and wait. Paul and Susan left for Brooklyn and their jobs and Lee and I went home. The doctor had my phone number in case of an emergency. All we could do was leave Mom in the hands of the doctors and in the hands of God.

It was a grueling night. Every time I closed my eyes I saw the lifeless body of Mom, blood streaming out of her stomach and doctors with no answers.

Throughout this ordeal I never ceased to pray for Mom's healing, but this night, remembering my mother's words to me weeks before the surgery, "Honey, if something goes wrong with the operation and I'm in a coma for more than three weeks, with no hope of recovery, please pull the plug", I prayed differently.

"Dear Jesus. I've been praying for you to heal Mom, bring her back to me, healthy. Don't let me lose her. But now I sincerely pray You do what You want. I don't want her to suffer. Give her peace, dear Lord and if You want to take her home with you, please do. I've been selfish, but I know You are with me and will give me the strength and courage I'll need in this crisis. Into Your hands, dear Jesus, I give you Mom. Do with her what You will, for You know best."

Tears rolled down my cheeks for the first time since I'd cried with Lee in the car, weeks before, only this time they were tears of peace. No longer was I afraid of Mom dying. She was in God's hands. Despite my grief and pain, His peace would be my foundation. Mom had been my rock all my life but I had forgotten who the ultimate rock is. The old hymn "On Christ the Solid Rock I Stand", reminded me we are all firmly in God's hand. He cares for us, grieves with us, but comforts, sustains and helps us through the valley of the shadow of death.

From that day on I feared not. With each trip to the hospital I felt a wonderful peace within me. I still hurt watching Mom suffer, but I knew God would give His strength to Mom, too.

Mom suffered a stroke that first night because her doctor had to give her vitamin K to clot her blood. Blood thinners were new to medicine and needed constant monitoring and this had not been done. The doctors wanted her blood thinned, but with testing they found that it had become too thin. She'd had no aneurysm. Her blood had become so thin she was bleeding internally. Vitamin K was the worst thing they could have given her because of the risk of stroke, but without it she would have bled to death.

A week later Mom was conscious and almost totally paralyzed on her right side, the side with which she writes. Also, the stroke had caused both her eyes to have blind spots in them. When Lee and I made our daily visits, Mom kept her eyes closed because the room would spin on her when she opened them, another side effect of the stroke.

Mom was depressed. I'd never seen her in such a state. She was almost without hope. My rock, here on earth, was shattered and I ached, but not for myself. I hurt for Mom and continued, with Lee always by my side, trying to help Mom from giving in to her depression.

When Mom wanted to talk about death, we did. One night all we talked about was her death; right down to what she wanted to be buried in. Many people, who are dying or believe they are, want to talk about death, but we onlookers are afraid it will upset them. Nothing upsets a person more than evading an issue. So we talked and Mom was comforted. We even joked about her death. It was one of the few times Mom laughed.

Mom's career was finished. She'd have to retire and she had never planned to, for she loved her work as secretary to the librarian at Ward Melville High School. This grieved her terribly. She fought against it, but in the days to come she slipped more and more into depression. I'd gone through these emotions, too, but it's more difficult when you've had a stroke because the brain damage physically affects your brain function. I continued to pray that God would help her climb out of her darkness. Mom still had her faith and I held on to my belief in Mom's faith and, more so, in the power of God.

As the weeks went by, with Mom working hard at her daily physical therapy, very hard because Paul and Susan's wedding was only a month away and Mom was determined to walk down the aisle, with Dad, to give Paul away, she began to improve. Love for her son motivated Mom as nothing else could.

Lee was vital to Mom's recuperation, too, for she would not let Mom get away with using her left hand. Lee made her use her right hand even if it meant taking an hour to eat a dish of ice cream, one of Mom's favorite foods. Mom was stubborn, but Lee was more so. It angered Mom, but she knew Lee was being tough out of love.

It was a slow process, but Mom was released on the Thursday before Paul & Susan's wedding. Mom walked shakily down the aisle with Paul and Dad, Paul holding both his parents more than they held him, but she did it. She even danced a slow dance with Paul at the reception. It was the beginning of a new life for my brother and Susan as it was the beginning of a new life for Mom. One that would take her time to adapt, one that would be difficult, but one that would end up with our church calling Mom their "miracle child", for even the doctors said she would never be well enough to live alone with Dad.

Chapter 5: 1982

Ten days after Mom's surgery I received a telephone call from Ruby, Grandpa Adickes' (Mom's step-dad) next door neighbor, telling me that Grandpa was acting strangely. He'd turned off his heat and the pipes in his house had frozen, breaking the heating system. She told me I'd better get in to check on him.

Lee and I took a Saturday off from visiting Mom and went to East Meadow to see Grandpa. This happened the end of March during Mom's first hospital stay and before I'd come to terms with her possible death. My mind was focused on Mom, more accurately, on my own selfish needs. The pressure I felt was overwhelming, but somehow there was a strength, deep within, keeping me from the feeling that I would collapse from the pressure that had increased my physical symptoms severely.

Grandpa greeted us with a smile, but he wasn't the man I'd remembered. Since Nana's death my family only saw him once a year and only for short visits. Grandpa was a quiet man, a loner and a devoted husband and had become more reclusive after Nana died.

We had spoken with him on the phone at Christmas and he did seem a bit forgetful, but he was eighty-one years old. In just a few months the change was unbelievable. He looked like the main character in the movie, "The Old Man and the Sea". Filthy white beard, dirty tattered clothing and stinking like a cesspool, Lee and I had trouble holding down our lunch.

The house smelled even worse and it was freezing. Though there was an electric heater by Grandpa's chair, it was off even though there was electric in the house. Gramps assured us he was warm. There was water, although it was cold, but no food in the refrigerator or the cupboards.

We tried to persuade Gramps to come home with us, but he said no, he was fine. I should have insisted, but had so much on my mind I foolishly trusted him and decided to leave him on the 'back burner', at least for now. Mom needed my time more, though I felt guilty as hell leaving Grandpa in his squalor.

The next weekend we returned to Grandpa's and found his situation much the same, except that he was a bit cleaner. Upon questioning he said he was fine and eating. Since he looked cleaner and seemed healthy, I decided that I could leave him for a while longer. Besides, he was adamant about leaving his house and I respected his wish to stay. Grandpa's mind was muddled, but he seemed to be holding his own.

I spoke with Ruby and explained my situation and she was very understanding. I found out that she and her husband were feeding Gramps a hot meal once a day, bathing him weekly and keeping an eye on him. So, for now, Grandpa could wait.

I was very appreciative of Ruby, who had always been a good neighbor. She was one of those people you loved instantly.

As Mom began to improve, during her second hospital stay, things got worse for Grandpa. Lee said she would quit her job so she could take care of Gramps and we decided to force him to come live with us. This time Gramps didn't fight us and with the help of my lawyer, a close friend of Mom's, Grandpa signed over his home to Lee and me and we withdrew all his money from the bank and put it in our account. It was quite a substantial amount; enough for us to buy a large hi-ranch house with a finished apartment downstairs. I bought a large house to accommodate my parents, too, for Mom's doctor told me that she'd never be able to live alone with Dad; both were too handicapped.

It took six weeks to find and close on the house, so Grandpa stayed in the living room of our one bedroom apartment, which contained a hi-riser. He moved in two days before Paul and Susan's wedding, but Lee and I never told anyone what we'd done until we were sure Mom was strong enough to know what had happened to her step-father. (Mom's biological father died when she was eight years old).

We hired a nurse's aide to sit with Grandpa when Mom was released from the hospital because for the first six weeks after her release, Lee went out to Mom's every weekday till one o'clock to help her and Dad. This time we put our feet down. I wasn't taking any chances on Mom's health. Mom was in worse shape now. Though much of the use of her right side had returned she was still weak and needed help with shopping, cleaning and cooking and Dad was too sick to help.

When Lee got home from taking care of Mom our aid left and Lee spent the remainder of the day caring for Gramps. I escaped all this because I had to work, but I still felt guilty.

By the time we moved into our house on July 15, 1982, Mom was making such remarkable improvement she refused to come live with us. Since she'd lost so much of her self-sufficiency, her house became the only thing she had to represent her independence. I understood and yielded because her health was improving.

Lee, Grandpa and I set up house in our beautiful home. It wasn't easy, but the alternative, according to the social worker in East Meadow, was to put Grandpa in a mental institution. A nursing home or adult facility was out of the question because Grandpa was healthy and needed only custodial care (feeding, washing and dressing). I couldn't bear the thought of my Grandpa in a state mental institution, nor could I bear the thought of the state getting all of his hard earned life's savings.

With Mom's miraculous improved health Lee only went out once during the week and we both went out each weekend. We could leave Grandpa alone for a couple of hours, now that he'd become accustomed to his new surroundings, but we'd get our nurse's aide when we were going to be gone long periods.

We "baby-proofed" the house so Grandpa would only have access to his room and the bathroom when we left him alone and at nights. When we slept he'd be awake. Grandpa had an insatiable appetite and the minute he knew Lee and I had gone to bed he'd make a beeline for the kitchen and eat everything in sight including the dry cat food we kept on the counter; he thought it was candy. Gramps was a handful, but a wonderful character. Pleasant and cooperative, he touched our hearts.

Chapter 6: 1983

The stress of the past year, along with the problems one can inherit going from financial struggling to instant, more than modestly well off, began to rock our marriage. Within the next year Lee and I were in serious trouble, again, growing further apart, trying to hold on to a love we both cherished, but fighting what seemed a losing battle.

I was now thirty-seven and Lee, twenty-seven. I was feeling the difference in our ages. A generation gap grew fast. The illness in my family certainly had its effect, for we were so busy taking care of Mom, Dad and Grandpa we had little time for each other. In my mind the needs of my ailing family took precedence over Lee and me. I'm not sure Lee felt exactly the same, but since we were so busy and tired, communication abated. Consequently, neither of us truly knew how the other was feeling.

Also, I now knew how hitting the age of thirty-five plus affects people. Maybe not all and certainly in different ways, but I felt a change taking place. Mid-life crisis some would call it. Whatever, it was a time for re-evaluation of my life, goals and values. Though they had stayed relatively constant, they had become more set and serious. Lee was into recapturing the fun she'd missed as a child. With the added responsibility of my family's needs, Lee was, once again, cheated. Though she handled the responsibility well, I was asking too much of her.

No one was all right or wrong. We were just in different frames of mind and not communicating well, so we steadily grew apart.

The very beginning of June I got a telephone call from Mom. I knew from her voice that something was terribly wrong and she got right to the point.

"Are you sitting down, honey?" Oh God, I thought, this is going to be real bad.

"Yes." I answered calmly, but my heart was beating fast.

"Jennifer is dead. They found her Wednesday morning, in her bed."

"Dear God!" I said, feeling completely numb. "What happened?"

"No one knows for sure. She called her mother on Friday night to tell her she wouldn't be home for Memorial Day weekend. She said she had a sore throat and was going to bed early. When she didn't turn up at work on Tuesday her friends just thought she'd made the weekend another day longer, but when she didn't show up on Wednesday they got worried and went to her apartment and found her in bed, dead."

"Oh Dear God," I said, feeling my throat choke. "Will they do an autopsy?"

"They can't. Apparently she died early Saturday morning and lay there four days. You know how frail she was. There was nothing left to autopsy. But the coroner said there was no sign of struggle. She died peacefully in her sleep. I guess either her heart or lungs gave out. It's really a miracle she lived thirty-eight years given her fragile condition."

Mom went on to tell me that the viewing would be on Friday and I told her I'd be there, forgetting about Lee and our marital troubles.

I hung up the phone and sat frozen. Jennifer, dead! The last fifteen years I'd only seen her at Christmas and once each summer. She'd been teaching grammar school at a Lutheran school in Boston. With all the hardships she'd fought and overcome in her short life, she'd made something of herself. She'd made an impact on others. I know that not a person in the world who had spent a couple of minutes with her, left without some positive feeling. Jennifer was a special woman. Now she was gone and my soul cried out for her.

I went to the sofa where Lee sat patiently waiting for the bad news and I told her what Mom had said. Lee held me tenderly, my tears finally flowing like a river and my body trembled from the aching sobs emerging.

On Friday night Lee drove us to Jennifer's viewing, picking up Mom along the way. I was crushed. I worried not for Jennifer's soul. She was a genuine Christian so I knew she was at peace with our Lord. Actually, when someone in Christ dies, your tears are for yourself and the loved ones left behind. I felt it a shame Jennifer had died so young, but felt no anger or confusion as to why God allowed her early departure. I grieved for her family and I grieved for my loss.

When I reached the funeral parlor I immediately saw Rebecca, sad, but bravely accepting what had happened to her youngest daughter.

I approached her, tears in my eyes and embraced her. I thought I was going to start sobbing, but when Rebecca said, "You've lost a good friend," the tears vanished. In her grief she was thinking of me. Knowing Rebecca's faith, her words came as no surprise. I loved her and felt closer to her than ever.

I saw Jennifer's older brother, Jack, a good man, but always getting into trouble and embraced him saying, "I've lost my best friend." He returned my words, tearfully, saying, "So have I."

The burial service was scheduled for the next morning. Mom said she wasn't up to it and apologized for not being able to come with me. I understood and I'm sure Rebecca understood Mom's fragile health and her emotions about Jennifer. Mom could identify more with Rebecca than I, for she was a mother and children aren't supposed to die before their parents.

Lee didn't come to the cemetery, either. At that point my failing marriage took a back seat to my need to see Jennifer's death through to the end and in many ways I was glad Lee didn't come, for I needed to be alone with the reality of Jennifer's death, the memory of our life and love and the nearness of her family. I was so devastated it was as if nothing existed outside of the agony Jennifer's death had brought.

I greeted Jennifer's family the next morning, said my farewell and waited, with the other mourners, outside the chapel while Jennifer's family said their good-byes.

I was holding up fine until I heard Rebecca wail, "Jennifer, Jennifer!" Over and over she cried out her name as she clung to the casket. Then my tears began to flow. From the funeral home to the cemetery, the procession stopping in front of Jennifer's house, I sobbed convulsively.

At the cemetery I gained my composure for a few minutes, until the minister began his final words. Again, more silently, I sobbed. My Jennifer was gone. I knew she was happy with our Lord, but I was filled with a void no other human could fill.

One by one we walked passed the coffin to say our final farewell. I kissed the lone flower, given to all the mourners and put it on Jennifer's coffin, softly saying, "Go with God, my dear friend. See you later."

As I walked to my car, crying, I felt a strong, yet gentle hand on my shoulder.

"How did you know Jennifer?" The woman asked.

I turned to see an elderly woman smiling warmly at me. I told her how I knew Jennifer. We walked for a while, her presence and words giving me comfort and then we parted. I'd never met Rebecca's sister till that moment, but I shall never forget her strength and faith which comforted me.

In my car, waiting for the hearse to lead us out of the cemetery, I sobbed more. Lord, I'd never cried this much in my entire life. I thought I'd never dry out.

Back at the church hall a handful of women from the church had prepared coffee and cake for the family and friends. I sat next to Rebecca, at her beckoning, composed now and talked of Jennifer, our years together and all the good times we had.

Jennifer was at 'home' and I was happy for her, but the ache in my heart would not leave.

Chapter 7: 1983-1984

The year following Jennifer's death was a stormy one. Just the year before, I'd gone through the crisis with Mom's illness and finally had reconciled myself to her eventual death. Mom had survived and was recovering wonderfully, but we all lived with the fact that, given her advanced stage of hardened arteries and her refusal to have the right carotid artery operation, lest she become more impaired, Mom could drop dead at any moment. Indeed, that's true of all of us, young or old, healthy or not, but Mom's odds were higher. Yet, I was calm, knowing the Lord was with us.

My marriage grew worse. Lee and I had our good moments, our loving moments, but there was always a wall between us. Neither of us believed in fighting and had had only a handful the first seven years of our marriage, but now fights were common and often severe. Then days, weeks would go by without us speaking to each other. Then we'd get close again. It was frustrating for both of us.

Jennifer's passing had a tremendous effect on me, positive and negative. On the negative side was the void her passing left and the guilt I felt. Many times I'd wanted to tell her I was gay, but my fear of losing her friendship, as I had lost Carrie's, kept me from confiding in Jennifer. How I could think she would desert me or even feel differently towards me because I was gay was beyond my comprehension. I wished she were alive so I could tell her.

On Christmas Eve I saw Rebecca at church. She and her husband had moved to Arizona (Jennifer had planned to go with them, but died two weeks before their scheduled move), but came back for Christmas. It was a joyous time of year and seeing Rebecca was wonderful, but painful. The emptiness in her eyes mirrored the void in mine.

In January of 1984 I dreamed of Jennifer, the first time in the eight months since her death. Many times I'd dreamed of my favorite movie stars and wakened wishing the dream would continue. However, my dream of Jennifer was quite different for it didn't need to continue. To me it wasn't an ordinary dream, but a vision from God. The Bible states that there is no communication with the dead. Visions are defined as, "something seen in a dream of a supernatural appearance that conveys a revelation." Despite what the Bible says on this subject, I believe I actually saw Jennifer.

I'm acutely aware that supernatural is a two-sided coin. One must know which supernatural power (God or Satan) is working, but I had no trouble discerning where this vision originated for it drew me closer to God and Satan doesn't work that way.

My vision began at my church. It was Christmas Eve service and as I walked to the entrance of the church I saw Jennifer standing before me. I ran to her and embraced her, feeling her frail body and humped back beneath my hands.

I asked her, "How are you?"

She answered, "I'm fine, but I'm not of this world anymore."

"I know." I replied sadly.

Jennifer smiled sweetly and continued, "But I'll always be with you, Jan."

We embraced again, her hump was gone and her fragile body was now sturdy. I was feeling her glorified body, as the Bible states will happen to those who die in Christ.

I awoke with a feeling of such peace and joy that I felt the great emptiness within me vanish.

However, there was still one hitch. One I thought I'd come to terms with years ago. According to the Church, Heaven would not be my final home. I was a lesbian, involved in a same gendered relationship. The peace I'd felt, years before, when I'd made my decision to be myself, feeling saved regardless of my sexual orientation, was being tested. Was my failing marriage God's way of trying to warn me to stop living gay or else my soul would be lost?

I prayed constantly, questioning God as to why He would damn my soul because I loved a woman. Again, God was silent. I changed my prayer as our marriage failed more and stopped asking God to heal us. Yet, the marriage would not destruct. Though the bad times outweighed the good, Lee and I just couldn't let go.

My love grew cold much of the time. Still, I couldn't call it quits. Was I fighting God? Rebelling, again?

Chapter 8: 1984-1985

By the middle of 1984 my marriage seemed to show signs of improvement. Perhaps this came about by an accident I had at the new job I had taken in April. I slipped on a section of wet floor in the company warehouse and when I went up I felt my right knee dislocate with a resounding 'pop'. This had happened every few years, a leftover from hitting my knee with the bowling ball when I was fourteen. Though extremely painful when it dislocated, it always went back in place and within a day I was back on my feet. This time, though, because of the pain I felt when it dislocated, I didn't realize the further damage done when I crashed on to the concrete floor, landing on my hip, shoulder and knee.

After twenty minutes of writhing in pain, no one in sight to help, I got to my feet and walked, slowly and painfully, back to my office. I knew something serious had happened because my knee had never hurt this much after dislocating. In addition, if felt as if everything was swimming around under my kneecap.

I wasn't back in my office more than twenty minutes, with a few employees running for ice, when Lee called. She asked how I was and, though I wanted to underestimate my condition, I couldn't lie to her. She told me she'd felt I was in trouble and that's why she'd called. Lee was always a bit psychic.

I told Lee I'd be home to get my ace bandage, but she insisted on picking me up because I would not be able to drive. I said "no" and we hung up. After telling my boss that I'd be back after lunch, I realized Lee was right. I could barely walk. To drive would have been suicidal.

Fifteen minutes after calling Lee, she arrived and drove me home. When we got inside, Lee demanded to see my knee. I told her it was "OK" and that I just needed to brace it and I'd return to work.

Lee persisted, seeing right through me and I showed her my knee. We went straight to the hospital emergency room for my knee was three times the size of the other.

The emergency room gave me crutches and said I had some liquid, possibly a little blood, on the knee and if it didn't abate by Monday I should see an orthopedic doctor. Lee knew my knee wouldn't recede so she made an appointment for the next day, Friday, where two Dixie cups of blood were tapped from my knee. She stayed in the room as my knee was tapped, running her fingers over my forehead. The love I felt coming from her meant the world to me and from that day on our marriage improved.

A second incident was to influence our marriage. Shortly before my knee surgery in 1985, I was watching the TV show "20/20" and it was talking about people who hadn't been able to leave their homes in years because of a disorder called "Panic or Anxiety Disorder". The show was a mirror of the physical symptoms I'd had for the past twenty-three years.

I went to the University Hospital in Stony Brook because they had an outpatient Psychiatric Clinic specializing in this disorder. Upon completion of a ten page inquiry, blood tests, heart tests and a consult with a psychiatrist, Lee by my side, I was diagnosed as a "panicker" and given Xanex, a controlled substance and also a prescription for a beta blocker to slow down my rapid heart rate. (I still take both to this day).

Years before I'd read a book on agoraphobia, which is Greek for "fear of the marketplace", i.e. crowds and I knew I had this. Research had progressed and discovered that the agoraphobic suffered from a physical disorder called panic, which caused us to become reclusive to one degree or another. Whether panic disorder originated in some kind of brain dysfunction or was caused by a chemical imbalance had not been pinpointed, but science was sure it was of physical origins. From the physical panic attacks, agoraphobia followed. Since I'd had these physical attacks for so long, my agoraphobia was severe, as was my physical panic disorder. In fact, no other patient in the clinic had experienced this ailment as long as I.

Finally knowing that my inability to function was not a mental problem (which I had never believed it was) made me so ecstatic, that if there'd been no medication I was still happy and felt I could continue my life with new confidence. Thank God, though, there was medication to help the disorder.

Over the next year, with Lee by my side, I saw the University psychiatrist every two months for two reasons. First, they had to establish and maintain the dosage of Xanex until I reached a level where the actual physical panic attacks were minimal, if not alleviated and second, to make sure how my emotional stability influenced or heightened the panic. Though the disorder is physical in origin, one's reaction to stress and one's emotional stability can affect the condition in a negative way.

It was established that I was mentally stable, but that the stresses in my life did aggravate the condition. Once I understood all the variables inherent with this disorder I was better able to fight the phobias that had built up over the years. After twenty-three years of undiagnosed, untreated physical panic, even with medication it would take hard work and time for the phobias to abate and some would always limit me.

Lee and I were so happy knowing that there was something physically wrong that had made me such a horror with which to live. It reassured Lee that my inability to function had not been due to lack of love for her.

It was a miracle! At the age of thirty-nine I felt as if my life was just beginning and I praised God for His miracle.

Chapter 9: 1985-1986

With the panic disorder medicated and under control my life became easier to handle. I became more productive at work, feeling well rather than ill. For the first time in my life I gained weight (going from 110 lbs to 130 lbs in six months). I was not cured, probably would never be, but the improvement was so great, 100% was not necessary. The phobias were still present, but most abated and I had more energy for other activities.

Outside of work I functioned better, too. Except for trips to New York City, Malls or traveling long distances with people, other than Lee, most of the out of home activities that had caused me physical debilitation continued to abate.

It washed over into my marriage and Lee and I seemed to get our act together again. The only thing that wore at both Lee and me was Grandpa's worsening condition. Since he'd broken his hip in February 1984, his senility progressed quickly. In addition, he was unable to do more than hobble around and we were forced to confine him to his room. We had to remove most of the furniture in his room because we feared he'd fall, as he'd done when he first broke his hip. When we'd put him in the wheelchair and bring him into the living room to watch TV, he was disinterested. We couldn't take our eyes off him for a minute, so determined was he to get out of the wheelchair and the house, despite his inability to walk more than a few steps.

We put a commode in his room, close to his bed and he knew how to use it, but he'd forget to open his fly or pull down his pants so we spent much time cleaning him and the floor. Soon we dressed him in a T-shirt and boxer shorts, hoping this would make it easier for him to excrete, but there were still accidents.

Grandpa had no interests anymore. All he wanted to do was escape. From what, we knew not. He'd hobble around his room calling for "them", which we believed meant us; he'd turn the hallway light switch on and off (the switch was just outside his door), bang his head against the wall, asking us to check 'this' (he was continually worried, especially about fire) and asking for more food (if we let him he'd eat till he burst). We tended to his physical needs, but there was little we could do to help him emotionally.

We felt terrible for the locked gate in front of his bedroom door, but there was no other way to protect him from doing more than he was capable. He was always hungry and we fed him plenty, but he began eating the fuzz from his blanket and many times, during the night hours when we slept and couldn't empty his commode, he began to ingest his own waste. Sometimes this made him sick, but there wasn't much we could do about this either.

By 1986 Lee and I did nothing but clean him and his room. No matter how much we cleaned we could not rid the house of the smell. Not just the aroma of waste, but the smell of a human being decomposing.

I worked eight hours a day, then came home to the work Lee had done all day, helping by cleaning any mess Grandpa made in his room while Lee cleaned him. I had no stomach for washing Grandpa. I soon developed a stomach for cleaning his waste-soiled room for Lee could not do everything. And we got used to the smell of death that permeated the house.

I prayed every night for God to take Grandpa home, but Gramps was the picture of health. At the time Lee and I were so worn out we'd kid that Grandpa would probably outlive us.

Our lives revolved around Gramps, again leaving little time for our marriage or us.

I never imagined that I could hold up under the pressure. Indeed, my panic medication was a great help because, instead of using my energy to fight the attacks, I had more strength to deal with what was happening with Grandpa. I knew, though, that our true strength came from God.

Through all the strain I kept constant contact with Jesus, asking for His guidance and strength. I knew I couldn't manufacture my endurance. It came from God and He held me up no matter how bad it got.

God gave Lee and me not only strength but a sense of humor. It was that humor that saved us from going absolutely insane.

* * * * * * * * *

In April I turned the big "4 0". I had always feared growing older, but lately, by virtue of my renewed relationship with Jesus, I felt good. All my life I'd feared death. Now my life was at least half over. I remembered when, at the age of fifteen, I told Mom, "You know, in five years I'll be twenty." How much, as teenagers, we want to be older. Then you blink your eyes and you're forty. I still felt fifteen, barring a few aches and pains brought about by injury and the aging process. Nevertheless, I welcomed mid life with a sense of humor and a resolution to make the next forty years, if God granted me such, more committed to my Savior and His plan for my life and the lives of others.

Lee faced my fortieth birthday with a sense of humor, too. She had a big party for me and decorated the house with streamers, all of which read, "Over the Hill" and a sign that read, "Guess who's 40: Jan". It was a wonderful day and with the improvement in our marriage, it marked the beginning of a new life.

Adding to our happiness was a phone call from Mom, on June 16th, telling us that Paul and Susan had become parents to a healthy baby boy. Two days later, phobias and all, Lee and I took the train to New York City to see my precious nephew, Adam. He was gorgeous. Paul and Susan were tired, but very happy. Mom, now Grandma, walked on a cloud from which she has still not descended.

* * * * * * * * * *

On June 2nd, while I was at work, Lee called. Something was wrong with Grandpa. He kept slumping toward his left side. Although that was the side of his bad hip, Lee was afraid Grandpa was having a stroke. I rushed home and we called an ambulance.

At the hospital emergency room, Grandpa's doctor examined him and then called the orthopedic surgeon who had operated on Grandpa's hip. After Dr. Kent, who was a wonderfully compassionate doctor, finished his examination, he told us Grandpa's hip was gone. He could operate again, but advised against it. Grandpa's advanced senility would make it impossible to rehabilitate him because he'd be unable to understand any instructions.

Kindly he looked at us and said, "It's time to put Gramps in a nursing home. You girls have done your job."

With tears of sadness, relief and thanks to God for taking the decision out of my hands, I gave Grandpa over to Dr. Kent.

Four years of taking care of Grandpa, watching him suffer and slowly die in front of us, was over. Good people who gave and would give Gramps loving care took the burden from Lee and me.

The same week I was fired from my job. Being fired is a traumatic event, financially and ego wise. Financially we had no worries and my ego was healthy enough to quickly heal. Besides, I was bone-weary tired, though I hadn't admitted it till now and needed a long, paid vacation.

Lee, as usual, was terribly happy I was unemployed. With Grandpa out of our hands and the summer ahead we looked forward to the long awaited alone time our marriage so desperately needed to relearn how to enjoy each other and to relearn how to communicate. It was a new beginning. A second chance for a marriage almost destroyed.

Chapter 10: 1986

My high hopes for a new beginning to our marriage quickly vanished. After four years of tending Grandpa, Lee and I had forgotten how to have fun together. We'd also completely lost the ability to communicate with each other, a thorn in our relationship from the beginning and the generation gap that had closed some in the last year began to grow at a faster pace.

I was deep into a time of introspection and change, or rather, growing values, beliefs and knowledge. Although still a clown, with a ribald, somewhat irreverent sense of humor, I continued to give more thought to my relationship with God and to the goals He wanted me to achieve in the years left of my life.

Lee, on the other hand, having had a childhood of physical and mental abuse, a childhood lost in the rearing of two younger brothers and now a marriage that, for the last four years was spent primarily back in the same role she had as a teenager, was not into the same frame of mind. She was free from caring for Grandpa and wanted a vacation from responsibility. I understood her needs, but neither agreed nor approved of her methods.

After a few weeks of unemployment I developed a lower back problem that left me virtually non-ambulatory. Lee's need to have fun couldn't be satisfied by me so she turned to the handful of friends (I use that word lightly) we had to fulfill her needs.

We drifted apart faster; Lee spending time with friends while I lay on the sofa nursing a bad back. Nothing helped it and by the fourth of July I was in such pain I finally broke down and went to a chiropractor, a healing person I'd feared and not believed in all my life. However, this doctor came highly recommended by a few people with whom I'd worked so I decided to give him a try. Though he was good and my fear and disbelief vanished, the healing process was slow. I had to rest much and do little of any activity.

Poor Lee! We'd had such high hopes, shattered now by my back. Yet, the back problem and its inhibiting effects was merely another straw breaking the backbone of our already weak marriage. The bottom line to our marital problems was, as it had always been, lack of communication. We had always been afraid to tell each other how and what we were feeling deep inside. Not about matters outside our relationship, but between us. When things bothered me concerning Lee, I kept them inside, afraid of hurting her. Lee had always had a hard time communicating her feelings. Unlike me, who would tell my life story to anyone who wanted to listen, Lee kept her gut feelings private. When we first met she told me everything that had happened to her, but how she truly felt about many of her experiences had not often surfaced.

In many ways Lee was like my brother Paul. He'd always kept his inner, gut feelings to himself. All too many people do. It's quite common no matter how you are raised, but can be very dangerous, not only to a marriage, but to the individual. The suppressed feelings build and build until they erupt and what I saw in Lee was a massive eruption.

Whenever I tried to confront Lee about my concern for her irresponsible behavior, an argument would ensure, followed by silence. There was no way to get through to her.

She was doing what she wanted and disagreed with my frame of mind as much as I did hers.

Then one day Lee opened up, letting me into her brain a little, only to heighten my fear for her. It also resurrected the fear that another time of rocky road for our marriage was beginning. At age forty I wasn't sure I could endure another siege of marital torment.

Lee was aware of her need to be less dependent on me. More accurately, she was feeling inadequate because she had never lived on her own. She'd left her mother's house at age eighteen to live with Dee and then went straight to me. Lee wanted to mature;

wanted to know that she could live and enjoy life through her own capabilities, without leaning on me. I knew she was capable of doing this, but one must have confidence in one's self and Lee lacked this.

In order to gain her sense of independence Lee wanted to get a room somewhere and fend for herself. This was not the best idea because it would have been a waste of money to pay for our house and a small apartment, too, so her plan went down the tubes because I would not agree to it.

Though I understood Lee's need to try her wings, I also felt it was a little late and unwise to be finding her independence in this manner. Besides, it would take more than the month Lee stipulated on living alone to learn and grow in self-sufficiency.

With this plan vetoed by me, another emerged when a gay friend of ours, some ten years Lee's junior, who had moved to New Jersey, invited Lee to spend a weekend with her. Lee asked if I would mind. Of course I didn't like the idea. I already felt Lee was tired of me, tired of living with a woman who had never been able to satisfy her needs. I was afraid Lee would turn to another woman. Jealousy wasn't the issue. Pure fear tormented me. Furthermore, I felt it was wrong for a gay, married woman to spend a weekend with another gay woman. It would be the same as if a husband visited a woman friend for a weekend. Yet, to say "no" would have been in vain. Lee had her mind set, scared though she was of being away from me. All I could do was hope that this trip would give Lee some confidence and help her straighten out her thinking.

Lee returned home Sunday night looking weary, but happy that she'd succeeded in having a nice time on her own. I was glad for her, but my fear would not leave. In just two days away from me there'd been a change I didn't like. Lee seemed distant and cocky. I thought maybe I was projecting my fears onto Lee and tried to be optimistic, but down in my gut I knew the change in Lee wasn't good. All I could do was watch my Lee start her trip to Hell and pray she would escape without our marriage and, more importantly, herself being totally destroyed.

Chapter 11: 1986

Three weeks later Lee went to Cally's for another New Jersey weekend visit. Still confined, most of the time, by my back pain, to a horizontal position, I was desolate.

I was losing Lee. This became quite apparent when her weekend visit turned into two weeks. She called twice, but I felt no love coming from her. My fear that Lee was losing herself intensified.

I was in bad emotional shape. Almost all day I'd listen to the country station on the radio, taping the saddest love songs, identifying with them. Occasionally I'd get out, but only for short periods because of my ailing back. My mood was a combination of depression, hostility, confusion and a lot of self-pity.

I prayed for God's help. Prayed He'd help Lee out of her crisis. It wasn't difficult to see that Lee was having an emotional burn out.

One part of me was loving and compassionate and I prayed God would give me His power to continue feeling this way. After all, I'd burned out sixteen years ago. We all deserve compassion during such times. Yet, my hostility was stronger and it put out the fire of my love for Lee. Indeed, I still loved her, but I couldn't feel "in love" and the loss of this feeling grieved me as much as everything else happening.

I'd spoken to no one concerning my marital problems until Lee's two week trip to New Jersey. After this it was impossible to hide our problems. Lee's mother and mine were aware of her absence and were worried, too.

I could talk openly with Mom, but Lee and I had never told her family we were gay so I had to be careful of my words. There was little to tell Lee's mother, anyway, since I didn't have a phone number to reach Lee and she called only twice. It was an awkward time.

Two weeks later, Lee called. She was returning the next day with Ronnie, another mutual gay friend of ours, who was driving her back home. I didn't know till Lee returned home that she had only stayed with Cally for two days because Cally's girlfriend was also staying with her and their constant fighting drove Lee to call Ronnie. Lee spent the remainder of the two weeks with Ronnie.

I was furious. Compassion went out the window. I was ready to chuck the whole marriage. With Cally I felt some security in Lee's fidelity, for Cally was femme and femme women weren't a turn on for Lee. However, Ronnie was on the butch side and, more terrifying, she was in to cocaine. It all worried me. Considering Lee's state of mind, her total avoidance of anything that had to do with me, which included both our families, she was capable of doing anything. There are a lot of things I can tolerate in marriage, but infidelity was not one of them.

My tenants, who were lesbians, only added to my fears. They thought Lee's behavior strange, too. Strange enough to ask if I thought she was cheating on me. I told them I was pretty sure she wasn't, but doubt clubbed at my insides.

When Lee and Ronnie stepped through my front door I wanted answers, but couldn't ask. Lee wanted her independence. I couldn't smother her, but I wanted to rant and rave and throw Ronnie out on her ass, especially when she told me how much Lee had missed me. At that statement, Lee in the bathroom, I was infuriated and more sure they'd had an affair. Ronnie was covering up. I tried to calm myself, knowing that I was letting my emotions get the better of me, but having little success.

That night, after Ronnie went back to Jersey, I asked Lee if she had had an affair with Ronnie or Cally. She denied both, saying she loved me very much, but needed time and space. She didn't know what was going on in her head and asked me to be patient and not leave her. I said I'd try. We talked quietly, each of us in tears and I told her she could do what she wanted. What else could I say?

For the remainder of the summer, Lee did her thing, seeing Ronnie now and then and getting closer to the two gay tenants in our downstairs apartment. They, too, had formed a friendship with Ronnie. I was, literally, the fifth wheel and my self-pity grew as fast as my anger.

Thank God I had to go to the panic clinic every month for medication maintenance, because my psychiatrist was the only objective person I could talk to about my problems with Lee and he was helpful. I tried to follow his advice to give Lee her space, let her get her much needed rebellion out of her system. He also helped me deal with my suspicions of infidelity, although he said it did sound as if it could be a real possibility. He helped me cope with Lee's possible infidelity in a realistic manner.

Lee was having a burn out and I ached for her. I wasn't completely selfish. I prayed for her healing as well as my own, but God seemed silent. Yet, I knew He was with all of us. Patience was never one of my virtues and God was working on this fault. I knew God would give me the answers I needed, the healing I needed, in His own time. Whatever the outcome, I trusted God's divine wisdom.

My prayers for God to heal my marriage ceased. I just told Him to take charge and do what He thought right.

I was at another crisis point in my life; a time of tremendous change for me. What kind of change, I was unaware. And it didn't end with the summer. It continued for the next year.

I'd had enough of Lee's burn out. She needed me to understand, but I was so angry I couldn't and, more accurately, wouldn't. She wanted independence and I gave it to her. We tried to be amiable with each other, but I never lifted a finger to help Lee. I felt she had to do it on her own. In the past, the more I tried to help the worse things got. Now I knew why. The more I had helped, the more helpless Lee felt. I had to withdraw and let Lee sink or swim, painful as that was for me to watch.

In August we had a bad scene that ended in us separating. We continued to live in the same house, since it was in both our names, but Lee moved into the spare bedroom. I promised Lee I would remain faithful. We were separated, but still married. It was agreed that we just live separately under the same roof.

Alone all summer, alone now, my crisis escalated along with Lee's. Each of us was fighting an enemy, not together as we'd done before, but alone.

I turned more and more to God. I felt God with me all the time. Everything I thought, felt and experienced was a prayer. God walked right by my side, feeling everything I did, knowing all my thoughts. He was the only person who understood and the only one I could lean on. Humans could try to comfort, but couldn't help. There was only God.

Chapter 12: 1986-2015

I thought I'd come close to hitting bottom other times in my life, but what I felt now made my other periods of terror, depression, loneliness and anguish seem mild in comparison.

My hospitalization when I was twelve, the years of arguing and broken bonds with Dad, my fear of cancer when I was seventeen, years of battling undiagnosed panic disorder, my burnout when I was twenty-four, my twenty year struggle coming out of the closet, the loss of Carrie's friendship, the loss of Dana, the heartbreak over Billy's suicide, the pain of Mom's illness, the debilitation of caring for Grandpa and the devastation of Jennifer's death all came to focus within my mind during the summer of 1986.

All these times of suffering were not forgotten. I'd merely gotten through them and time had healed the pain. But my problems with Lee and our marriage were a present reality. A reality I had no idea how it would be resolved. So, it seemed to me that this was the lowest point in my life.

I felt totally drained; totally out of control. I had felt that way during the other crises, but I was now forty years old. I was more mature and wiser. I should have had more control over my situation, emotions and behavior. However, I felt less control than ever before.

Yet, at the same time, I felt the presence of God more than at any other time in my life. I didn't feel any surge of great emotion as I had when I'd counseled at the Billy Graham Crusade. It was a quiet feeling, passive in nature, but I felt more loved by my Lord, more in touch with Him and more trusting in His wisdom and power; God would take care of Lee, our marriage and me, His way.

Though the pain from my problems didn't magically vanish, my life was becoming less dominated by negative emotions with each passing day. I began to function more normally, shedding my summer of self-pity and depression. Despite the sadness and worry present, I felt something comforting me, giving me the wisdom to perceive my problems not as debilitating, but as a challenge that would lead me closer to genuine peace. That something I felt was God.

My back began to heal faster and in February 1987 I was able to return to work. Lee was already working a few months by this time and was acting more responsibly. She'd broken all relationships with the gay "friends" she'd leaned on and, since I still withdrew most all my help from her, Lee was facing her problems independently. She was growing in a positive manner, slowly, as I was and by August 1987 we were back together as a married couple.

In October of 1989 I got another job at a radio station. Shortly after I started I was able to get Lee a job there as the receptionist, stationed right outside the door of my office. Working together was great and the people at the station were family; they knew we were married and couldn't care less. Life was looking up until Lee ruptured her Achilles heel in 1991 and had to quit. It was during this time that I began to realize that Lee had the symptoms of diabetes. She would not go to the doctor, but when it was determined she needed surgery on her heel, the blood tests verified my suspicion. Surgery was pushed off for two months, until her sugar level was under control and that injured her heel more. Her position at the station was filled and Lee had to stay home while I continued to work long hours. This strained our relationship and in August of 1992 I knew our marriage was over and so did Lee. I could not 'kick' Lee out, for the house was in both our names, but she moved into the spare bedroom and we lived in platonic peaceful co-habitation. Lee took an accounting correspondence course while she waited for her father to make their attic into an apartment for her.

By April 1994 Lee had finished her accounting course and her Dad had finished the apartment. When I came home from work Lee's room was empty; she had left. I was simultaneously happy and sad. Falling out of love is not easy, either.

EPILOGUE

My brother Paul and his wife celebrated 33 years of marriage in 2015. My nephew, Adam, graduated college and has worked in Washington, D.C. for the last 6 years.

Gramps died in 1990 and two months later my Dad died. By God's power I had forgiven Dad eight years before he died and was at peace. Mom continued to live alone and was doing well. I'd visit her almost every weekend and it was a joy. Mom died in 2001; I was at her side as she went home to Jesus. She was just shy of her 83rd birthday. She'd lived the last 19 years of her life building our Church's library to be one of the largest in the North East. The Church renamed the library after her and her picture hangs inside with a page long synopsis of how she built this library from a couple of dozen books. She lived her last 19 years in service to our Lord and Savior and to His glory, never wasting one minute.

I have lived a single and celibate life since my divorce. The responsibilities of marriage hindered my ability to work for LGBT inclusion and affirmation, as I would have liked. I continue to encourage gay love and marriage.

I worked full time as a full charge bookkeeper until 2006 when I decided I wanted to move back to where I grew up. I knew it would be hard to get a job, but Mom left Paul and me a substantial inheritance and I just wanted to return to Trinity Lutheran Church.

I did find a part-time bookkeeping job for a year, but left to pursue trying to start an MCC (Metropolitan Community Church) on Long Island. I found a minister and a few people, but plans fell through because the few people interested were miles apart. It was not to be. However, I found an MCC on the internet, located in Pensacola, Florida and listened to their sermons each week and became friends with the minister.

The minister of Trinity Lutheran was all for my project of a "Homosexuality and the Bible" discussion group, which began the end of 2006 and continued for a year and one half. We had the faithful seven, all gay affirming, straight and gay, but we disbanded because no one else was joining us, even though a couple of dozen applauded our efforts. It was a big disappointment for me, but I had done much research which I used to tape a Public broadcasting television show for another year and one half. I was more passionate than ever in helping gay and straight people who struggled with the issue of homosexuality and the Bible and remain so to this day.

On December 31, 2008 I got a call from Lee, precipitated by an unexpected and tragic death in her family and from that day on we have been the best of friends. She lives with her parents and takes care of them and is an active member of her church. She has many burdens, but is always ready to listen to mine or anyone else's with a cheerful, loving attitude.

Looking back I can now clearly see how I had gotten through the bad times. How I'd had the strength to push myself. How I had lifted myself from depression. How I had the strength never to even once consider suicide. I knew how I'd done it. I HADN'T! God had given me the power to overcome the evil in my life. Though my faith was weak, God never left me. His strong, but gentle hand had guided me through the valleys, tenaciously trying to instruct me. It took a long time, but I'm a stubborn person. I was so grateful to God for His patience and grateful that He'd allowed me to go through hellish times because I was now more clearly seeing Heaven. Whether you believe in God or not, it is the Almighty who helps you. Many are unaware of this and more are too full of pride to accept the fact that God helps you even if you have rejected Him. God loves all of us and hopes that we will come to Him and find truth and the only peace that is genuine and guaranteed.

BOOK FOUR: Gay Affirmation: Scripture & Homosexuality

What does the Bible say about homosexuality?

I hope what I say here will help you understand that the BIBLE says NOTHING of a condemning nature about homosexual love/marriage, which I define as a SELF-SACRIFICING, LOVING, COMMITTED, MONOGAMOUS, LIFE-LONG UNION OF TWO NON-BLOOD RELATED PEOPLE.

Let me preface all I am going to say with this: THOUGH THE BIBIE IS INSPIRED BY GOD, THE WRITERS WERE NOT GIVEN SCIENTIFIC INFORMATION IN ADVANCE OF THEIR TIME.

"All Scripture is inspired by God and profitable for teaching, for reproof, for correction and for training in righteousness, that the man of God may be complete, equipped for every good work." 2 Timothy 3:16-17.

GENESIS 19: 1-32 (King James Bible)

"All the men in Sodom" wanted sex with the two male visitors, whom were not known to be angels. Many believe the sin that destroyed Sodom was homosexuality. This is wrong!

The sexual sin we see depicted in this account was sinful and it was male/male sex, but it was not homosexuality. It was gang rape by heterosexual men and rape IS a sin. Remember, Lot offered his daughters to these gang bangers which reveal volumes about the sexual orientation of the men of Sodom. Even Lot knew these men were heterosexual and that the only reason they wanted to have sex with the visiting men was to bring shame to them; shame that far surpassed the raping of a woman, given woman's lowly status in biblical time.

Sodom was NOT destroyed by God because of this attempted rape. God was going to destroy Sodom BEFORE the attempted male/male rape occurred. Read Genesis Chapter 18 and see for yourself. Abraham was related to Lot, but did not live in Sodom. Abraham feared for Lot and began bargaining with God. Verse 23: "suppose there are 50 righteous (meaning right with God) people in Sodom. Will you (God) destroy the city?" God said He would spare the city for 50 righteous people. This continued as 50 could not be found or 40 or even 10. Abraham knew Sodom was doomed. That's how Genesis Chapter 18 ends. Only Lot and his family (6 in all) would be spared, but they had to leave Sodom.

Sodom was a wicked city, non righteous and full of every sin; legions of non-sexual sins and consensual and non-consensual sexual sins Let us not confuse the word "consensual" as ALWAYS meaning moral in God's eyes. Lord knows, I've had consensual sex with dozens of women, but ALL, until I married my wife, was sinful because it was lustful and promiscuous. TO EQUATE LUSTFUL CONSENSUAL SEXUAL BEHAVIOR WITH SELF-SACRIFICING, LOVING, COMMITTED, MONOGAMOUS, LIFE-LONG MARRIAGE IS A HUGE STRETCH OF THE IMAGINATION AND IS QUITE ERRONEOUS IN THOUGHT.

The people of Sodom were idol worshippers who would not bow to the God of Creation. THIS is why God destroyed Sodom and the visitors came to warn Lot and his family to leave this wicked city so they would not perish, too.

Male/male sexual behavior was not THE SIN that destroyed Sodom. It was the TOTAL unrighteousness of worshipping idols instead of the true God that God found so detestable that He destroyed the entire city. Ezekiel 16: 49-50 will explain more clearly: "Behold, this was the iniquity of thy sister Sodom; pride, fullness of bread and abundance of idleness was in her and in her daughters, neither did she strengthen the hand of the poor and needy. And they were haughty and committed abomination before me; therefore I took them away as I saw good."

This "clobber" passage holds absolutely NO evidence that homosexual sex within a loving relationship is a sin, for the Sodom account depicts violent sex ONLY. So chuck this Sodom account out as a condemnation of ALL homosexual behavior. Those who won't are assuming much and reading into the Sodom account that which is NOT there. It is pure fabrication on the part of anti-gay Christians.

JUDGES 19:22-26 (King James Bible)

Discard this as a condemnation of homosexuality for it is speaking about male/male rape in an almost identical version as in Genesis 19 (Sodom). It has nothing to do with homosexuality at all!

The Bible labels the actions of the men in these accounts, which is RAPE, as horrific and vile. These two accounts illustrate how little sense it makes to make biblical judgments based on homosexual gang rape and use them as a BLANKET condemnation of mutual loving, self-sacrificing, monogamous, and unrelated by blood, same gender love/marriage. To carry this BLANKET LOGIC consistently, one would have to condemn heterosexual love/marriage, too, for in this passage the men DID give up on raping the male visitors and raped the concubine of the owner of the house the entire night; yet, no anti-gay Christian condemns ALL heterosexuality because of this vile rape of a woman. They will bring up the Creation Account and Jude, verse 5-7, but this is a ploy to confuse you, as I will explain later.

The truth is, homosexuality was not the case nor should it be nor was it meant to be, per Scripture.

LEVITICUS 18:22 and LEVITICUS 20:13 (King James Bible)

Leviticus 18:22 reads: "Do not lie with a man as one lies with a woman; this is detestable.

Leviticus 20:13 reads: "If a man lies with a man as one lies with a woman, both of them have done what is detestable. They must be put to death; their blood will be on their own heads."

The first passage is the condemnation. The second passage is the penalty.

If God's Laws are for ALL people, for ALL times then ALL 600 plus Laws in Leviticus should be obeyed today. However, anti-gay Christians make exceptions, stating that many of these Laws were temporary and situational; that many were about culturally "clean" and "unclean" issues that no longer apply in today's society. I agree.

However, we cannot dismiss the importance of Leviticus, then and now, even though much of it was situational and temporary and given to the Jewish people, believers in the one true God, to separate them from pagans who worshipped many idols (i.e. gods) and who were engaging in legions of sin, non-sexual and sexual. A veritable orgy was going on; heterosexual and homosexual sexual behaviors, all of which was sinful because it was lustful, excessive and part of pagan worship of false gods. This was forbidden for the Hebrews.

As we read in the book of Exodus, when Moses went up the mountain to receive God's Ten Commandments, he returned to the Hebrews and found then engaging in idol worship, just like the pagans from whom God had freed them. To overlook this leads to misunderstanding of what Levitical Law is referring and to whom. It was written to the Jewish people who had been slaves in Egypt for centuries and had witnessed Egypt's pagan culture. The Law of Moses (Leviticus) was given by God during the time the Jews had fled from slavery in Egypt, as accounted in the book of EXODUS, a pagan land, to live in the land of Canaan, another pagan land. THE JEW'S ONLY FRAME OF REFERENCE TO SAME GENDER SEXUAL BEHAVIOR WAS GANG RAPE AND SHRINE PROSTITUTION. God did not want His chosen people to behave like pagans.

We would be foolish to ignore the universal moral laws included in Leviticus. However, there is no distinction between ceremonial, ritual or moral laws in the original manuscripts. Break one law and you break them all. The penalty of "death" or "communal ostracism" is used in each category within these laws. For example: engaging in sex while a woman has her period, the requirement that males be circumcised, breaking the Sabbath and a law that forbade cursing one's parents. We don't adhere to the first three as even a sin in our Church Doctrine and the last one carried the death penalty. The true moral, universal law is Leviticus 19: 1-17 which contains the Ten Commandments that had been given to Moses in the book of Exodus, BEFORE the Law of Moses in Leviticus.

Historians tell us that our model of loving, life-long same gender marriage did not exist in pagan cultures. Therefore, it is not reasonable that the author of Leviticus intended to prohibit a form of same gender union that did not exist at the time (i.e.

INFORMATON IN ADVANCE OF THEIR TIME).
Nevertheless, anti-gay Christians stick to their belief that same gender loving, committed relationships DID exist in those times and WAS known by the people of those times and was condemned by God with NO valid historical or BIBLICAL evidence.

One must understand that though the Bible has historical information, it is not a complete book of history. In order to understand what the inspired writers of the Bible were speaking one must go outside the Bible and research the history of the times. Anti-gay Christians do not do this thoroughly.

In Moses' time and all through the Bible, women were seen as less than men. This was not just in pagan cultures, but in the Hebrew culture, too. There was a gender hierarchy and men were on the top tier.

With this firmly in your mind, these two passages in Leviticus CLEARLY are a condemnation of some kind of sexual immorality DIRECTED AT MEN ONLY. Anti-gay Christians will argue that the passages include females, but if you read the passages after each, in Leviticus, which speak of bestiality, the law is specifically directed at BOTH male and female, putting to rest the anti-gay's inclusion of women in Leviticus 18:22 & 20:13.

Deuteronomy 23: 17-18 is where I believe we find a probable clue as to what these two passages are truly speaking and to whom. It states: "There shall be no whore of the daughters of Israel nor sodomites of the sons of Israel. Thou shall not bring the hire of a whore or the price of a dog into the house of the Lord thy God for any vow, for even both these are abomination unto the Lord thy God."

It is clear that this passage is referring to male and female prostitution. The word "sodomite" is a translation of the Hebrew word "Qadesh" which means MALE CULT PROSTITUTE". "Qadeshah" is Hebrew for FEMALE CULT PROSTITUTE. (Strong's Concordance). The word "DOG" is a derogatory word for a Shrine Prostitute.

One can clearly see, in Deuteronomy 23:17-18, that BOTH male and female prostitution was condemned. "Whore" referred to woman prostitutes and "sodomites" referred to male prostitutes. It was part of their pagan religious rituals. Men had sex with other men because they believed this was the offering demanded by their pagan god(s).

QADESH/QADESHAH IS NEVER USED, IN SCRIPTURE, TO MEAN HOMOSEXUALITY! The world of the biblical writers had nothing that remotely resembles the mutual loving, committed gay marriages we know today! Modern translators imported their beliefs into Scripture that did not exist in biblical times. DO NOT BE DECEIVED BY THEIR WORDS! We do not take the Bible's condemnation of heterosexual temple prostitution and conclude that heterosexual marriage is a sin; why would we do this with gay people?

These two Levitical passages (18:22 & 20:13) ARE focusing on male/male prostitution, Shrine or otherwise and not homosexuality.

Female prostitution was first mentioned in Genesis 38: 15-24 and well known among the Jews. NOW God was addressing the fact that male prostitution was equally detestable in His sight and we can include behavior outside of religious rituals or cult practices within the Temple, although that is the primary emphasis.

If something carries the death penalty, as in Leviticus 20:13, it is extremely important to God. If you were to make a list of all the offenses given in Leviticus for which the death penalty is stated, you will find every one of them is forbidden in Deuteronomy, with the exception of one.

Deuteronomy specifically forbids male prostitution and Leviticus does not: or does it, in Leviticus 18:22 & 20:13? If this is true, wouldn't God put commands against other kinds of idolatry in the same place? Wouldn't fortunetelling, wizardry and sacrifices to Moloch be mentioned? Read Leviticus Chapter 20 and you will see these are all mentioned. Could this be more than a coincidence? I think not. Leviticus 18 and 20 are NOT speaking of homosexuality; they speak of male/male prostitution. The world of this time was acutely aware of female prostitution, shine or otherwise. One can find more evidence of female prostitution in Genesis 38:13-34, Leviticus 19:29, 21:7 & 9.

PROSTITUTION IS DESTESTABLE IN GOD'S EYES AND SINCE THE SUBJECT OF MALE/MALE PROSTITUTION HAD NOT BEEN ADDRESSED BEFORE LEVITICUS, IT WAS TIME TO DO SO.

To use Leviticus 18:22 and 20:13 as a condemnation of ALL homosexuality is pure misinterpretation at best and pure prejudice at worst.

Sadly, the majority of Christians embrace this erroneous "blanket" logic when applying these passages to gay people. They refuse to see the truth of Scripture; that our sexuality helps us grow in Christ-like love and mutuality. These condemnations of male/male rape and prostitution do not cast one shadow of judgment or thought on faithful gay loving marriage.

To amplify what I have said I would like to list other passages in the Old Testament which add more evidence to what I have addressed in my interpretation of Leviticus. (Translations in parenthesis).

I Kings 14:24: "and there were also sodomites (i.e. male cult prostitutes) in the land and they did according to all the abominations of the nations which the Lord cast out before the children of Israel."

I Kings 15:12: "and he (i.e. Asa in verse 11) took away the sodomites (i.e. male cult prostitutes) out of the land and removed all the idols that his fathers had made."

2nd Kings 23:7: "And he broke down the houses of the sodomites (i.e. male cult prostitutes) that were by the house of the Lord, where the women wove hanging for the grove." "Grove" refers to the outdoors where pagans also gathered to worship their gods.

"Thou shalt not plant thee a GROVE OF ANY TREES near unto the altar of the LORD thy GOD, which thou shalt make unto thee." Deuteronomy 16:21.

CRUCIAL TO UNDERSTANDING: in every passage where SODOMITE occurs in the Bible, it is coupled with idolatry and/or prostitution. It is the male equivalent to "WHORE" which is a female Shrine (or street) prostitute. References to Sodom and sodomites run from Genesis to Revelation and NONE mean homosexual/homosexuality.

Anti-gay Christians WILL focus on Jude verses 5-7 to prove their condemnation of ALL homosexual behavior, but Jude is speaking of the male/male attempted rape in the Sodom and Judges accounts. The two male visitors in each account were actually angels disguised as men, but no one knew this. All we know was that the accounts were condemning RAPE! If one sees more than RAPE, as anti-gay Christians do, some reading comprehension is greatly needed.

Emphasis on male prostitution does not negate God's condemnation on female prostitution; both are equally detestable to God. However, in a culture where men were believed superior to women, above the law so to speak, God had to bring us humans back to the reality that MEN were NOT above HIS Law. Leviticus 18:22 and 20:13 accomplished this. It and the other passages from 1st & 2nd Kings and Jude, have NOTHING to do with committed, faithful, non-cultic marriage between two men or two women.

Before heading over to the New Testament passages, let me give a brief introduction. The New Testament is written in Greek. Why, when the Old Testament was written in Hebrew? By the time of the New Testament, many Jews couldn't speak or read Hebrew. Greek had become the language of the world. Around 300 B.C. the Septuagint was finished; the Greek translation of the Hebrew Old Testament. Since the Gospel was being spread to the Gentiles, it was a great missionary tool for the early Christians, for now the Gentiles could read God's Word in their own tongue and the Jews understood, too.

I TIMOTHY 1: 9 & 10 (King James Bible)

"knowing this, that the law is not made for a righteous man, but for the lawless and disobedient, for the ungodly and for sinners, for unholy and profane, for murderers of fathers and murderers of mothers, for manslayers, for whoremongers, FOR THEM THAT DEFILE THEMSELVES WITH MANKIND (ARSENOKOITAI), for men stealers, for liars, for perjured persons and if there be any other thing that is contrary to sound doctrine."

I CORINTHIANS 6: 9 & 10 (King James Bible)
"Know ye not that the unrighteous shall not inherit the kingdom of God? Be not deceived; neither fornicators, nor idolaters, nor adulterers, NOR EFFEMINATE (MALAKOI), NOR ABUSERES OF THEMSELVES WITH MANKIND (ARSENOKOITAI) will inherit the kingdom of God."

I'm lumping these two passages together and putting them before Romans because they are a LIST of sins that will keep one out of Heaven if unrepented (i.e. acknowledged and confessed to God that you have committed these sins and want to turn from them) and they, basically, say the same thing and in the same way. Paul, the author, lists sins to teach the Church in Corinth and Ephesus (I Timothy) that because they are forgiven by Christ does not give them a license to sin. These sinful behaviors are to be an example of UNRIGHTEOUS behaviors.

Paul's reference to same-gender sexual behavior makes sense when we see it in historical context, which was within a culture of promiscuity, exploitive, cultic, pederastic same gender sexual behaviors prominent in Paul's time and culture. We don't need to be scholars to see that theses behaviors are inconsistent with God's gracious purposes for love, marriage and sexuality. To use these passages about growing in faithfulness to God to exclude committed gay people from loving and marrying is Bible abuse. God's intent for marriage is to help people grow into Christ-like love and self-giving. This interpretation does not ignore or water down or discount these passages as truth.

The people of Corinth were predominantly Gentiles who worshipped many pagan gods and the people of Ephesus (1st Timothy) were, also, mostly pagan Gentiles. Neither was familiar with the Torah which contains the Law of Moses (i.e. Leviticus). THIS IS IMPERITIVE TO KNOW in order to understand these two passages for, as with the book of Romans, Paul had to preach the Gospel of Jesus to an audience containing Gentiles who knew nothing about the Law of Moses.

The book of TIMOTHY, who was a convert of Paul's, was written by Paul to Timothy and Corinthians was written by Paul to the Church in Corinth. Paul was a converted Jew. A Pharisee and, as such, spent his life studying the Law of God. Paul was an expert on the Law before he came to follow Jesus as the Messiah.

Anti-gay Christians focus on three words: arsenokoitai, malakoi and porneia, which are the only words essential in understanding what these two passages are speaking.

The word PORNEIA was used to refer to ALL forms of sexual immorality; same gender or opposite. Ancient word meanings are not as CLEAR as anti-gay Christians would argue. Porneia and fornicators were also used to refer to male prostitutes. Modern day pornography comes from this word and no one with half a brain would say pornography is God approved. Those who engage in making porn movies are prostitutes. Those who watch these kinds of movies are engaging in immorality by virtue of mental prostitution.

As one can see by my capitalized words in these two passages, they are a translation of Paul's Greek words. Problem with all Bible translations after the mid 1800's is that the newer translators used the word HOMOSEXUAL in place of the original Greek words, which were a translation from the original Hebrew words in Leviticus 18:22 and 20:13. Essential point being: ALL speak of male/male prostitution predominantly found in pagan Shine/Temple worship. The usage of the word HOMOSEXUAL, which would include female/female sexual behavior, is an error in translation. Even though female prostitution was going on within the pagan Shrine religious worship, it is not given mention in these two passages, so we cannot embellish Scripture to suite our prejudices.

Arsenokoitai is a mixture of two Greek words: "arseno" and "koitai". "Arseno" is Greek for MALE and "koitai" is Greek for BED or sexual behavior. Paul uses this word to describe what is sinful in God's eyes (male/male prostitution) and condemned in Leviticus 18:22 and 20:13 (for the Jewish audience) and to those who had no knowledge of the Torah and its moral Laws (i.e. Gentiles to whom Paul spoke.)

Malakoi had many different meanings in Bible times. Soft cloth and ill health are the predominant meanings you will find in the Bible and in non-biblical historical writings of the time.

ANTI-GAY CHRISTIANS interpret malakoi as meaning the male partner who is being penetrated by another male, explaining that in Paul's time and in the time of the writing of Leviticus, the penetration of a male by another male was seen as the penetrated male being passive like a woman and in the culture of the world at that time, to be male and associated with anything female was detestable to THEIR definition of norms of culture and roles of male and female. Yet, anti-gay Christians insist these two words refer to both male and female same gender sexual behavior – homosexuality. How anyone can think this, when these two words are clearly speaking of males only, is playing with Scripture to reinforce their own prejudice against homosexuals.

Another anti-gay Christian argument is, "Then fornication (which biblically is a word used for prostitution) is OK as long as it's within a loving, committed, monogamous, life-long relationship." This is another trap anti-gays use. If you mean prostitution, fornication IS a sin. Fornication means only one thing to anti-gay people: sex without heterosexual marriage.

There are senior citizens living in loving, monogamous relationships without the benefit of marriage because if they were to "legally" marry their social security benefits would be reduced significantly enough to render them unable to financially survive as a couple. Is it sinful for them to enter into fornication of this nature? I'd say "NO" because it is not prostitution.

Marriage needs only the blessing of God. The legal aspect of marriage was different in biblical days. Marriages were arranged; affection and love did not enter until the 1st century A.D. Most biblical marriages were loveless. Are loveless, arranged marriages pleasing to God? I'd think long and hard on this question.

ROMAN 1: 26 & 27 (King James Bible)

"For this cause God gave them up unto vile affections; for even their women did change the natural use into that which is against nature. And likewise also the men, leaving the natural use of the woman, burned in their lust one toward another; men with men working that which is unseemly and receiving in themselves that recompense of their error which was meet."

One cannot take few lines out of the Bible and draw conclusions without reading what came before and after the passage in order to understand to whom and to what it is referring.

This passage refers to pagans, those who worshipped creatures instead of the Creator. Knowledge of 1st century A.D. Greco/Roman culture, which would also apply to the verses in I Corinthians and I Timothy, is ESSENTIAL in understanding Romans 1 for it was written to the Gentiles, not the Jews (Romans 1:13). It is in this oversight that anti-gay Christians make their error. KEEP THIS IN MIND OR YOU WILL MAKE THE SAME ERROR.

Anti-gay Christians believe the people of Paul's day were aware of same gender LOVING relationships and that they were included in Paul's inspired condemnation of same gender sexual relations in Romans 1: 26 & 27. This is pure fabrication. We cannot ASSUME such loving same gender relationships existed. Specific mention would have to be made, as it is for heterosexual relations/relationships; very few of which were marriages of LOVE. Jacob is one specific example of loving a woman and marrying her, but most marriages, especially in the Old Testament were arranged; no love involved. Even Jesus said nothing about these loveless, arranged marriages. Is the silence of Jesus denoting blessing or condemnation?

Paul's words on same gender sexual behavior are not even close to a condemnation of homosexuality, as anti-gay Christians would have one believe. This passage is not describing loving, committed, self-sacrificing, life-long sexual relations between same gender people. Note Paul's use of the word LUST. Nevertheless, anti-gay Christians base their belief on one two word phrase that Paul used in verse 26 & 27 of Romans 1 to "seal the deal" on ALL same gender sexual behavior, including love and that phrase is: "both men and women exchanged NATURAL RELATIONS."

Here is where anti-gay Christians go astray. They do not see that Paul's audience was both Jew and Gentile, so Paul had to teach in a way that each group would understand. The Jews understood the Law of Moses and worshipped GOD as the only Creator, but the Gentiles did not. The Gentiles believed in living consistently with the laws of nature as they understood it. The Jews believed in living consistently with the Law of God, given to Moses.

Paul had to explain what salvation in Christ meant to each group and this was a challenge. God's standard is perfection and no one can achieve this. It is by God's Grace, alone, that we are saved through belief in Jesus the Christ. Part of believing IS acknowledging and confessing our sins (known and unknown) and wanting to turn from our sins. Our sins keep us from a pure relationship with God and only through belief in Jesus as Lord and Savior can we be reconciled to God the Father. Now, this is NOT a license to sin. As we follow in Jesus' Will, our will to follow Christ and obey His Will, will increase by the work of His Holy Spirit who comes to live in us when we accept the Holy Spirit's truth that Jesus is Lord and Savior. Our "acceptance" does not come from our own ability, but by the work of the Holy Spirit in us. We can reject this truth.

Here is what anti-gay Christians fail to see and what I have briefly touched on earlier. The words of Romans, Chapter 1, were directed ONLY at the Gentiles: "That I might have some fruit among you also, even as among other Gentiles." Romans 1:13. THIS IS IGNORED BY ANTI-GAY CHRISTIANS AND IS A SERIOUS ERROR IN INTERPRETING GOD'S WORD.

The words "nature" and "natural" in Romans 1: 26 & 27 were directed at the Gentiles, whose philosophy was Stoicism. Their definition and understanding of "nature" and "natural" was not the same as the Jews. Converting Gentiles, who did not believe in one God, Creator of all, as the Jews believed, created a barrier in Paul's preaching of Jesus as Savior of ALL.

One cannot just discuss the Bible without looking outside the Bible to verify what I have said, for the Bible is not a complete history book, though it is historically true. The Stoic philosophy began around 300 B.C. and was pervasive in Paul's Greco-Roman times. THIS IS CRUCIAL IN UNDERSTANDING Romans 1: 18-32.

Paul brilliantly appeals to the Gentiles, who knew nothing of the Old Testament, using an analogy and/or metaphor. He begins by stating that God made Himself known in ALL of Creation. One can either accept the Creator (God), which is natural or reject Him, which is unnatural.

Every behavior described in Romans 1: 26 & 27 is seen as unnatural by Stoic Gentiles. They see both genders having no self control, lustfully motivated and sexually immoral by being outside of the male dominated social and sexual roles and by being non-reproductive.

One must also recognize the 1st century gender hierarchy in order to understand Romans 1: 26 & 27 correctly. Women submitted to everything. This was accepted as natural. Women were to submit in marriage, family, culture, government and, most importantly, sex. Men were the "natural" active sexual partner (the penetrator) and women the "natural" passive sexual partner (the penetrated). For a man to deviate from this and be placed in the role of a woman was degrading. It was against THEIR definition of nature/natural relations, even if the male was the active partner (penetrator) in sex with another man.

In Romans 1: 26 & 27, women were behaving unnaturally, too, though the Bible does not go into detail on how. We can only make an educated guess: they were having non-procreative sex; exchanging their passive for active sex roles. They may well have been having sex with another man in which the woman was in the active role, anally penetrating the male; they were having sex with other women. All of which was unnatural by cultural and Stoic definitions of male and female roles. All we know is that the motivation and behavior of the women was the same as for men, which went against cultural laws of morality. (Also, very similar to the culture of the Jews).

Romans 1:26 & 27 is not a strong position of God's condemnation of homosexuality when one factors in the Stoic philosophy of morality during this time and the cultural hierarchy of men. Paul's inspired genius in using SEX and the phrase "exchanging natural relations" helped the Gentiles understand that it is unnatural NOT to believe in God.

This Stoic mentality still exists in the 21st Century, on the issue of homosexuality and on the belief that "man is the Head of woman"; that no woman should be allowed be an ordained minister and other issues we are debating today, on the basis that the Bible says so. But, I digress. Let's get back to homosexuality.

In the 20th and 21st century it is not unnatural for women to be active, sexually or otherwise or for a man to be passive, sexually or otherwise. It might amaze one to know that not all homosexual men want anal penetration. Heterosexual couples engage in non-penetrative sexual behavior without it being deemed the sin it was in Paul's time.

Paul spoke of men and women of his time exchanging the norm – the natural roles of passive and active as seen through the eyes of the Stoic culture's moral beliefs and the Jewish cultural beliefs, too. Paul is addressing this and NOT homosexuality.

The "due penalty" (recompense) for such sexual immorality was stated, in 1987 by Jerry Falwell who said death from AIDS was today's "due penalty" (recompense) and I quote: "God says that homosexuality is a perverted lifestyle. Those engaged in it will receive, in their own person, due penalty'. God is bringing judgment against homosexuals through AIDS."

Jerry Falwell did not do his homework, for AIDS originated among people in third world countries who were infected through contact with the chimpanzee family, who were infected with a virus almost identical to AIDS and the people hunted and ate these animals thereby ingesting the virus which mutated and spread to other humans through sex or other bodily secretions.

We misuse this passage in Romans 1: 26 & 27. Certainly, in the 1980's, AIDS came to light in the gay male population, but one must remember that men have what I call "the curse of testosterone" and will be more sexually active than women. Therefore, gay men will have more sex than two women or a heterosexual couple and are at a higher risk. However, AIDS was later found in the heterosexual population, too, the result of sexual promiscuity.

Let's put the 'blame' where it belongs – unknowingly infected people who spread AIDS through sexual promiscuity, regardless of sexual orientation.

IN SUMMARY: When you factor in the Stoic philosophy prevalent in Paul's day, it changes the entire dynamics and interpretation of what Paul is trying to teach as sin, which was the unnatural worship of a 'god' i.e. Nature, who is not THE GOD of ALL CREATION. Paul is teaching worship of the one and only Creator using a subject that would grab the attention of the listeners and what better way than SEX.

Now let's move on to the Creation Account which is the foundation for all arguments against homosexuality – the alleged "gotcha".

Anti-gay Christians will say: "Many who affirm homosexuality end up denying Genesis, Chapters 1 and 2 as real because they contradict each other. I DO NOT BELIEVE THIS WAY! They are no myth; they are real and they DO NOT contradict themselves. One is a quick narrative and the other more detailed.

The anti-gay comeback to those like me, who DO believe Genesis, Chapter 1 & 2 are literal history is: "If you accept that the creation account in Genesis is literal history then you MUST also accept what the creation account and the rest of Scripture, based on this creation account, teaches about God's gift of sex being limited to one man and one woman within marriage." Really? Let's dig deeper.

God DID create only one man and one woman, first as companions. Sexuality came second in the 1st blessing from God "to be fruitful and multiply". There was no other way to populate the Earth. One must look at Genesis 1 & 2 WITHIN the context of "in the beginning" (speaking of the beginning of mankind for God has no beginning or end.)

Beginnings are just that, literally. Whether it is the Bible or a novel, there is more to the "beginning" than meets the eye. We know God created one male and one female, but we can't assume that God had no intention of same gender, sexually attracted people entering His World, approving of their love or that homosexuality is a result of sin.

Remember, Eve was created first for companionship; sex came second and it was heterosexual or God would have had to continually and supernaturally create humanity. This does not mean God condemns sex between same gender couples in marriage. Let us not assume that which is not stated. It was **information in advance of the times**. It is not mentioned because it would not produce children. Adam and Eve had to procreate; as the world grew in population this was NOT totally necessary for a marriage, but love is and even love was absent in most Biblical marriages, especially in the Old Testament.

God's Creation is not presented as a finished product. It leaves room for further creative developments. God's world is "good", but it never says "perfect"; in need of development. This can be seen after Adam and Eve sinned and God "cursed" them. Genesis 3:16: "Unto the woman he said, I will greatly multiply thy sorrow and thy conception." HUH? I thought there was no sorrow in Eden before sin.

God did not create a static world. There are many consistencies, but God created a world with certain openness with respect to its future. This correlates well with actual history of a developing NATURAL ORDER across the centuries – new animals, mountain ranges and most obviously – races. None of which is brought about by sin; same with homosexuals. God's order is not fixed in stone. It is still in the process of BECOMING.

Some would counter that the presence of sin and its ill effects in developments in creation have not always been good. Thus, other types of sexual relations are "unnatural" and against God's Will. Using this logic, since Adam and Eve were created one "race", to be other would be unnatural and, therefore a sin.

Genesis 2:18 states, "the two shall become one flesh". Sexual relations and reproduction is not the only meaning of "one flesh." According to anti-gay Christians one can only become one flesh in a marriage between one man and one woman for procreation and for pleasure. Though pleasure is not mentioned in Genesis, it is real for without pleasure in sex there would be no desire for sex and no reproduction.

To quote anti-gay belief: "The purpose of sexual activity includes the celebration of the unique "one flesh" relationship that exists only between one man and one woman in marriage because woman was made from Adams's side (rib) so that's the only way it can be. Any sexual activity outside the context of one man and one woman, within marriage, is a perverted and sinful use of what God intended sexual activity to be." (Sorry all single, celibate people, gay or straight – you can not be considered "one flesh" by this definition. Hang on – you can still be "one flesh" and remain celibate as I will explain shortly.)

I must inject one more point to heterosexual sexual relations. The vagina of a woman is FIRST and FOREMOST the avenue through which a child is born.

My definition of marriage, based on the Creation account, goes beyond the physical aspect. Humans are bodies and spirits. Clinging or cleaving (Genesis 2:24) includes sexual communion along with spiritual and emotional union. Bodies and spirits are involved in helping us grow into a deep, encompassing communion with a beloved partner. Marriage is designed to help our human love grow into the image of God. Our loving God wants us to experience the joy, passion and mystery of this growth into the divine image. God blesses us with the gifts of love, sexuality and marriage in order to help us grow more deeply into the image of Christ's self-giving love which is what marriage is.

Is this not a more biblically accurate description of marriage? Marriage is not just physical. Marriage is spirit followed by physical. One is attracted to the physical, but falls in love with the soul of a person. I surely did with my wife. No scientist has or ever will be able to solve the mystery of why we fall in love with whom we do. The Bible doesn't answer this.

Yet, those who condemn love/marriage between same gender couples continue to focus on the physical, the "one flesh" as making marriage a blessing in God's sight, equating one flesh as physical only. I see this as putting God's concept of marriage into a box.

To be "one flesh" is the result of leaving and cleaving and this is MUCH more than just a sexual union. This is about giving and receiving; joining and responding. This is emotional; this is about love and care and attention. Only as we leave and cleave and develop closeness in ALL these ways can there be the kind of physical union that's right, ideal and nourishing. This union should last as long as we live, be you straight or gay.

Now, my fellow celibates, here's how you and I experience "one flesh" while remaining celibate.

I am one flesh with my mother, my brother, a dear straight or gay male friend, a dear straight or gay female friend. We are one flesh NOT because of sexual attraction or sexual behavior, but by virtue of the spiritual love we have for each other as companions. This is what is being spoken of in Genesis as "one flesh". Adam had a companion first and they became married. I, 100%, doubt sex was what Adam meant when he said "flesh of my flesh". Adam saw another human as a companion first; not a sex object.

Anti-gay Christian belief on same gender sexuality lacks academic integrity. The negative response to same sex behavior, especially between males, has traceable roots in the social and sexual status of women throughout history, which plays an essential role in our understanding of what the Bible IS or IS NOT saying about homosexuality.

Recently we have heard anti-gay Christian's use the word "complementarity" to reinforce the Genesis account that ONLY one man and one woman can attain this in marriage.

The dictionary defines the word "compliment" as something that "completes". With the exception of procreation, which is NOT what makes a couple complimentary (complete), two men or two women are equally complimentary.

Emotionally, two women are more complimentary, as are two men. In heterosexual marriage, each partner needs to bond, as companions, with their own gender, thus the "boys night out" and the "girls night out".

Hormonally, two women are more complimentary, as are two men. Most, not all, women need emotion first before having sex and most, not all, men are driven by sex first and emotion second.

Physically, two women or two men are more complimentary. Men arouse faster than women. Men can quickly achieve orgasm by penetrating ANY orifice. Women need more time to achieve orgasm and most do not by vaginal penetration alone.

We hear about the "G" spot in women as reinforcement for penal/vaginal intercourse; however, that "G" spot, which is the size of a pen point, is located in a woman's vagina that an erect penis cannot directly hit. Only fingers can do this for they are flexible.

We have also heard of men's prostate gland as part of their sexual pleasure. This gland, which is the size of a walnut, is located at the back end of the penis and is stimulated best by anal penetration. Just ask any man who has had his prostate gland examined and massaged and you will find that it is done anally by a doctor's finger and has been found to be pleasurable. If anal penetration was not sexually pleasurable, one must ask why is the prostate gland located in a place where it can be stimulated anally. If one is to be honest, male/male anal penetration is more complementary.

Many straight men would say to be anally penetrated by their female spouse would be homosexual, but it is no more homosexual than a straight woman achieving orgasm by her husband's digital or oral massage of the clitoris, which is the primary way in which women achieve orgasm.

So let us not assume that male to female sex is the best in pleasure, emotionally or physically. That is determined by the orientation of each person.

My point in being so sexually graphic is: heterosexual sex is not all it's built to be, unless you are heterosexual and then it's lacking the essentials of physical differences between the two genders.

Anti-gay Christians like using the comparison of a plug and socket to represent penal/vaginal intercourse. It is a limited view of sexual behavior because it depicts one type of sexual relations which is predominantly more satisfying for men than women and the only 'natural' way to reproduce and the reason God created two genders. The belief of anti-gays that same gender partners "do not fit" is illogical for if they didn't "fit" gay sex would not be pleasurable and IT IS!

Human sexuality is more complicated than what is written and understood in the Bible, in biblical and modern times. There are many ways human anatomy can work for sexual pleasure apart from the limited vaginal penetration by a penis.

God created the human body to allow different ways of sexual satisfaction. So can we use the idea of "parts that fit" as a logical argument against same gender sex? NO!

Therefore, complementarity is NOT a word I would use to describe heterosexual sex as the ONLY way to have sex or to become "one flesh". There is no biblical record that lists anatomy as a condition for marriage.

In Galatians 3:28 we see that ALL these sexual rules are not part of the Kingdom of God, for there is no hierarchy in Heaven nor is their marriage or sex.

We say in the Lord's Prayer, which Jesus taught us to pray and part of that prayer states, "Your Kingdom come, your will be done on Earth as it is in Heaven." We are praying for God's Kingdom to come more fully to Earth. In God's Kingdom ALL systems of hierarchies are gone. ALL are equal. SIN brought inequality into this world. This was not God's intent. God's Word wants us to erase division and power relationships, sexual and otherwise. But we have not and sex, even within a loving marriage can turn into an act of power, dominance and subjugation in and out of the bedroom. ACTIVE AND PASSIVE ARE ACTUALLY WORDS FOR DOMINANCE AND SUBJUGATION, neither of which belongs in a marriage.

Anti-gay Christians quote Jesus, in Matthew 19, to prove male/female sex is the ONLY God ordained sex. They do not understand what was going on in that passage. Jesus DID (Matthew 19:3) quote from Genesis because he was talking to people who were trying to TRAP Him and Jesus turns their question around on them for divorcing their wives for trivial reasons. Jesus was condemning this practice and NOT homosexuality.

When a couple is in love and married, what they do in the bedroom is not sin as long as each partner wants certain sexual behaviors in their lovemaking and that behavior is self-sacrificing and non-violent.

When we sinned we ruined all this equality and love and the battle of the sexes entered as did our battle with affirming same gender, loving sexual relationships.

God blessed many marriages which contained one man and more than one woman: Abraham was married to his half sister (incest) and had sexual relations with Hagar, his wife's maid (adultery). David had many wives. Both Abraham and David were Godly patriarchs blessed by God. These two examples should give one pause to reflect on the evolution of marriage in terms of God's blessing or condemnation.

Anti-gay Christians continue on this "love" issue by bringing into the equation the fact that if we affirm homosexual love and marriage we should also affirm other sexual relationships, such as incest and polygamy, adultery and bestiality, as long as they take place within a loving marital relationship. This is a weak argument because incest was acceptable in God's sight until HE condemned it in the Levitical Laws. Adultery is CLEARLY condemned as a sin in the Ten Commandments, which precede the Levitical Laws. Polygamy, though allowed by God for many generations (for populating the Earth), is not a blessed union by virtue of the Creation Account of ONLY two people in a marriage, but there is more. In marriage a person is to give 100% of him/her self to his/her spouse and that would be impossible to do with more than one spouse. As for bestiality, it is an obvious sin because it would be inter-species sex and in Genesis 2 God had the animal's parade before Adam so he could find a companion who was "suitable" for him and no animal was. Only another human would be "suitable". Using bestiality is truly asinine and disgusting.

Are you listening to these anti-gay Christians and do you believe their erroneous interpretation of the Bible on gay love/marriage?

I believe the Bible supports gay love and marriage, without twisting any portion of Scripture.

Many denominations of the Church foolishly cling to traditional condemnations, as they have with other prejudices, but the Church has been wrong before. LGBT's lives and faith have been broken by misunderstanding and sometimes, malicious interpretation of the Bible.

The CLEAR message of the GOSPEL of JESUS is pushed to the background among such homophobic misinterpretation of Scripture.

LOVE is what Jesus preached and lived. Love of God and love of our neighbors.

* * * * * * * * * *

I hope and pray that by telling you my life story and what I have written in BOOK FOUR will help you find the truth that I knew was in the Bible when I was a teenager, decades before anything positive was preached or written on homosexuality; when gay people were believed, by society AND the Church to be mentally ill, freaks and sinners bound for Hell. I know I have not answered all your questions; no pro or anti-gay writer can. That is why there is always a question and answer time when anyone speaks on this issue.

You can contact me, privately, on Facebook or email me at mamasgirl422@verizon.net.

BIBLIOGRAPHY

Achtemeier, Mark: "The Bible's YES to Same-sexed marriage". Westminster John Knox Press. 2014

Baldock, Kathy: "Walking the Bridgeless Canyon". Canyonwalker Press. 2014

Barefoot, Scott & Starr, Richard: "Forgive Us Our Sins". Northwestern Publishing House 2013

Eckstein, Tom: "Bearing Their Burden". Lulu, Inc. 2010

Helminiak, Daniel A.: "What the Bible Really Says About Homosexuality". Alamo Square Press 1994

Perry, Troy: "The Lord Is My Shepherd and He Knows I'm Gay". Nash Publishing 1972

Made in the USA
Monee, IL
03 September 2022